D1326804

WOMEN IN INDUSTRY AND TECHNOLOGY

FROM PREHISTORY

TO THE PRESENT DAY

museum of
LONDON

WOMEN IN INDUSTRY AND TECHNOLOGY

FROM PREHISTORY

TO THE PRESENT DAY

CURRENT RESEARCH AND THE MUSEUM EXPERIENCE

PROCEEDINGS FROM THE 1994 WHAM CONFERENCE

Edited by

Amanda Devonshire and Barbara Wood

5855

A (DEV)

THE PAUL HAMLYN LIBRARY

First published in Great Britain in 1996 by the Museum of London, 150 London Wall,
London EC2Y 5HN

Copyright © 1996 Museum of London

The right of the contributors to be identified as authors of this work has been
asserted by them in accordance with the Copyright, Designs and Patents Act, 1988.

All rights reserved. This publication may not be reproduced, stored in a retrieval
system, or transmitted, in any form or by any means, electronic, mechanical,
photocopying, recording or otherwise, without the prior permission of the publisher.

ISBN 0 904818 74 8

604.820941 DEV

Project Manager Suzie Burt
Editorial Suzie Burt, Mandi Gomez, Doreen Palamartschuk, Chris Parker
Designer Donna Hughes
Formatting Concise Artisans
Photographers John Chase, Richard Stroud, Torla Evans
Indexer Dorothy Frame

Printed and bound in Great Britain by Biddles

CONTENTS

PREFACE

In 1994, the organisation Women Heritage and Museums (WHAM) celebrated its tenth anniversary. In that decade much had been achieved (see the essay by Kirby on p305) and although recent conferences had been on a small scale, it was felt that both the existence of the group and its activities should be recognised and celebrated. Consequently, the conference which is published here took place at the Museum of London over two days, 20–21 May 1994.

WHAM has always acted primarily as a transmitter and co-ordinator of information between museum workers, those interested in women's past and those seeking a more balanced presentation of history. It also provides a link between academics and museums. The membership of WHAM reflects this, including curators, academics, amateur historians, workers in the heritage industry, students, social historians and archaeologists. We intended that this conference would appeal to the wide range of membership.

Aware that in the current climate it is often difficult to justify time away from workstations unless the activity can be directly related to work underway, we aimed to provide a programme which was tightly arranged with a specific purpose. We intended to facilitate an exchange of information and debate between those researching history and those who interpret and present it to the public. With a broad spread of papers covering periods from prehistoric to contemporary collecting, the conference took on these issues from the perspectives of current research and the museum experience. It provided rapid access to recent research for museum workers, particularly those who individually cover a range of periods in their work. It was a chance to look critically at how museums interpret objects, encouraging new ways of using existing collections and considering how objects and information are interpreted to museum visitors. Among the academic delegates particularly we hoped to raise an awareness of the potential of material culture and encourage its use in their research, while also providing them with an understanding of the application and interpretation of their work by museum professionals.

The subject of industry and technology was chosen partly because of the increase in current work in this area but also because it was relevant across the widest timespan covered by museums. From Prehistory to contemporary collecting, the papers ranged from women toolmakers in the Bronze Age (Sørensen) to women's work in the London Docklands (Hostettler), and covered heavy and light industries (for example Geddes, Preece, Gater and Davin), as well as production from the home base (Sharpe, Atkinson). The unusual drawing together of vastly different historical periods and specialisms appears to have been successful, attracting 150 delegates of varied backgrounds and interests, including some from North America, Sweden and Slovenia.

The conference recognised the often unexplored commonality between periods. Prehistoric collections, for example, only reflect the social history of an earlier age. This element has become particularly apparent to us as the book has been drawn together. Themes such as metalworking may be traced through the book from Bronze Age metalsmiths (Sørensen); medieval bell-founders (Geddes) and pewter traders (Weinstein) to the needle-makers of this century (Werner and Jones). Similarly, the papers looking at exhibition techniques emphasise that throughout museums, representations of women are often confined

to the domestic setting and the roles of mother, cook, wife etc (Butler, Holgate, Taziker, Wood).

The aims of the conference were reflected in its structure. Sessions were defined by general historical periods and each included a keynote paper presenting an overview of women's work. Subsequent papers looked at specific industries, with a final contribution in each session directly considering the presentation of evidence through museum interpretation. A total of thirty-seven papers was given, with speakers from academic, museum and heritage backgrounds. Speakers represented a wide range of museums, from the National Museums of Scotland (Kidd) to smaller institutions such as the Trowbridge Museum (Wigley). As ever, there were papers given at the conference which it was not possible to include in the final publication, in this case contributions from Dr Caroline Barron, Jason Doherty, Margaret Ehrenberg, Phillippa Glanville, Jane Middleton, Gaby Porter, Fiona Talbot and Sue Wilkinson. Some of these authors have published work elsewhere and the bibliographies for the relevant chapters include references which cover the areas which they discussed. However, there remained two important gaps, and we are grateful to Beverley Butler ('Virginia Woolf, Madonna and Me: Searching for Role-models and Women's Presence in Museums and Heritage') and Judith Stevenson ('Working Women in Medieval London') for so effectively filling them at short notice.

In the main, this book reflects the struc-ture of the conference. It is intended to provide both an introduction to women's work in particular periods and the means to begin specific research through the references in the sources section. This section includes not only bibliographic references but also notes of relevant collections, archives and exhibitions. We hope that it will be used as a first point of reference for anyone with an interest in the role of women in industry, the role of the museum as interpreter of information and women's history generally. We hope to see further studies which will build on the work of the contributors to this publication, resulting in both more links between the worlds of academia and museums and similarly structured studies relating to other areas of women's lives.

Finally, we would like to thank all those who have helped to make this project a success. For help with the original conference, thanks to the WHAM Committee, particularly Margaret Brooks, Karen Fielder and Beverley Butler, also thanks to Julie Carr. For support during the length of the project to Adam Toth and Philip Burton. Both book and conference have been helped enormously by the staff of the Museum of London, notably Judith Stevenson, Roz Sherris and Jonathan Cotton. Particular thanks should go to Nick Merriman for his support of the proposal for joint publication (WHAM/Museum of London) of the proceedings of the conference and to Suzie Burt, Museum of London Publications Officer; Donna Hughes, Designer; John Chase and Richard Stroud, photographers; and to Doreen Palamartschuk, editorial assistant. Thanks also to Rob Pecks for additions to the contemporary source section, and to all the contributors for their co-operation, patience and support.

Amanda Devonshire
Barbara Wood

FOREWORD

The tenth anniversary conference of WHAM which took place at the Museum of London in 1994 took as its theme 'Women in Industry and Technology'. This collection of papers is a permanent record of a successful and inspirational meeting. It will be of interest not only to museum professionals but also to every museum visitor who enjoys the study of history and wishes to learn more about the past and the way in which it is interpreted in displays and exhibitions.

Publications of conference proceedings are both more and less than the actual events which they record. A printed version cannot reflect fully the value of debate, whether it takes place in the formal context of a discussion session in the lecture theatre or more casually over coffee during the breaks in proceedings, but to counter that weakness, a volume of collected papers reaches a far wider audience than the meeting itself and ensures that the conference has a continuing and evolving influence on research and scholarship. Furthermore, a printed record can present a far more balanced overview of the event than is possible at the time. In this particular case, the number of speakers and length of time available dictated that simultaneous sessions had to take place in different locations. No single conference delegate, therefore, was able to appreciate the whole chronological sweep of the subject, from earliest Prehistory to the present, as it is set out in this collection.

The grouping of the chapters is chronological, and the principal aim of the book is to provide the reader with an insight into what we know of the contribution of women to industrial and technological processes in the past, using both general theory and specific examples. A timeframe which ranges from the

Palaeolithic to the twentieth century cannot hope to do justice equally to all those vastly different periods, and even the most cursory glance at the list of contents will indicate how heavily this book is biased towards the post-medieval period, and in particular the nineteenth and twentieth centuries.

The inclusion of Prehistory and the Roman period, the domain of the archaeologist rather than the social historian, has a special value in emphasising the importance of understanding the nature of primary evidence. As an archaeologist specialising in the Roman period, I envy the wonderfully detailed and precise sources available to historians of more recent periods, but at the same time I am conscious of the fact that the severe limitations of the material remains of the past, defined to a great extent by the survival of stone, metal and ceramics and the decay of organic substances, are at least wholly independent of gender. If we follow tradition and attribute weapons to males and jewellery to females, that is our decision; the objects themselves do not try to manipulate our thinking as do so many historical documents, and the archaeologist therefore has less excuse for sexual stereotyping than his or her historian colleagues.

The limitations of archaeological evidence, however frustrating they may be, also free the imagination in a way which is both liberating and dangerous. Students of early periods are virtually obliged to devise imaginative hypotheses which can all too easily be taken as factual by those who have not grasped the incomplete and biased nature of the raw data. But our colleagues who are able to cite specific and well-documented evidence for particular situations and events in

the more recent past must also exercise care, for those events or situations, however 'real' they may be, will define only one reality out of many; consciousness of the under representation of women, and our determination to correct it, should make us especially sensitive to other imbalances and prejudices, some of which are mentioned in the chapters which follow. Enough has already been written elsewhere about the historical biases which operate against certain social classes and ethnic groups to underline this. Complete objectivity and even-handedness is ultimately unattainable by human beings, but that should not prevent us from working towards it to the best of our ability.

The written evidence relating to the medieval and modern periods is in any case a mixed blessing, for it is of varying quality and can be as patchy and incomplete in its way as the archaeologist's flints and potsherds, even when it is not deliberately misleading. The most illuminating insights often result from comparisons of different periods or places, for example, an observation made not only in several of the chapters dealing with women in wartime but also in those dealing with aspects of the fourteenth and fifteenth centuries: namely the fact that women have been permitted to encroach upon 'masculine' skills and responsibilities at times when war or pestilence has reduced the availability of male labour, only to be forced back into the domestic sphere as soon as the population imbalance has been redressed.

When we come to very recent times, an additional source of evidence is available in the form of oral history. The vivid quotations from the personal stories of women who took part in the two World Wars of the twentieth century, or of those who remember the hardships and achievements of industrial processes now irrevocably lost through technological and social change, will probably leave the strongest impression of all upon every reader of this book.

Apart from the overall chronological survey of the subject of women in industry there is a subsidiary theme, the 'museum experience'. This addresses the obstacles and choices which face the curator as he or she attempts to interpret a vision of the past, derived from scholarly research, in a way which both informs and entertains the museum visitor. Again, there are great differences between work focused on recent and more remote periods. We can almost guarantee that any museum visitor of mature years will have at least a passing interest in a display about the Second World War as well as some personal knowledge and understanding of the subject, but the technology of flint-knapping is by any standards a specialised matter, and few of those who wander into a gallery of prehistoric artefacts will find it easy to identify closely and immediately with their forebears from the Stone Ages. The curator of archaeology has a greater gulf of experience and understanding to span.

Only another museum curator can fully understand just how difficult it is to translate published academic research into the concrete form of a museum gallery. Some of the problems of presentation and interpretation are addressed here in several papers which record the creation of new exhibitions or review specific displays, but they are concerned only with the central theme of representing women fairly. The daunting constraints imposed by the actual content of collections, restrictions of space, conservation requirements, design styles, security and safety regulations and of course financial limitations are barely mentioned, for many of the conference delegates were people who worked in museums, and these multifarious problems are part of the texture of their everyday lives which have been taken as read by the contributors. The general reader therefore needs to be reminded that the intellectual agonies of interpretation form only one aspect of the hard travail which transforms abstract concept into completed showcase.

The complexities of intellectual debate do not lend themselves easily to presentation in a museum gallery. One of the subtle revolutions in scholarship over the last generation or so is that it has become increasingly acceptable in academic writing to present alternative hypotheses which fit the same set of evidence without necessarily deciding on one or the other as 'correct'. Not all the scholars of both sexes who rightly take advantage of this new freedom and openness realise that its origins lie in feminist thinking, with its flexibility and its need to challenge traditional approaches, particularly the rigid and often confrontational power strategies of some male academics. The presentation of alternative or multiple hypotheses is thus an important advance in scholarly research. It is quite simple to achieve in written work, whether academic or popular, but within the physical framework of an exhibition gallery it is likely to be well nigh impossible. Too often we are obliged to face a simple either/or choice because the facilities simply do not exist for us to display a range of options.

It is all too easy, when forced into making specific choices, to interpret the past as we should like it to have been. We may sneer at outmoded phrases like 'Man the Hunter' or deplore the recurring image of the female knitter by the fireside, but if those stereotypes turn out to be true, or even to be one facet of the truth, we have to face up to the fact. While we do not assume, as an earlier generation of scholars did, that all graves with weapons are those of men and all those with jewellery, women, if independent and open-minded research confirms the male warrior and the bedizened lady of leisure, we must, however regretfully, consign our visions of fierce Amazons and docile house-husbands to the realms of fantasy. Everyone concerned with women's history hopes to find inspiring examples of female power, authority and independence in the past. They will indeed find some, and should take pains to make them better known, but there was no Golden Age, and ultimately we must remember that we do not need even a single example of a politically powerful woman to justify our determination to see the female half of the human race given proper attention and respect in our vision of history.

All of this leads me to wonder whether curators are in some danger of over-interpreting the past. In our eagerness to entertain the museum visitor and make museums friendly and colourful places, we are perhaps underestimating both the imagination and the intelligence of the public. The efforts of museum curators and other academics should be focused upon educating the general public to think for themselves, to be willing to reject what they are told by 'experts' and go straight to the basic evidence itself, but only to do so from an informed

position. To achieve this, they must learn above all to understand the nature of archaeological and historical evidence, its strengths and weaknesses, and the careful and consistent way in which it should be used. Perhaps the current popularity of models and reconstructions is not ultimately the best way ahead. If we simply tell people what to think, whether by means of words, pictures or shop-window set-pieces, we are failing to learn the most fundamental, valuable and lasting lesson of feminism, which is that accepted knowledge is not necessarily true.

In its ten years of existence, the group Women and Heritage in Museums has made a very significant contribution to historical research and its presentation in museums. This collection of papers reflects something of that enthusiasm and vision, but it is very much a record of work in progress. There are still far more problems than solutions, but the dynamism and application revealed in the chapters which follow augur well for the future.

Catherine Johns

PART 1

WOMEN IN INDUSTRY AND TECHNOLOGY

THE CONFERENCE IN CONTEXT

Virginia Woolf, Madonna and Me :

VIRGINIA WOOLF, MADONNA AND ME:
SEARCHING FOR ROLE-MODELS AND WOMEN'S PRESENCE IN MUSEUMS AND HERITAGE

Beverley Butler

It was the decade of Backlash and Miss Whiplash. A decade which saw Greenham Women at the wire and Princess Diana at the publishers. A decade which saw the rise and fall of Indira Gandhi and Winnie Mandela, and of Margaret Thatcher removed by 'treachery with a smile on its face'. Hillary Clinton vied for Presidential Partner while iron curtains were pulled aside and walls came down for Raisa Gorbachev to visit Downing Street. Annie Lennox and Aretha Franklin sang 'Sisters are doin' it for themselves' while Madonna was expressing herself in more Material Girl fashion.

In true post-modern style the media role-models came thick and fast for women young and old to try on for size, and if reality had become just a little too hard to handle there were some fictitious females who offered some alternative lifestyles. At the flicks we suffered Michael Douglas's attempts to work through some 'post-feminist' male angst in a series of revamped male fantasies, while Sally Potter's adaptation of *Orlando* and Jane Campion's *The Piano* showed that feminist agendas were not over yet ... 'Della seeks Binnie' runs an advert in the pages of *Loot*,[1] while Silver Moon, the women's bookshop in Charing Cross Road, London, stocks T-shirts which read FREE BETH JORDACHE,[2] references to the lesbian chic which has run through British soap operas, from the former male preserve of the Queen Vic in the East End of London to Liverpool's Brookside via the once sleepy rural idyll of Beckindale.[3] A *bricolage* at once breathtaking and loaded. Add political correctness, Neil Lyndon and Camille Paglia, and lie back for that *fin-de-siècle* feeling! Perhaps our own biographies in those ten years will prove just as fascinating and fickle?

It was not that women did more or less in the decade 1984–1994 than at any other time, but that the struggle for women's rights and wrongs is now news. It was in these Modern Times that Women, Heritage and Museums (WHAM) was born and nurtured. It rose in resistance and has laboured through periods of unpopularity to make it into the 1990s and to our tenth-anniversary celebrations.

My 'Problematic' here relates to the representation and misrepresentation of women, or more specifically to the response and relationship of the museum world to the wider media-inspired representation and misrepresentation of women; how 'Women' as a grouping – the gender, the sex, the presence – can populate the museum.

In this paper I intend to survey current research and developments in museum studies, including the WHAM tenth-anniversary conference, to look at these critically, while placing them in the context of the wider influences of the media, women's history, feminism, and personal biography. Any reading of women and museums highlights the connections and interactions between these elements.

MAKING CONNECTIONS: The Search for Role-models

While the media and popular culture offer us the whole gamut of women's experience it has been to academia that museums have traditionally looked for their role-models and reference points. In the case of museology and women it has been to feminism and women's studies that critiques have looked. However, with the recent hype surrounding 'post-feminist' politics one could be forgiven for thinking academia had transgressed into the world of pure entertainment. Media shows have projected American feminists such as Camille Paglia and Naomi Wolf as potential role-models. Spats between icons such as Germaine Greer and Suzanne Moore have proved how dedicated the press are to seeking out (or eking out?) dissension in the ranks. Misrepresentations abound! That's entertainment! The viewers and readers at home are left with a pick'n'mix of different varieties of feminisms from liberal to lesbian, Christian to anarchist, Marxist to meta-physical, psychoanalytical to socialist, radical-separatist to existential. With the naming of the so-called 'Cosmo', 'Third Wave', 'Do me', 'Pod' feminists, it appears that the 1990s has it all![4]

Behind the bright lights, the make-overs and the glamour, the influence of a feminist profile has forced both public and private institutions to address 'women's issues'. The ten years since the founding of WHAM have also seen vast increases in the number of books on women's history and in opportunities to pursue women's studies. No one would claim that the struggle for equality is over; in some areas it is only just beginning, while in others it has suffered a serious setback or been reversed. However, the contemporary focus upon women (although mere lip-service in some situations), has led to new connections being formed.

The projects of feminism have been as varied as feminists themselves: feminism as a meta-narrative; feminism as action emanating from the 1970s women's movement; feminism as critique; as personal; as political; feminism as historical, international and cross-cultural. Women have looked back to the past as Goddesses and to the future as Cyberfeminists. These many different, and sometimes conflicting methodologies, have been and continue to be employed to identify and challenge women's oppression.

Museum studies, or museology, is notorious for its raiding of other disciplines for suitable theories, paradigms and practice; the approaches and methodologies of certain feminisms have been utilised in this way.[5] I choose to begin where many others have begun; with an icon, a founding sister of feminism, Virginia Woolf, who in 1929 in the British Museum pondered this same problematic of the representation and misrepresentation of women. Woolf's attention was directed towards women and literature as she surveyed the rows of books in the British Museum's Reading Room. She could just as easily have been surveying the rows of objects in the nearby galleries, or just about any other museum for that matter! She comments: 'A very queer, composite being thus emerges. Imaginatively she [woman] is of the highest importance, practically she is completely insignificant. She pervades poetry from cover to cover; she is all but absent from history'.[6]

Nowhere is this more pertinent than in the 'truthful', 'objective' museum space, where the poverty of representation of women is more pernicious than fiction, and where the portrayal of women has traditionally been riddled with inaccuracies. With honourable exceptions, critics have indicated how museum role-models have been fixed by these binaries and have existed as stereotypes within the domestic sphere.[7] Woman is ever the muse and never the historical 'subject'. She is always the angel and never the worker.[8] These are the polarities which fix women's experience in the museum space. Always she is objectified but we have few objects to interpret her own history. It is not that women necessarily need to come out of the kitchen, be it Georgian, Edwardian or MFI, but that they need to be truthfully represented in this sphere and their role in other spheres recognised, re-evaluated and reaffirmed.

Near to the British Museum, in my office in Gordon Square (I must admit this is a shared space rather than exclusively 'a room of one's own'), I am able to commune with the heritage and spirits of some of the most inspiring and inspired women: those who were committed to achieving equality and positive representation for women.[9] Across the square a blue plaque testifies to, and makes connection with, the presence of Virginia Woolf, who shared the space ninety years earlier. The building, 50 Gordon Square, now functions as a careers office for University College London. Would Virginia, who so often wrote about women and professions, be pleased I wondered? How many women, I asked, would be inspired to carve a career in the arts, in the sciences, in technology and industry before the day, the term, the year, the next decade is out?

Another thought: how many women were inspired into museum work? Be warned! The titles of just a couple of articles written on the job prospects for women in museums sum up the severe obstacles to equal opportunities in this particular profession. 'Where are All the Women Museum Directors?' asked Terry Trucco in *Artnews*,[10] while Kendall Taylor wrote of 'Risking It: Women as Museum Leaders', in *Museum News*.[11] The only connection with women comes in the use of the term the 'feminisation of museum work'.[12] This is of course a reference to poor standards rather than any commitment to women, as Skjoth comments: 'In some countries women form a majority of museum professionals. The catch is that their salaries and other conditions of employment are considered insufficient by men'.[13] The changing nature of work, the trend towards part-time, job-share and temporary contracts create both opportunities for flexible working and potential difficulties for fair employment.[14] Women (whether curators, cleaners or attendants) form the largest percentage of this new type of worker, therefore these are issues which are key agendas in debates regarding employment equality in the future.[15]

In a museum culture where identity and professional status are increasingly linked to job-titles and subject specialisms, WHAM by its very existence has transgressed the mainstream by daring to claim an identity based upon gender lines. Furthermore, in the choice of 'Industry and Technology' as the subject of its tenth-anniversary conference, WHAM has threatened the traditional composite outlined by Woolf. The presence of women, whether in the gallery or in the boardroom, still remains an anomaly, highlighting an irony running through many women's careers, but perhaps best expressed in a classic comment from Marcia Tucker, formerly of the Whitney Museum of American Art, currently Director of the New Museum of Contemporary Art:

> **I am now one of a minority of women directors in the field but not one who was chosen to be a director. Finding virtually no place for my being and my ideas within the existing museological framework, I chose to establish a museum. This made me both privileged *and* marginalised at the same time, since I had to create the institution in order to work in it.** [16]

REPRESENTATION AND ROLE-MODELS
IN WOMEN'S HISTORY AND FEMINISM

For those of us who remain simply marginalised and underprivileged when it comes to the prospects of creating our own institution, our connection here is in the element of autobiography, of *égo-histoire*, of the personal which is fused with the political, which leads many women to stray from the mainstream in order to find a relevant, useable and empowering history. How many women were drawn to museum work because of some revelatory museum experience which spoke to them? May I assume that this wasn't the case? Personal experience and biography is the key to understanding the emotional investment of museum workers and their further commitment to raise questions, offer research and critiques to make museum work and representations in the gallery space more democratic and less oppressive. Recent volumes on gender issues in museums have highlighted the need to include 'testimonials, accounts of role-models …'.[17]

Just as Virginia Woolf forms part of my own personal search to find reference points and role-models, it is with this sense of making connections between one's own history, women's/feminist history and that of the museum that the aspirations of WHAM and the WHAM conference can be placed. It is part of the spirit of a growing impetus to populate the past, to search back into women's history, and into the physical environment and heritage. I find myself standing side by side with heroines of my own discovery, all of whom open possibilities in one's own life. Feminism and women's history have given us icons to empower (Dale Spender in her 1982 study, *Women of Ideas* …, set up a line from Aphra Behn to Adrienne Rich), ordinary lives to remember and hidden histories to reclaim from the condescension of patriarchal history (for example through the approaches of Sheila Rowbotham and Deidre Beddoe).[18]

Alternative perspectives enable us to cast an eye over museum history and to see that behind every 'great' museum moment in the store, in the gallery, in the office, were the spirits and presence of women. Women may be ordinary, extraordinary, audacious, radical, inspirational, typical or atypical by their example and their very presence, they recast the history of museums. Taylor has researched into the 'Pioneering Efforts of Early Museum Women'.[19] A line of collectors and benefactors, and women museum workers emerges from her work; from women with wealth, power and connections such as Lizzie Bliss, Mrs Cornelius J. Sullivan and Abby Aldrich Rockefeller, who founded the Museum of Modern Art to women such as Catherine Lemmon Manning, curator of the Smithsonian Institution's division of philately between 1912 and 1951, known as 'the first lady of philately'. This approach to populating the museum is also apparent in other research.[20]

Woolf herself had a similar notion of bearing witness, of seeking to commemorate the women who went before when she exhorted women to lay a wreath at the graveside of Aphra Behn, seeing and acknowledging 'the experience of the mass is behind the single voice'.[21] This ritual performance of remembering is of key importance to a more truthful representation of women; the potential to 'make safe' or defuse the radicalism of our icons is a process Patricia West warns against in her paper, 'Gender Politics and the "Invention of Tradition": The Museumification of Louisa May Alcott's Orchard House'.[22]

While the aforementioned approaches continue to be used, the idea of a simple celebration of women, of feminism for feminism's sake, has been effected by the self-reflexive nature of current intellectualism. For example, the ahistoricity of treating gender as if this was the unifying factor has been exposed; issues of class, race, sexuality, ethnicity and historical context showed the inadequacy of this line.[23] The Eurocentric feminist world view has been qualified by those whose personal biographies testify to an alternative experience. Newer developments in Eco-feminism, Black feminism and non-aligned feminism suggest ways in which all women can take on critiques and move towards a relevancy for all.

These have ranged from the drawing out of absences and the deconstruction of sexist images to debates on essentialism, separatism, gender, culture and nature – all have been played out in the museum space. The recent volume of *Gender and History* is a collection of papers on women and museums which engage in all of these debates and methodologies.[24]

On a further level both feminism and museum studies have engaged in the wider discourses of structuralism, of psychoanalysis, of semiology and of post-modernity. For example, the work of the so-called 'post-modern feminists', the French theorists Kristeva, Cixous and Irigaray have taken on the desire to rethink the aspirations of women, to think non-binary and to link women's oppression to oppression in general. Irigaray has questioned the validity of equality as the goal of feminism and has posited sexual difference as the agenda of our age.[25] All these works have application to the museum space. Creative agendas have revolved around the theory and practice of 'écriture féminine'. The interest in interdisciplinary areas such as those of cultural studies, contemporary studies, public histories and in specific agendas like those of representation, of power, of empire and of gender have led to intense analysis of cultural forms, including that of the museum.[26]

ROLE-MODELS AND REPRESENTATION IN MUSEUMS

The registering of these advances in heritage and museums has been complex. The academic research work of the kind brought together at WHAM's tenth-anniversary conference is likely to find its way into museum displays whether this is in women's role in prehistoric technologies; early modern craftwork, medieval heavy metal industries, the coalmining industry or modern industry. The centrality of women's political protests, from food riots to Greenham Common, via the suffrage women, is similarly likely to be acknowledged in displays of social history.

More problematic, to my mind, is the acknowledgement of women's experiences. At least in museum displays women stand shoulder to shoulder with men, women flex their muscles at the pattern wheel, and sisters carry the banners alongside their fraternal comrades. Such equality is to be welcomed. But it cannot be denied that, with honourable exceptions, museums insist on tackling themes which ensure 'equality' remains the norm; moreover, when it comes down to individual experience, men win hands down. Women are 'put in' to exhibitions; exhibitions are rarely built around them. Their inclusion could be lost tomorrow or disappear to other agendas in identity politics unless exhibitions deal specifically with gender.

There are now a number of museums devoted exclusively to women which open the way for positive representations of women: the Women's Museum at Aarhus, Denmark formed in 1982; the Cumbe Women's Museum in Ecuador; Le Musée de la Femme, France; Frauen-Museum, Germany in Bonn and Wiesbaden; the Museum of the Mother, Greece; Daughters of the American Revolution Museum, Washington, DC; the National Museum of Women in the Arts, Washington, DC, and the Women's Heritage Museum, Palo Alto.[27] There is also a Museum of Women's Art planned to open in the near future in Britain.

Yet the discovery has been made that not any representation will do. Rather, there is a need to take forward the element that connects all feminisms − that of *critique* − a factor which has come out of the various conferences held on women and museums. The museum as medium may not have the immediacy, the responsiveness of TV, film and/or the dynamic of popular culture, but it can still grapple with the best of them. The museum culture is able to tap into outside influences and shared culture − to collect Hillary Clinton's makeover bill, Madonna's bra, Margaret Thatcher's handbag, Suzanne Moore's stilettos, wire-cutters from Greenham − to see museums not only as a cultural form responsive to the agendas for women historically but contemporaneously and with an eye to the future. In terms of its choice of representations of women, the museum, as an institution entrusted with cultural continuity, has a capacity and a responsibility to be discerning.

The commentary from *Our Sister's London: Feminist Walking Tours* shows that misinformation as well as misrepresentation goes on:

> **On its [Gordon Square's] east side, at no. 50, a plaque commemorates the 'Bloomsbury group', the intellectual and artistic circle of which Virginia Woolf and her sister Vanessa Bell were members. In fact, both sisters, along with their brothers Thoby and Adrian, lived at no. 46, where a plaque commemorates the later residence of economist John Maynard Keynes.**[29]

Feeling rather as if I had been had for making my pilgrimage to the wrong door, I stopped instead outside number 46. This is now University College London's snack bar. Looking for a presence, for role-models, one can do no better than to begin with ourselves. The hope is not only for equality, difference and relevancy, but for something I hold dear, the ongoing commitment to critique and intellectual freedom. Be on guard against women being put back into the kitchen!

The project in the museum space has begun. The history, the experience, the precedents, the exhibitions, the personalities, the role-models, begin to populate the museum. The aims of WHAM and the presence of women gathered for the tenth-anniversary conference marked a significant moment in this process and underlined how women as visitors, as museum workers, as historical and contemporary 'subject', can claim a place and can seek equal *representation*, not simply *objectification*, in the museum space.

ENDNOTES

1 'EastEnders' storyline 1994–5, BBC. Della and Binnie were the first two lesbian characters to be found in this British soap opera 'EastEnders', which is set in the fictional working-class borough of Walford in the East End of London.

2 'Brookside' storyline 1994–5, Channel 4. Continuing this so-called media fixation with 'lesbian chic', the soap opera 'Brookside', set in the suburbs of Liverpool, created its own dyke icon in the character of Beth Jordache. Beth's death at the height of her fight for justice against domestic violence led many sceptics to believe the media are fickle in their fleeting fascinations and lesbian characters expendable when they become too problematic.

3 'Emmerdale' storyline 1994–5, ITV Carlton. The ultimate sign of same-sex relationships gaining media attention must be the inclusion of lesbian characters in the once quiet rural idyll of Emmerdale set in the fictional northern farming community of Beckindale. As with the other British soaps, there is a thin line between 'issue TV' taking a stand and the need to bump up the viewing figures by spicing up storylines!

4 Television was not the only medium keen to jump on to the feminist-hype bandwagon. 'A new generation of women thinkers – are embracing sex (and men). Call them "do me" feminists,' announced *Esquire* magazine in their February 1994 cover story. The *Observer* newspaper's guide to the 'A–Z of the '90s Part I' comments, 'The magazine *Esquire* discovered feminists championing no-regret, no-guilt sexual liberation and contrasted them with the supposedly prudish Seventies feminists. The article was illustrated with kittenish poses by Naomi Wolf, Third Wave leader Rebecca Walker ...' An exasperated Susan Faludi suggested her own catchphrase for revisionists – 'pod feminists' – after the sci-fi classic *Invasion of the Body Snatchers*.

5. Jones, S. and Pay, S., 1990; Jones, S., 1990; Jones, S., 1991; Wilkinson, S. et al, 1991.

6 Woolf, V., 1992, p56.

7 Porter, G., 1988; Porter, G., 1991; Horne, D., 1984.

8 Porter, G., 1986.

9 Sturtevant, K., 1990, pp7–20.

10 Trucco, T., 1976.

11 Taylor, K., 1985.

12 Cummings, A., 1991, p143.

13 Skjoth, 1991, p125.

14 *Museums Journal*, October 1994.

15 Hewitt, P., 1993; Blyton, P., 1985; Leighton, P. and Syrett, 1989.

16 Tucker, M., 1994, p51.

17 Glaser, J.R. and Zenetou, A.A., 1994, pxiii.

18 Rowbotham, S., 1973; Beddoe, D., 1993.

19 Taylor, K., 1994.

20 Braz Texeira, M., 1991; Dublin, T., Grey Osterud, N. and Parr, J., 1994; Campbell, M.S., 1990; des Portes, E. and Raffin, A., 1991; Glaser, J.R. and Zenetou, A.A., 1994.

21 Woolf, V., 1992, p86.

22 West, P., 1994, pp456–67.

23 Tong, R., 1989.

24 Dublin, T., Grey Osterud, N. and Parr, J., 1994.

25 Irigaray, L., 1985.

26 Bennett, T., 1995; Sherman, D. and Rogoff, I., 1994.

27 *Museum*, 1991.

28 Glaser, J.R. and Zenetou, A.A., 1994; Higonnet, A., 1994; Dublin, T., Grey Osterud, N. and Parr, J., 1994.

29 Sturtevant, K., 1990, p17.

PART 2

WOMEN IN INDUSTRY AND TECHNOLOGY

CHAPTER 1

WOMEN IN PREHISTORY

MISTAKEN ABOUT EVE?
FINDING AND REPRESENTING WOMEN IN THE OLD STONE AGE

Jill Cook

As the term Palaeolithic or Old Stone Age implies, our understanding of some two and a half million years of early human Prehistory is based to a great extent on the character and technology of stone tools. These predominate in the artefact inventories and records of this time period and it is assumed that they were utilised for a variety of tasks ranging from food procurement and butchery to the manufacture of equipment made from non-lithic materials. It is possible to say a great deal about how such stone tools were made and, occasionally, what they were used for, but, contrary to the impressions given by many book and museum diagrams and illustrations, the archaeological record reveals nothing about who would have carried out such technological activities. This involves insights into the social lives of our early Prehistoric ancestors which are difficult, and at times, impossible, to infer from the palimpsest of evidence available. As a result, the roles of both women and men in Palaeolithic technology are represented on the basis of current values and assumptions and, by recourse, to theories derived from various fields of anthropology and biology. These palaeoanthropological models of social/behavioural evolution reflect the values and bias of the contemporary societies from which they emerge[1] and transform archaeological data into circumstantial evidence to support opinions which are inevitably debatable. In view of this, it would seem helpful to outline the partial skeleton of known facts in order to compare what is known from existing evidence and what is imagined before considering whether it is possible to engender[2] the technology of the Palaeolithic.

BECOMING HUMAN

The evolutionary lines leading to the modern great apes and anatomically modern humans diverged from a common ancestor five to six million years ago. From limited fossil evidence and a well-dated trail of footprints discovered at Laetolil, Tanzania,[3] it is clear that the major anatomical changes which distinguish humans from apes and enable upright walking (bipedalism) had occurred by at least four million years ago. Although these earliest hominids (australopithecines) may have utilised sticks and stones during their daily activities, the oldest recognised, deliberately manufactured tools date from approximately 2.4 million years ago and were probably produced by a larger-brained species of *Homo*. However, the appearance of an archaeological record may only inform us that people were part of the landscape and, where the earliest traces of human activity are concerned, even this can be problematic. At a most basic level, determining the products of nature from those of human manufacture can be difficult and controversial.[4] Even if artefacts can be certainly identified, they may have been moved from their place of deposition, modified during transportation, separated from the associated material, redeposited and reassociated with items from a different source and/or date. In such circumstances, no behavioural information can be ascertained and it is only the character of the artefacts and their possible age which are accessible.

Material found *in situ* is obviously more useful but may vary enormously in character from discrete clusters incorporating a small number of pieces occurring in isolated scatters or, in groups over a wide area, to high density concentrations containing thousands of artefacts such as Olorgesailie,[5] a 400–700,000-year-old site in Kenya, or Bilzingsleben near Erfurt in Germany, where 350,000-year-old implements and numerous animal bones occur around a thermal spring.[6] Across this range, there will also be varying degrees of disturbance and states of preservation of organic materials such as animal bones. Over the last twenty years, research projects aimed at discerning early human strategies have focused on high-density sites such as FLK (Zinjanthropus) in Olduvai Gorge, Tanzania[7] and FxJj50 at Koobi-Fora, Kenya.[8] Discerning particular activities at such sites can be problematic because the processes involved in their accumulation may not be entirely human.[9] Further, human use of a site may have been episodic and spread over a long period and the concentrations may have been modified by natural factors after deposition. Consequently, the questions addressed tend to be concerned with broad behaviours, such as whether meat was obtained by hunting or scavenging, how carcasses were butchered, where raw materials were obtained, whether sites were occupied seasonally and were bases for groups or transitory camps and whether they were points for central or multiple-place foraging. The individual, whether male or female, is subsumed within these general questions about human activities. Away from or within these concentrations, 'snapshots'[10] or, 'precise moments in time'[11] may occasionally be achieved where discrete scatters of waste flakes can be fitted back together to provide a blow-by-blow account of the reduction of a block of raw material by a single toolmaker to produce one or more implements in a matter of minutes as at FxJj50[8], or the 450,000-year-old

English sites of High Lodge, Suffolk[12] and Boxgrove, Sussex.[13] However, there is nothing in this or the broader studies which will reveal the sex of the knapper. As a result, women's work during the Lower and Middle Palaeolithic has been deduced by recourse to anthropological theories with an admixture of ethnographic parallels and comparisons from primate behavioural studies. The results provide the easily and often justly criticised pictures which illustrate books and museum panels. Understanding the origin of these theories helps in evaluating them and reveals an area of research and communication which requires some new insight from the archaeological side.

BEHAVIOURAL EVOLUTION

Two complementary models of human behavioural evolution have held sway over the last fifty years. Their roots may be traced back into the nineteenth century. They are epitomised by the well-known labels 'Man the Toolmaker'[14] and 'Man the Hunter'.[15] Both enshrine tool use and manufacture as the critical factor in social/behavioural evolution, favouring not only the development of human adaptive strategies but also selection for bipedalism. These models suggest that as forests contracted and savannah grasslands spread in response to climatic change, some primates were driven to finding food on the ground. With hands free to make tools and brandish them as weapons, the slower biped could be a more successful predator. An adaptation to hunting was then assumed to result. These models offered pictures of the imagined lives of our early ancestors which reinforced the male imperative in human evolution. This imperative had deep roots.[16] Darwinism had challenged the biblical creation story but, as Elizabeth Gamble noted in 1894, Darwin ignored facts which he himself adduced about the mental capacities of women and the relative capabilities of the sexes and the advancement of his theories did nothing to shake theological dogma on the natural inferiority of women. A century later, Stonehouse[17] has suggested that this mental block may have stemmed from a misunderstanding of the female role in reproduction which encouraged the view that men were the givers of life and embodied courageous creativity and innovation, while women were simply nurturers. Drawing on the ideas of social theorists such as Spencer and Malthus and reflecting contemporary Victorian *laissez-faire*, self-help values, the followers of Darwin certainly presented human evolution as a competitive struggle for the survival of the fittest male individuals.[18]

The 'Man the Toolmaker/Hunter' models have helped to sustain such concepts even by their titles. Hunting and the technology of its equipment are regarded as male pursuits in modern Western societies and the use of the term 'Man' although simply a translation of the generic *Homo*, is loaded with active versus passive, emotional versus rational connotations[19] which have undoubtedly blinkered perceptions of social evolution and the role of women in technological and cultural activities to the extent that: 'were it not for the fortunate fact that daughters as well as sons inherit their father's genes, the mates of contemporary men would have to be female apes'.[20]

To counteract this view, female-centred interpretations of early human evolution have promoted either female control and adaptation of male

FIG. 1
Palaeolithic woman at work. Illustration by Worthington G. Smith, c. 1887

behaviour, or the need to carry and defend young as a stimulus both to bipedalism and the innovation of tool use by women.[22] The models of 'Woman the Gatherer/Innovator/ Selector of co-operative mates to ensure survival' have become the new face of social palaeoanthropology. However, there are good reasons to be as cautious about these versions of the evolution story as their male-centred predecessors.

As noted above, there is an apparent gap between the appearance of human physiology about four million years ago and the first recognisable signs of an adaptive strategy which requires consistent, patterned effort in making and using tools (technology) in order to sustain life. It is true that improvised or expedient tool use may not survive or be visible in the archaeological record. However, the paucity of evidence for technological activities among our earliest bipedal ancestors undermines the prominent engendered theories of behavioural evolution and their derivatives which attempt to explain physiological changes such as bipedalism, variation in body size between the sexes (sexual dimorphism) and reduction in male canine teeth size, by reference to assumed tool-using adaptive strategies. Furthermore, just as stone artefacts, even when associated with bone debris, cannot be taken as unequivocal evidence of male hunting, they are equally uninformative about our activities. Recent biological research[23] indicates that bipedalism seems to have been a physical adaptation to help regulate body temperature which, in addition to hairlessness, would enable hominids to forage for food for longer periods of the day, so making them more effective predators. Trinkaus[24] also notes that few anatomical characteristics of recent humans can be regarded as the results of the selective pressures of a predatory existence. Consequently, the significance of tool using/making and hunting as assumed in both the male-and female-centred theories of physical and social evolution may have been misconstrued and may offer a misleading view of sex roles in technology. The 'selfish genes' of evolution[25] seem to have been motivated by factors other than subsistence and culture *sensu lato*. Consequently, the origins of the latter are still challenging us for an explanation.[26]

Even when toolmaking and using are clearly represented in the archaeological record (from about two to four million years ago in Africa; one million in Asia and about 500,000 years ago in Europe), it is impossible to say whether there was any sexual division of labour. Clearly, women, as well as men, could and probably did make and use stone tools. This was accepted as long ago as 1887 when John Allen Brown used a picture of a woman flint-knapper by Worthington Smith to illustrate his book on artefacts from north-west Middlesex (Fig. 1). Smith[27] subsequently added more pictures of women, as well as men and women knapping in his own volume although as hunting erroneously came to be understood as the main subsistence activity of early humans, so toolmaking was depicted as a skill passed from father to son,[28] and this view still turns up as, for example, in the otherwise novel 'Flints and Stones' exhibition held at Newcastle-upon-Tyne Museum of Antiquities in 1994. Such depictions minimise the role of women and are misleading. Stone artefacts, even when associated with bone debris, cannot be taken as unequivocal evidence of male hunting[29] nor can it be assumed that women would simply have been responsible for their own needs at base camp. The latter assumption implies that women may have been less mobile than men and that artefact and bone concentrations represent camps where repetitive, interruptible and non-dangerous tasks were carried out by females. Although such male–female task separation has occurred in some recent societies,[30] it is not universal and other models such as independent male and female feeding strategies[31] may offer better explanations for the differences observed between contemporary sites and tool assemblages during the Lower and Middle Palaeolithic. Testing new and more imaginative hypotheses will require the 'development of sound methods for reliable inference'[32] and this may be easier for the more recent period of the Upper Palaeolithic when we are dealing with anatomically modern humans and societies in which 'gender roles and engendered meanings are most likely to have been at work'.[33]

THE UPPER PALAEOLITHIC

Within the general narrative of human evolution, the appearance of fully modern humans heralds the introduction of art and symbolic behaviour, as well as increasingly sophisticated technology, subsistence activities and social organisation. In Europe, the former characteristics are apparent from an early stage, about 34,000 years ago, as modern humans replaced older communities of Neanderthals, whereas the latter characteristics have a slower transition, becoming most evident during the Magdalenian period, between approximately 16,500 and 10,000 years ago. Sites of this period frequently contain tool kits consisting of diverse lithic artefacts, as well as a wide range of equipment made from bone, antler and ivory. In some instances, as at the site of Pincevent, Seine-et-Marne, France,[34] the distribution and organisation of the artefacts suggest the possible use of areas for specialist activities while the refitting of pieces within and between scatters indicates the movement of materials and possibly people around the site. How to question whether these activity areas may be the products of male or female labour is problematic, particularly if stereotyping of sex roles is to

FIG. 2
Female profile engraved
on the base of a lamp,
220mm long. From the
cave of Courbet, France.
c. 12,500 years old
(BM 1864. 12-26. 1124)

be avoided. Indeed, it may be possible only to acknowledge the possibility of a division of labour rather than attempt to define its affects.

Conkey[35] notes this problem in her consideration of Cueto de la Miña, a rock shelter and cave on the Cantabrian coast of Spain. Within the Upper Palaeolithic, Magdalenian level B at this site, there is an extensive bone and antler working industry producing perforated harpoons, needles, awls, batons, perforated deer teeth and shells. Such an assemblage implies not only distant foraging for some of the raw materials but also provides indirect evidence for the processing of hides, vegetable materials, sewing and the production of cordage (string) from animal sinew, hair and vegetable fibres. Cordage was an essential product for use as harpoon lines, sewing thread, netting and necklace thread, as well as having numerous other functions such as in traps or for tying things together. For Conkey, this ignored aspect of Palaeolithic technology could be women's work, but she sees a problem in giving credence to what might be regarded as a stereotypical, enclosing and homogenising role.[36] However, there is some support for her view from the cave site of Courbet in the Aveyron Valley, Penne (Tarn), France. This site contained a Magdalenian assemblage about 12,500 years old.[37] As at Cueto de la Miña, bone and antler artefacts are numerous and include barbed points, fishing equipment, awls, needles, perforated teeth, bone pendants and ivory beads. Among the art objects, there are two engravings of female profiles (Fig. 2)[38] and this form is repeated both in a tiny figurine 24mm high[39] and ivory beads (Fig. 3). A short distance upstream on the opposite bank of the river, a similar assemblage from the rock shelter of Fontalès includes a stylised female engraving, pendants and needles,[40] whereas the nearer shelter of Montastruc[41] contains distinctive material although close in age. Here, the needles are lacking, the personal ornaments include roundels[42] and a fine cut-out (*contour decoupé*) horse head[43] of a kind absent from the other sites. The ivory beads are circular,[44] the only female engraving is stylistically distinctive[45] and there is a small baton engraved with fish which might be considered to have a masculine, phallic form.[46] The cave of La Magdeleine[47] with its wall engravings of reclining female figures is also situated in this valley. The similarities and differences between the ornaments and artefacts and the male and female representations within these sites are only casually observed here but they none the less suggest that localities within the Aveyron Valley may be

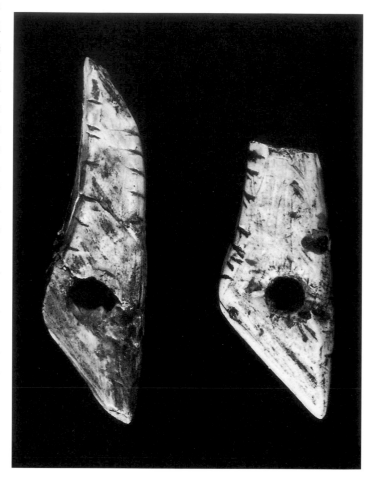

FIG. 3
Ivory beads, 25mm high, echoing the form of the female profile shown in Fig. 2. From the cave of Courbet, France. (BM1864. 12-26. 894, 895)

linked and/or segregated for particular reasons. Traditionally such variations might be explained as ethnic or cultural in origin but they could also be connected and separated by sex roles which may in turn be related to technological and subsistence activities. As such, they would be appropriate candidates for detailed questioning and inference building from this angle. Working outwards from female representations of a different kind also suggests that women may have had active working lives during the earlier part of the Upper Palaeolithic.

SEX OR SELF-IMAGE?

Female figurines and bas-reliefs of the earlier Upper Palaeolithic, between approximately 30,000 and 18,000 years ago, are still often popularly referred to as Venuses. This label sums up the manner in which they have been regarded as erotic images, fertility goddesses, icons of motherhood, totems and items of exchange or communication. As such, they are an example of what Spector[48] has described as 'history subordinated by taxonomic device'[49] which allows them to be regarded as the products of men made for the use of men or the whole community. Looked at individually, these figures can be seen to be representations of individual women,[50] young, mature, obese, slim, pregnant, not pregnant, giving birth, nude, clothed, wearing personal ornaments or without. Many of these figures such as the renowned Willendorf statuette from Austria,[51] the French figures from Brassempouy, Landes,[52] or Lespugue, Haute-Garonne[53] have been described as stylised, exaggerated or distorted, because, observed straight on, the breasts and stomachs appear to be rounded too far forward and the hips and thighs laterally expanded. The upper quadrants of the buttocks just below the waists are high and rounded, while the upper parts of the trunks are narrow and too short in length by comparison with the depth of the buttocks. Viewed from above, these supposed distortions fall into perspective. The foreshortening of the trunk is no longer evident and the form of the breasts and hips appear as they would to a woman looking down or, over her shoulder, at her own body. If this is correct, it would also explain the absence of faces from many figures, the minimal arms and vague hands. If these are images of women made by and for women and/or a wider audience, it would suggest that women were skilled in working soft stone, ivory and bone using stone, bone and antler tools and, by extension, that they may also have made the necklaces, bracelets and clothing to be seen on the same figures. It would also imply that women had well defined roles within the technological, social and ritual lives of their communities, echoing the possibilities suggested by the later sites in the Aveyron Valley and inviting similar questions as to the significance that sites such as Laussel in the Dordogne, France, which contains both male and female bas-reliefs,[54] had in relation to its neighbours.

CONCLUSIONS

Archaeological evidence for the roles of women and men in the technology of the Palaeolithic period is minimal. Theories developed by social anthropologists ignore the limitations of archaeological knowledge and tend to stereotype and homogenise the past in a manner which denies both the behavioural and cultural diversity evident through time and space. The stories they offer about what women did during the Palaeolithic period are matters of opinion and prejudice but we can at least evaluate their fidelity to the facts and we would be poorer without them.[55] Within the museum, as pictures, these stories add vivacity to the empiricism of timescales, tools and ornaments, but perhaps we have gone too far and have begun to mask the intrinsic interest and diversity of ancient artefacts with well-worn clichés which no longer serve a purpose. Perhaps if we were to return to displaying objects within the framework of place and time,[56] we might begin to exhibit the empirical arguments from which we may offer new identities and construct fresh stories of how women and men organised their lives and spent their time. Shortcomings aside, at least archaeology is now beginning to agree with Mark Twain's Adam that it is 'mistaken about Eve…' for, 'it is better to live outside the Garden with her than inside it without her…'.[57] because, 'wheresoever she was, there was Eden'.[58]

ACKNOWLEDGEMENTS

My thanks are due to all those museum visitors, friends and colleagues who have inadvertantly contributed to this paper through informal discussions and especially to A.C. Welté with whom I have collaborated in research on the Courbet material. I am also particularly indebted to the late Professor R. J.C. Atkinson who taught me about the nature and limitations of archaeological evidence and whose lessons have always been so valuable in approaching problems of the kind discussed in this paper. I am also grateful to the Trustees of the British Museum for permission to publish figures 2 & 3.

ENDNOTES

1 Landau, M., 1991.

2 Gero, J. M. and Conkey, M. W., 1991.

3 Leakey, M. D. and Hay, R. L., 1979.

4 Johnson, L. L., 1978; Roebroeks, W. and Van Kolfschoten, T., 1994.

5 Isaac, G. L., 1977.

6 Mania, D. and Weber, T., 1986.

7 Bunn, H. T., 1986; Bunn, H. T. and Kroll, E. M., 1986; Leakey, M. D., 1971; Potts, R., 1988.

8 Bunn, H. T. et al, 1980; Isaac, G. L., 1976; Isaac, G. L. in Leakey, M. D. and Leakey, R. E. F., 1978.

9 Behrensmeyer, K. A., 1987; Binford, L. R., 1981, 1985, 1987; Schick, K. D. and Toth, N., 1993; Stern, N., 1993, *inter alia*.

10 Stern, N., 1993.

11 Roe, D. A., 1980.

12 Ashton, N. M. et al, 1992; Cook, J. and Ashton, N. M., 1991.

13 Roberts, M. B., 1986.

14 Oakley, K. P., 1957, 1949; Washburn, S. L., 1960.

15 Washburn, S. L. and Lancaster, C. S., 1968; Pfeiffer, J., 1978.

16 Gross, M. and Averill, M. B., 1983; Harding, S., 1986; Hubbard, B., 1983; Stonehouse, J., 1994.

17 Stonehouse, J., 1994.

18 Gross, M. and Averill, M. B., 1983; Hubbard, B., 1983.

19 Fee, E., 1981; Nixon, L., 1994; Slocum, S., 1975.

20 Harding, S., 1986, p97.

21 Knight, C., 1991.

22 Dahlberg, F., 1981; Ehrenberg, M., 1989; Gross, M. and Averill, M. B., 1983; Longino, H. and Doell, H., 1983; Slocum, S., 1975; Tanner, N. and Zihlman, A., 1976; Zihlman, A., 1978, 1981.

23 Wheeler, P. E., 1992a, 1992b, 1994.

24 Trinkhaus, E., 1987.

25 Dawkins, R., 1976.

26 Kuper, A., 1994

27 Smith, W. G., 1894.

28 Oakley, K. P., 1949.

29 Binford, L. R., 1985; Longino, H and Doell, H., 1983; Gero, J. M., 1991.

30 Brown, J. A., 1970; Gough, K., 1975.

31 Binford, L. R., 1985.

32 Ibid, p325.

33 Conkey, M. W., 1991, p57.

34 Leroi-Gourhan, A. and Brézillon, M., 1972.

35 Conkey, M. W., 1991.

36 Ibid, p81.

37 Cook, J. and Welté, A-C., in press; Owen, R., 1869.

38 Alaux, J-F., 1972; Cook, J. and Welté, A-C., 1992.

39 Ladier, E., 1988.

40 Darasse, P. and Guffroy, S., 1960.

41 De L'Isle, P., 1867.

42 Sieveking, A., 1987, nos 618–22.

43 Ibid, no. 617.

44 Ladier, E. and Welté, A-C., 1994.

45 Sieveking, A., 1987, no. 566.

46 Ibid, no. 554.

47 Lautier, J. and Bessac, J., 1976.

48 Spector, J. D., 1991.

49 Ibid, p388.

50 Duhard, J-P., 1991; Rice, P. C., 1980.

51 Delporte, H., 1993, fig. 128.

52 Ibid, figs 2–16.

53 Ibid, figs 19, 20.

54 Delporte, H., 1993, pp59–65.

55 Landau, M., 1991, p184.

56 Walsh, K., 1992, pp148–59.

57 Twain, M., 1904, p89.

58 Twain, M., 1906, p109.

WOMEN AS/AND METALWORKERS
Marie-Louise Stig Sørenson

BACKGROUND

'Women as Metalworkers' was the title originally suggested for this contribution. On initially agreeing to cover this topic, I took for granted that the interest indicated should be accepted on its own terms. The title asked indirectly for a different interpretation of Prehistory, and I thought that this need should be respected and satisfied irrespective of its implications, rather than challenged. At a deeper level I also neglected to question whether it is constructive to change the aims of an engendered analysis as a result of exercising it within different contexts of the discipline. On further reflection dissatisfaction with the topic arose and conflicts became apparent. As they are indicative of different ways of approaching engendering the past they are worth outlining as a preamble to this paper.

The wording was in particular felt to be unsatisfactory due to the manner in which it would constrain analysis of women in Prehistory. In fact, it introduced an obvious bias of interpretation. A different version of the topic, namely 'Women and Metalworkers' was therefore developed. This, it was felt, altered in subtle but significant ways the agenda and in doing so it created intellectual space for manoeuvring. The research topics indicated, and analytical procedures needed, differ for the two titles; but both would at present be entirely plausible as themes in museum exhibitions. We can approach, analyse, and display the women of Prehistory in a variety of ways, including different feminist versions. There are several potential voices and different agendas. To illustrate the differences arising from such varied approaches the thinking and the potential answers that the two versions of the title can produce will be briefly outlined. As I personally find the second version the more constructive I will concentrate on discussing women *and* metalworkers in terms of bronze metalworking in the Bronze Age of northern and western Europe.

WOMEN AS METALWORKERS

The topic of 'Women *as* Metalworkers' implies that we know that women were metalworkers and the research topic must accordingly be the analysis of women in that capacity rather than researching their involvement with the technology. In procedural terms this would primarily mean actually finding these women in the archaeological record, or finding the signs of metalworking activities among women. In short, this is about making women visible in a part of the archaeological record that hitherto has been denied them. This suggests that the male association assumed by earlier research can be or has already been challenged and that this aspect of Prehistory is ready for reinterpretation. The first impression of this agenda is that this would be extremely satisfactory.

If, however, these propositions are looked at more critically then certain weaknesses emerge. Metal and the various technologies it involves have certainly uncritically been assumed to be a male affair. The first version of the title suggests that we can now reject this association and propose an alternative feministic interpretation. But can we, or rather, what are the consequences of doing so?

The male association is clearly weak. It is not rooted in data analysis, nor generally supported by any particular evidence, although there may be a few archaeological indications such as supposedly male graves with apparently bronze-working tools. Thus, the assumption of male association comes from outside the archaeological data rather than being generated by them. One root is ethnographic studies, which show that metalworking procedures are predominantly male activities.[1] Another is found in contemporary male stereotypes and in particular the gender associations drawn during the industrial period and the prominent image of male blacksmiths from earlier periods. Both reasons can be criticised. The ethnographic analogies for metalworkers come from cultural contexts which otherwise have very little in common with the European Bronze Age, and they are in no way conclusive either about the general organisation of metalworking or about the gender association of the activities. The male stereotypes, among other weaknesses, are so obviously decontextualised that they have no value whatsoever. In addition, iron technology, to which these stereotypes and analogies relate, is an activity substantially different from bronze working, and it is only known ethnographically from societies that are organised very differently from those of the European Bronze Age.

The assumption that metalworkers in the Bronze Age were necessarily males can therefore be rejected and challenged relatively easily; but is it equally easy to put women in their place, or must we for now conclude – and I should like to stress that this in itself is an important and constructive result – that we do not know how metalworking activities were gendered, and therefore should not aim to state whether the metalworkers were male or female?

The call for critical awareness concerning assumptions used, stereotypes and biases should, if consistently applied, also make us accept that based on present archaeological data it can not be established whether women were metalworkers in the sense that the title originally proposes. This negative answer is, however, possibly a result of the way the topic – despite its contrary intentions – was worded. I believe that the thinking arising from and the assumptions embedded in this version of the title (and many similar topics) to some extent will lead us down a blind alley. In particular it will reproduce sexist views of labour organisation that may be both andro- and ethnocentric, and it will force us either to propose unsupportable conclusions or, alternatively, to appear unable to reach an engendered understanding of this important aspect of Bronze Age society.

On this basis I found that a more constructive, in a way more ambitious, approach would consist of considering women *and* metalworkers. This approach by its very nature can not produce as absolute and as easily presentable results as the first can; but I trust that modern museums find it possible to communicate and activate an engendered understanding of the past rather than being satisfied with simple cartoon versions of its social organisation.

WOMEN AND METALWORKERS

If, as an alternative strategy, the topic is approached in terms of women and metalworkers, then we start from a point of knowing that both of these groups existed, and that in their co-existence they must in different ways have influenced each other. It is furthermore possible to investigate these relationships further, and in particular to explore how and in which ways the various activities and production sequences involved in metalworking affected women's lives. The central question of this approach becomes how women integrated with the social and material aspect of this important technology. In terms of a feminist archaeology the obvious strength of this manner of investigation is that the prehistoric women can be maintained centrally in our research independently of whether they were the metalworkers. By avoiding the absolutism of the first formulation, this approach erases the risk of failure. Centralising women in this manner, and securing their presence in our research agendas and interpretations of the past, will, however, have certain costs. Primarily, this approach will be less about taking over the past or of replacing men. Prehistoric women will not necessarily emerge from it as equal to men in the past, but they will share if not take the centre stage in the analysis. In other words a Prehistory of extremes, where women either 'are' or 'are-not' (which can produce very effective politicised interpretations), is replaced by a multicoloured past in which women participate by definition but are not guaranteed access to all roles and values.

The following brief outline of how these issues can be explored through the data has taken its inspiration from an analytical procedure or 'investigation mentality' used by Conkey.[2] Her discussion of the Magdalenian Period aims to break a similar deadlock in our attempts at redefining the role of women in the Palaeolithic. The aim is not to establish women in particular roles or to assign them special characteristics but rather to reach an engendered engagement with the technology in question.

For the present purpose this means understanding the range of activities involved in metalworking, and how at different levels they constitute contexts which interact with gender politics. Metalworking involves a range of more or less centralised activities from prospecting, producing firewood and charcoal, to shaping and decorating the objects. Unless we have reason to believe that all of these activities were rigidly circumscribed and detached from other activities and that they were carried out by isolated male-exclusive groups then they would habitually overlap, interrelate, clash with, be dependent on etc — in various ways relate to — a range of other activities. To the extent the society had sexual division of labour, gender roles and ideological norms, these activities would have a gender element. The limited scope of this paper, allows only an explorative consideration of these issues and the following will therefore be restricted to a discussion based on the moulds used for the casting of bronze objects.

ENGENDERING BRONZE WORKING

Our understanding of prehistoric bronze working, both in terms of activities involved, technological knowledge and the organisation of its production, is generally reached through investigations of the remains of the finished objects and the instruments used in their production. While the former are habitually associated with humans in burials, the latter and for the present purpose more important type of evidence, is rarely directly associated with individuals. The itinerant smiths that Childe and others described[3] are therefore largely a theoretical construct. There are in fact very few graves where conventional ideas of the meaning of gravegoods make it possible to describe them as being of smiths. There are therefore no obvious correlations between items such as moulds and men or women. The 'maleness' of these objects and the activities in which they were involved is assumed.

With regard to exhibitions on technology and the desire to engender museum displays, another issue of importance is that items such as moulds are visually rather boring and indistinct. Their importance is as evidence and this cannot be immediately observed. Even their function needs mediation through texts, figures or reconstructions. As broken, indistinct parts of general settlement debris they are a substantial challenge to the museum designers. They are important, but they do not speak for themselves. So far, museum displays typically use these objects passively. Moulds may be involved as part of a theme on technology, but there is generally little attempt at empowering the public's understanding of their social importance and they have remained absent from an engendered past or even gender-sympathetic displays.

Despite what is shown in most museums the find contexts of moulds do in fact place them solidly within the living society. Recent settlement excavations in northern and western Europe have increasingly demonstrated the presence of mould fragments, crucibles etc, as part of the settlement matrix and in the later part of the Bronze Age particularly as part of the general midden refuse.[4] These Bronze Age settlements at the same time do not seem to be structured according to specific activity areas, and the impression gained is rather of metalworking being included as a regular but not clearly structured activity within the settlement area generally but outside the structures themselves. This suggests that metalworking was not spatially differentiated from other ongoing activities within the life of the settle-ments, nor did it involve structures, such as hearths, that were permanently maintained and marked as separate entities.

This simple and well-known observation has two important implications. First, it challenges the model of the wandering bronzesmith,[5] and it places metalworking activities within the group.[6] While the former model was thought of, and possibly rightly so, in terms of males, the latter interpretation has no such implication. Second, being a local, regular activity it would impinge on everyone in the settlement, redirecting labour away from other tasks while the casting was done. In the small-scale, extended-family situation, documented by the settlement evidence, it is highly likely that women as well as men were involved in this project. The casting would furthermore have interfered with other activities, as it cannot be broken up into different stages but must be conducted in one event. Negotiation of the event would therefore have taken place as part of its planning, and in that its relationship to a range of unrelated but potentially interfering activities would be of importance.

Another interesting aspect of the moulds, which has unexpected implications for gender, is that they are generally made of clay, often apparently from local sources and with little preparation. Clay and clay-related activities, at the same time, are usually assumed to be domestic activities and these are most often associated with women. So should this mean that women shaped the moulds, and thus in effect decided upon the appearance of bronze objects? If not, then males made the moulds, but does it then follow that men produced all the objects made by similar simple techniques from the same local clay sources, such as loom weights and ovens? This would involve males in traditional domestic activities. Or did men and women produce different categories of things from the same material? If so, how was this decided upon, how did this affect the prospecting for clay sources and bringing it to the settlement area, and how was the firing of these different categories of objects planned?

The practical aspects of the fabrication of moulds, together with the logic inherent in the assumptions we have been using, show clearly that the gender association of the moulds and their use could have been constructed in different ways. One extreme could be caused by contemporary gender ideology rigidly assigning gendered value to the objects, their associated technologies and their use, while another could have arisen from the cultural merging of the value (and the production) of different clay items due to their interdependence in the practical processes.

To conclude, the very simple evidence provided by the material and technology of the moulds suggests a number of possible alternative relationships that would all, but in different ways, have affected people's ideational as well as practical understanding and experience of the contemporary gender ideology. The alternatives can be outlined as follows:

IF CLAY TECHNOLOGIES ARE WOMEN'S WORK

THEN **Women shaped the moulds**
 Women designed the types

THEREFORE **Women worked with firing**
 Women did prospecting
 Women made objects used by males

IF MEN SHAPED THE MOULDS

THEN **Clay technologies were not exclusively women's domain**
 Men designed the types
 Men made objects used by women

THEREFORE **Men participated in domestic activities**

IF HOWEVER   CLAY TECHNOLOGIES ARE NOT GENDER-EXCLUSIVE

    THEN   **Different stages of the production were gender exclusive**

    OR

    THERE WAS   **No gendered division of labour**

    THEREFORE **The production was dependent on the co-operation of gender groups**
The planning of production involved negotiation around gender divisions and ideologies.

CONCLUSION

In conclusion I should like to propose that this simple exercise in engendering our thinking about an aspect of bronze technology suggests that this activity probably was a team effort, and that in different ways it affected the whole settlement population. More importantly, however, this paper also demonstrates the danger of enclosure created by certain ways of wording our aims. Our task should not be to demonstrate that women were present in (Pre)history, nor should we painstakingly try to appropriate certain practices and technologies as women's. Rather, knowing that both women and men were present, we should aim to explore and understand how the organisation of these various productive technologies affected both men and women and their relationship. Such approaches would secure but not predict women's presence in the past and it should make it possible to include apparently non-gendered items, such as clay moulds, in our exploration of gender relations of the past. Through this appropriate sources available for gender research would expand vastly.

ENDNOTES

1   Rowlands, M., 1971.

2   Conkey, M. V., 1991.

3   Childe, V. G., 1940, p118.

4   Needham, S. P. and Sørensen, M. L. S., 1988.

5   Childe, V. G., 1940.

6   Pearce, S., 1983.

WOT! NO DINOSAURS?

INTERPRETATION OF PREHISTORY AND A NEW GALLERY AT THE MUSEUM OF LONDON

Barbara Wood

Presented at the 1994 WHAM conference, this paper discussed museum presentations of 'Women in Industry and Technology' with particular reference to the Museum of London's original Prehistoric Gallery which opened in 1976 and the plans for a major redesign which had then reached the early stages of on-site construction. As the new exhibition has since opened (November 1994), the latter part of this discussion now considers the gallery as it currently exists.

'Wot! No Dinosaurs?'; a flippant title, or the reaction of many visitors to an exhibition about human 'Prehistory'?

In visitor research carried out at the Museum of London in 1992, prior to the closure of the original gallery, when asked, 'Can you tell us what you associate with the word "prehistoric"?', nearly thirty per cent of visitors replied, 'Dinosaurs'. Additionally, six per cent replied. 'Animals or monsters', other answers included 'Bones', 'Barbarism', 'Jungles', and 'The Flintstones', as well as a minority of more accurate responses.[1] Unfortunately, as dinosaurs were extinct sixty-three million years before recognisable human beings existed, they did not feature in the galleries of the Museum which were (and are) devoted to the human and social history of the area now approximately defined by the M25 motorway. The answers given to this question were of particular concern as the respondents were replying after, and not before, they had visited the Museum.

Once it becomes clear that there are no dinosaurs on offer, it may be expected that visitor expectations of a prehistoric gallery in terms of entertainment, or even educational value, will be low.[2] It is likely that any ideas of what the gallery will be about will focus on dinosaurs, rocks, geology and 'man the hunter',[3] if on anything at all.[4] This general lack of pre-visit knowledge was unintentionally summarised by remarks made by the teacher leading a group of 'A' Level students to the Museum of London who was heard to advise them: 'The museum is chronological, the first gallery is prehistoric ... don't spend too much time in there; it's just about geology ...'

We can be clear that the majority of visitors to our museums have no concept of how long humans like ourselves have existed, or where and how they lived. The reasons for this lack of pre-visit knowledge may be many, but one current cause for concern is the lack of inclusion of Prehistory within the National Curriculum in its present form. Although possible to work within history syllabus options such as 'Invaders and Settlers' or within technology and art modules, this presupposes that teachers possess relevant knowledge. Having themselves been educated in a system which frequently excludes Prehistory we can clearly not assume that this will happen. Unlike other historical periods which acquire some kind of familiarity through costume dramas on television and stage, or the 'good old days' which grandparents may remember, Prehistory is a period which many people do not know existed. Before we can begin to consider how prehistoric galleries interpret the role of women with reference to the earliest technologies, it may therefore be relevant to first consider how, or even if, women are presented within such exhibitions.

A consideration of some of the images of women which have appeared in museum galleries and both academic and popular books provides an interesting starting point. From the earliest attempts at artistic representations

FIG. 1
'An Acheulian family in the Thames Valley'.
Sarah Platts-Mills
(The Museum of London)
1976

of prehistoric life, right up to images commissioned over the last few years, a consistency can be seen in artwork design, apparent in the unchanging basic structure of social groups and in the roles and importance implied for each sex within that group. The importance of individuals and the tasks they perform, suggestions of power, subservience, value, even intelligence are conveyed to the viewer both explicitly and implicitly.

The images of a Palaeolithic family group, featured in many museums and popular books, and intended to depict the life of our immediate ancestor *Homo erectus* provide a simple example. The pictures are frequently very similar, showing an extended family group, with many (perhaps too many) activities taking place. A large number of such images exists, but here I have taken as an example two which were commissioned by the Museum of London. Consider the messages being conveyed by these pictures. The first (Fig. 1) is an illustration used in the original Museum gallery in 1976. A group is centred around two male figures who by their positioning within the image, size and involvement in focused activity dominate the group. One is in the process of making a tool or weapon, an activity which suggests strength, skill and acquired learning. Similarly the second seems to be removing meat from an animal, presumably to provide food for the other group members. The woman remains behind the men, and appears slightly smaller. She's shown breastfeeding, an exercise not requiring this kind of learning and expertise, a mother in a domestic setting. Compare this with the second image (Fig. 2), an illustration commissioned for the book *Prehistoric London* in 1990.[5] Note the placing of individuals and the similarity of the activities in which they are engaged. The attention of the viewer is still focused upon a male toolmaker. The female is shown breastfeeding a child, again sitting at a lower level and placed behind the male figure. This typical Palaeolithic domestic scene can be traced in both literature and exhibitions right up to the present, with numerous examples.[6] Images of other prehistoric periods may be similarly deconstructed.

However, it is not necessarily that the ideas of the curators who commission such images remain unchanged, or that new thinking and information have not been included. There are women (and also children) included to a much greater extent in the later image. Rather, what is lacking may be an understanding by the curators of the information which they are supplying to their audience. Women are present, and although there is a 'breastfeeding woman' in her usual position, women are active in other roles. One is shown gathering foodstuffs in a sack, and one is helping to carry the results of a hunting expedition. However, they frequently remain unnoticed because their presence is unexpected and because they are placed on the periphery, away from the focus of attention. As visitors or readers skim across images, implicit messages are not enough. In order to suggest interpretations, information must be explicit.

Once the visual representations of Prehistory are brought into question, it becomes clear, particularly as the majority of visitors are unlikely to read much exhibition text,[7] how a misrepresentation is created and perpetuated.

In larger-scale representations women are frequently seriously under-represented or disappear completely. A view of the Iron Age hill fort at

FIG. 2
'Swanscombe 350,000BC. Early Hunters in the Thames Valley'. *Derek Lucas* (The Museum of London) 1990

Maiden Castle in Dorset, published in the children's book *Now Then. Digging up the Past*,[8] showed thirty-seven figures. If we assume that the women will be perceived as the figures shown wearing dresses and the men trousers, there are eight figures who cannot be identified. Of the remainder, there are twenty-two men thatching, fighting, riding horses, looking after animals, digging or 'striding purposefully', and one boy who is running and waving a stick. Of the seven figures who will, at first glance, be perceived as female, two stand close by two men who are seemingly in conversation; the women are turned away both from this focus and from each other. Another two walk alone, carrying buckets and a sack; two stand in the distance apparently chatting to single male figures; one stands alone in a doorway. Not only are they in a minority, but their activities are clearly less active and for five women, solitary, suggesting less involvement and importance.

When women appear alone they often perpetuate the ideas of European male archaeologists of the earlier twentieth century, who drew on the lives of 'primitive' peoples (as they perceived them) in other parts of the world for models to suggest how prehistoric societies might have functioned. Women may be shown weaving, cooking, occupied with mirrors, jewellery and, of course, children. Their activities are described with adjectives and passive language. By contrast men appear in active roles: hunting, farming, chopping wood and making tools. Likewise the language used to describe their activities is also active, employing verbs. This use of language, first perhaps evident in textbooks, creeps into museum text and labels.

Where women and men appear together, relationships and the importance of individuals are made obvious, whether intentionally or not, by the stature and position of figures and by the objects which they hold. The models of prehistoric (and later) families displayed at Jewry Wall Museum in Leicester are a well-known example. Within these families, men may be placed forward of the women and appear larger, as in the Bronze Age group. They may look confidently outwards, while the attention of women is directed towards children and partners as in the Mesolithic, Neolithic and Bronze Age families. Men carry weapons or the tools of activities undertaken outside the home, such as a fishing spear, while women carry children, or tools with domestic connotations, spindle, bucket or a small basket of grain.

Focusing the discussion on to the subject of 'Industry and Technology', it can be difficult to find references to women at all in the displays and text devoted to the traditional 'industries' of Prehistory, these usually being exhibited as stone, bronze and iron working. Women do appear in displays about pottery, although this has sometimes been justified by the irrational reasoning that women were producers of pottery because they have more patience than men. However, their patience is obviously limited, as it is often the men who are pictured firing pottery. Women also appear weaving, a task which is never given the value it would have merited in societies where cloth was the result of many hours of labour; but they are very rarely seen to be doing anything connected with the objects which form the bulk of our displays, stone and metal technologies. The recently opened gallery 'Comers in. Early Settlement in the Huddersfield District' at the Tolson Memorial Museum in Huddersfield included a figure of a Mesolithic woman knapping flint. This image was considered so unusual that it achieved national press coverage through the pages of the *Museums Journal*.[9] However, there is nothing in the archaeological evidence to suggest that she would have been unusual in any way in her own time.

Stone and metal are important, and, with the addition of pottery, they are almost the only remains of the material culture of prehistoric times and form the core of our displays. Chelmsford Museum, for example, headlines part of its recently-refurbished Prehistoric Gallery 'Metal!'. How do we start to make women part of displays dealing with these subjects and how do we encourage interest in such exhibits?

Perhaps we should start by confirming that we do not have evidence for who made anything in Prehistory. The allocation of responsibilities or acquiring of skills may have had as much to do with rites of passage, superstition, age, family 'trade', or tribal specialisation as with gender.

A brief example which illustrates how little we may know of those cultures that we have the responsibility to present, comes from the Iñupiaq people of Alaska.[10] Although both men and women hunt, track, handle dogs etc, and while the skill or information which one person can provide is more important than that person's sex, there are gendered divisions of labour in what Bodenhorn describes as 'subsistence activities'. Men, for example, will make and maintain tools and equipment although women may also own and purchase tools. Men are responsible for hunting, for although women may sometimes hunt they are primarily responsible for processing the meat and hide of the captured animals.

While a less than perceptive observer with current Western preconceptions would perhaps place greater value on the male role, the Iñupiaq do not perceive a difference in the value of the tasks involved or a difference in the value of the contribution of male or female. The roles are of equal merit and importance, for how could one activity exist without the other and why would one exist without the other? The values of a different people, whether ancient or modern are not necessarily the same as our own, nor are roles always simply divided into useful – less useful; important – unimportant; valued – not of value.

To focus on the Prehistoric Gallery in the Museum of London: until its closure in May 1994 the displays were essentially those created in 1976 when the Museum opened. The gallery presented a chronothematic history of the period of settlement in the London area before the Roman foundation of Londinium in AD 50. The objects were used as illustrations of that story. The gallery was very well received when the Museum opened, but obviously over the last two decades ideas and theories have changed and new information has become available. Our knowledge of prehistoric activity in the area now covered by London has expanded dramatically through the work of field archaeologists, while research considering the use of galleries by visitors is available to inform exhibition construction and design.

Tracking studies carried out in the old gallery in August 1991[11] showed that a quarter of the people who entered the Prehistoric Gallery walked straight through, perhaps drawn by the unintended focal point: a full-size statue of a Roman soldier at the entrance to the Roman Gallery. Only one-third of visitors to the Museum spent any time in the Prehistoric Gallery and of these only one-tenth spent more than ten minutes. Only ten per cent of visitors looked at any case for over three minutes.

It was assumed that the reason for these figures was partly due to a lack of structure within the gallery and the lack of a clear route for use. The figures may also reflect the often 'typological' approach to the display of unfamiliar material compounded by the large amount of text (approximately 10,000 words) on the walls, which perhaps combined to put off the many visitors who were encountering Prehistory for the first time.

When the curators working on the gallery began to look afresh as new displays were considered, many issues were discussed. Looking at the old displays, our gallery presented many of the traditional views of Prehistory and had probably contributed to some strange ideas of prehistoric life. 'Settlers by the Thames', an exhibit which included a Mesolithic shelter, was an obvious example. Intended to be a section of a model of a shelter, it actually looked like impractical accommodation for very small people, as it contained full-size arrows and tools. The Bronze Age 'loom' had also caused confusion. Described as 'dismantled', and with no image to explain either construction or use, it looked like a bundle of sticks – which is what it was! Language was dated, using terms such as 'man' and 'mankind', and as far as people were featured, women and men remained in traditional roles. Such an awareness of the gallery was not confined to the curators. Comment slips returned by visitors mentioned outdated language and the absence of women.

As the aims and objectives of the new exhibition were considered, there was a clear recognition of the difficulties of presenting Prehistory as discussed above. Hopefully aware of the problems and with the knowledge that this was only the second of fourteen galleries that the visitor might see, we were concerned to clearly define the intended aims and objectives of the gallery. These will be summarised elsewhere[12] but one of the most important was to show viable and fully functioning societies. A Prehistory which included women, children and older people as well as men and to show those usually under-represented groups in positive and active roles.

In an attempt to achieve the stated aims, the new gallery has been divided into two parts. Unable to change the existing 'corridor' shape and function of the gallery, we have endeavoured to use this form in a more structured way. Believing that a chronological approach to Prehistory is the clearest form of presentation for visitors, one side of the gallery is now used to tell the 'narrative' of the history of settlement in London, while the inner wall has become a central thread dealing with technologies.

Commissioned especially for the gallery, new models and artwork now intersperse full-size dioramas and object-based cases, adding life and context. All models and images were discussed and researched at length with the artists involved. The numbers of figures and their gender, age and positioning were individually considered, as were activities, clothing and even hairstyles. These discussions threw up many challenges as we attempted to show a Prehistory with more positive gender images. For example, most of the women in the gallery are now shown wearing dresses. This has already provoked some interesting questions. In fact, after experiments by artists and modelmakers and discussion among the curators, it seemed the only way to make immediately clear the male and female figures.

The dioramas contain both original and replica objects in an attempt to put back the missing materials of Prehistory; textiles, wood, grasses, animal products and foodstuffs. We have tried to make links to the past by illustrating that the full range of materials and technologies familiar to us today were available then, even if used in different ways. Within the 'Technology' sections we have been more explicit, with modern equivalents placed alongside ancient objects. For example, a beer glass is displayed with a Bronze Age beaker, a Swiss army knife with a flint hand axe and some crushed aluminium cans with an ancient hoard of scrap metal. 'Touch' sections provide an extra dimension of experience.

All the cases have titles. 'Masterpieces in Metal' is the only point where text may seem, at first sight, gender-specific. This is a case devoted to particularly impressive examples of metalwork. After much thought, we could think of no feasible alternative to 'Masterpieces'. However, we hope that even here there is a balance achieved. As in the rest of the gallery, there is no presumption made about who made these objects and, apart from the case title, no gender-specific terminology. Included are beautiful armrings, pins and brooches as well as swords and daggers. Any item could have been used by either sex.

From the use of painted backgrounds, lighting and a sound track of bird song to create a precise atmosphere, to the images of the people of Prehistory, this gallery will, we hope, begin to make connections for visitors between the present and the past. Modern photographs and maps locate the excavated sites around which the gallery is based and many visitors recognise familiar streets or landmarks. We have tried to bring the past alive with illustrations which show the people of Prehistory as individuals. We hope that the images we have used show our ancestors as intelligent and focused.

FIG. 3
'Early People in the Thames Valley'. *Derek Lucas* (The Museum of London) 1994

Finally, an important element in the process of involving our visitors is a panel set at the beginning of the gallery entitled 'Can you believe what we say?' This is an attempt to speak directly to the visitor. Using both images and text, we describe how archaeology deals with only 'shreds' of evidence. We are only interpreting fragmentary remains. Other people, including the visitor, may interpret information differently. Here we are also able to make the point that interpretation has often reflected the experiences of the curator, archaeologist or illustrator. As an example, three images are used to show how women have been marginalised and stereotyped in earlier archaeological interpretations. We also acknowledge the biases and preoccupations of our own time.

This approach has been echoed around the gallery. We have tried to present the evidence we have and then interpret it. Where there is more than one possible explanation, alternatives are given. Questions are also raised, encouraging the visitor to formulate his or her own opinions.

As the visitor leaves the gallery a final panel asks the question, 'Now what does Prehistory mean to you?' In contrast to the entrance, which is dominated by a 'noble savage', Raquel Welch in fur bikini, an 'apeman' and dinosaurs as 'stereotypes' of Prehistory, this panel uses figures chosen from the artwork used in the gallery to try and emphasise the point that Prehistory is the history of real people.

We have tried hard to question our language, our presentation and the people who we put in our gallery. We hope that we now show women, children and older people in active and positive roles. There even appears a new and hopefully improved version of the Palaeolithic group as discussed above! (Fig. 3).

Today no one would suggest that there is only one view of the past, and evidence is open to many interpretations. However, we are still presented in our museums with societies which are little more than reflections of the experiences of a European man of the nineteenth or twentieth century. The possibilities are far more interesting and our displays should attempt to portray this. What really were the values of prehistoric people and how can we judge? It is up to those presenting Prehistory to stop perpetuating ideas for which there is no basis. We need to think about what a display will tell an audience, and question the information that visitors will take away with them. Whatever is in a case or on a panel is what will be believed. Take a second look at how collections are used. Particularly with Prehistory, we must work with the collections we already have, but perhaps we should be using them in different ways.

ACKNOWLEDGEMENTS

With thanks to Jonathan Cotton and Judith Stevenson for reading drafts of this paper and for useful discussion.

ENDNOTES

1   Unpublished visitor research, Museum of London, 1992.

2   Merriman, N., 1991.

3   Unpublished visitor research, Museum of London, 1992.

4   David R. Prince and R. T. Schadla-Hall, 'The Image of the Museum: a Case Study of Kingston upon Hull', *Museums Journal*, 85(2), pp39–45.

5   Merriman, N., 1990, p10.

6   See, for example: Stephen Green and Elizabeth Walker, *Early Modern Hunters in Wales*, figs 4, 5, National Museum of Wales, 1991; Alex Morrison, *Early Man in Britain and Ireland*, jacket illustration of 'Starr Carr 8th Millennium' by Alan Sorrell, Croom Helm, London, 1980; Murial Goaman with illustrations by Frank Hampson, *Through the Ages: Food*, a Ladybird Easy-Reading book, Wills and Hepworth Ltd, Loughborough, 1968, p9; Marjorie Maitland Howard, Henry Hodges and Edward Pyddoke, *Ancient Britons*, John Baker, London, 1969, pp13, 25.

7   For summaries of work see: Pearce, S., 1990; Victor Kanel and Pinchal Tamir, 'Different Labels – Different Learnings', *Curator*, 34/1, 1991.

8   Francis Pryor with David Collison, *Now Then. Digging up the Past*, B. T. Batsford Ltd, London, p21.

9   'Openings', *Museums Journal*, February 1994, p22.

10   Bodenhorn, B., 1993.

11   Unpublished visitor research, Museum of London, 1991.

12   Cotton, J., forthcoming; Cotton, J. and Wood, B., forthcoming.

CHAPTER 2

FRAGMENTARY EVIDENCE FROM ROMAN BRITAIN

THE ACTRESS AND THE BISHOP:
EVIDENCE FOR WORKING WOMEN IN ROMAN BRITAIN
Lindsay Allason-Jones

An apology is due for the title of this paper. It is usually possible to resist the temptation to use facetious titles but on this occasion the temptation was too great, as there are only two pieces of epigraphic evidence for women working in Roman Britain: one is a piece of graffiti from Leicester which refers to one Verecunda, actress and girlfriend of Lucius, a gladiator;[1] the other an altar dedicated by Diodora, a priestess of the cult of Heracles of Tyre at Corbridge.[2] Is this a full picture of the work pattern of the women in Roman Britain? It would seem unlikely that the women living in Roman Britain were either unemployed or employed only at the extremes of the saints and sinners spectrum. For a more balanced view we must look for evidence elsewhere.

First, what is the evidence for working women in other parts of the Roman Empire? A number of women are recorded at Pompeii with an indication of their professions. Unfortunately, much of this evidence comes from graffiti, so again this will not provide a very balanced view. Women working in the textile industry are well attested – at least ten female weavers are mentioned at Pompeii while three more are listed as working as laundresses in a fuller's shop. Three women bakers are mentioned, although it is not clear if they made the bread or sold it. Also in the food industry were Capella Bacchis, Prima and Edoné who were waitresses, although Capella Bacchis and Prima had a sideline in prostitution.[3] A woman called both Palmyra and Sitifera served at the counter of Ermes.[4]

Some of the working women recorded at Pompeii were in positions of some responsibility. Ascula and Pherusa were tavern owners and would have employed others,[5] while Fortunata, Caprasia, Pollia and Asellina were manageresses of thermopolia – taverns specialising in hot drinks.[6] One woman, called Faustilla, referred to on the walls of a gambling den, was a moneylender.[7]

Priestesses are also mentioned, although the evidence for their existence tends to be via altars rather than graffiti – Eumachia, for example, was designated as a public priestess while Biria was referred to as a prophetess.[8] Six other priestesses are known by name from Pompeii, three of whom served the goddess Ceres.

As much of the evidence from Pompeii comes from graffiti on the walls of public houses and brothels it is hardly surprising that at least sixty-three prostitutes and madams are recorded. Clearly Pompeii, although adding a few professions, such as weavers and waitresses, to the list of those undertaken by women in the Roman Empire, is not going to help the picture to any great extent – there is still a bias towards the two career extremes, although it does, perhaps, put Britain into perspective. If the sources are graffiti and altars, one should not be surprised if the professions referred to are prostitutes and priestesses.

Sculpture on the Italian mainland in the first century AD has provided more detail than that from Britain between the first and fourth centuries, and from Ostia a more balanced picture begins to emerge. The Via Ostiensis sarcophagus illustrates a children's nurse and a terracotta relief from the Isola Sacra indicates an *obstetrix*.[9] Barmaids are still to be found, as on the Isola Sacra sarcophagus, but the Ostia Episcopo relief gives evidence of a vegetable seller, the Via della Foce relief offers a poultry seller while a female shoemaker may be indicated on another relief.[10]

Tombstones at Ostia also provide extra information: we get references to Abudia Megiste, who sold grains and pulses at the Middle Stairs; Pollecla, who sold barley on the Via Nova; Atinia Tyrannis, who sold seed goods at the Porta Triumphalis; and Aurelia Nais, who sold fish in the warehouses of Galba.[11] Unnamed but still recorded are female sellers of purple, sellers of ointments, a bean seller, a seller of bottles, a dealer in resins, a fisherwoman and another baker.

A source of information which is always worth trawling is Justinian's *Digest*. This may not always give names, but it does reveal whole groups of workers whose activities were regulated by law. For example, it is from the *Digest* that we learn that in the *familia rustica* there were women whose function it was to cook food other than bread for the slaves, while others just baked the bread.[12] There were also female slaves and freedwomen called *lanipendi* who portioned out the work for spinning women and supervised the spinning, weaving and clothes making and, by implication, there were women employed in these pursuits.[13] The spinners (*lanificae*) are also mentioned in the *Digest* in the legacy of an estate where they are among the *instrumenta* – that is, they were part of the owner's equipment, as were the maids who made clothing for his slaves.

Many of the women mentioned in the *Digest* are slaves or freedwomen; in particular, weavers, repairers of garments, maids and the *focariae* – the women who kept the fires going for bakers, fullers, etc – could be either slaves or freedwomen.

Roman literature also pads out the information. Plautus, for example, discusses the women who made and applied cosmetics, and Servius refers to a female hairdresser.[14] An Italian tombstone also mentions a hairdresser and is decorated with a comb and a hairpin.[15]

Soranus and Tacitus both mention wet-nurses, midwives, nannies and the like. Tacitus made some adverse comments about the Romans' use of wet-nurses and was firmly of the belief that Roman women should follow the Celtic practice of suckling their own children.[16] Soranus presumes the use of wet-nurses and his list of the essential virtues of the perfect wet-nurse includes details as to the shape and condition of her breasts, physical condition and moral character, and particularly recommended that she be a Greek 'so that the infant should become accustomed to the best speech'.[17] Wet-nurses were either slaves or freedwomen and their contract usually lasted for two years, during which time they might either live in the mother's house or take the child into their own home. Wet-nurses often continued in the role of nanny after the child had been weaned. Despite Tacitus's dislike of the practice, the tombstone of the wet-nurse Severina from Cologne indicates that wet-nursing was known in the north-west provinces as well as in the Mediterranean area.[18]

Midwives were also a widespread phenomenon and several of Italian and Gallic origin are known by name, such as Claudia Trophima and Poblicia Aphe.[19] Soranus also gave instructions concerning a good midwife and listed among their attributes short fingernails and long fingers as well as strength of body and mind.[20] As Roman medical practices developed so the role of the midwife was extended – often midwives were well-read women who had trained in many branches of female medicine and treated various gynaecological conditions as well as attending at births. At Metz in Germany a tombstone records the career of a female doctor and references in Juvenal and Martial suggest that she was not unusual.[21]

The evidence of the law codes makes it clear a woman could learn skills while a slave – those listed include spinning, weaving, midwifery and metalworking – and continue to practice her craft after manumission. There was some argument among the legal profession as to whether a former slave could set up in business in direct competition with her former owner. The jurist Papinian pronounced that, in his opinion, 'a freedwoman is not considered ungrateful because she practices her trade against the wishes of her patron'.[22]

Keith Bradley, in his survey of child labour in the Roman world, has looked at apprentice documents which survive from Roman Egypt. In these children are handed over to a master craftsman for a specific period of time in order to learn a trade. A number of these are girls, some as young as one to four years old. In Britain we do not have any apprentice documents but it is possible that Mercatilla — the freedwoman and foster daughter of Magnius, who died at the age of eighteen months at Bath — may have been the subject of a similar deal.[23]

Documentary evidence surviving in Italy and Egypt indicates both girls and boys being apprenticed at the later age of twelve or thirteen, but only the sons and daughters of those of freed status or slaves: freeborn girls, even from the poorest families, do not appear to have been trained for a career in any formal way. Free women seem to have been expected to adapt themselves to be helpful in the family business. Little evidence has been found for free women working in a Mediterranean province except as priestesses, or rather, little evidence for working women making their free status clear.

Where does this leave us in Britain? The epigraphic evidence is still confined to the inscriptions of Verecunda and Diodora; what other evidence is there?

Justinian's *Digest* provides one scrap, albeit a bizarre scrap. It refers to an anonymous female slave of Marcus Cocceius Firmus, centurion of the Second Legion Augusta at Auchendavy.[24] She was condemned to cook for the convicts at the salt mines as punishment for an unspecified crime. While serving out her sentence she was captured by 'bandits of an alien race' and sold. Cocceius Firmus bought her back but took the Imperial Treasury to court to sue for the repurchase price on the grounds that the State should have taken better care of his property while she was in its charge. This case is usually quoted to prove that centurions could own slaves, but in the context of this discussion it can be taken as evidence for female cooks in Britain, even if not voluntary cooks.

Illustrations of women working on mosaics, wall painting and pottery etc, can be ambiguous. If one takes the view that such objects were produced according to pattern books then one can argue that any illustrations can only be evidence for activities having taken place at the source of the design rather than necessarily at the findspot. However, it is unlikely that such illustrations would have been totally alien to the purchasers. Regrettably, none of the activists illustrated on Romano-British mosaics can be identified as a working mortal woman, as opposed to a working deity, but the pot from Water Newton showing a female acrobat should not be forgotten.[25]

There has been much discussion as to the validity of assigning occupation on the grounds of skeletal evidence, but the implication that Romano-British women led active lives with a great deal of lifting and physical work, which took its toll on their bone structure, is supported by the appearance of nodules on the vertebrae, which are the result of using the spine in carrying out heavy tasks. Signs of arthritis in the necks of women found at Cirencester have been interpreted as the result of carrying heavy weights, such as water pots or fuel, on their heads.[26] Squatting facets on ankle joints, noted at Trentholme Drive, York, suggest long hours spent squatting over cooking fires or other work. One woman at York presented a badly healed right femur and an unusual variation in her lumbar vertebrae. Calvin Wells suggested that this implied that she had been a professional acrobat.[27]

This leads into that dangerous area known as 'presumption'. This is the area where imagination takes over from evidence.

Literature makes a number of references to bath attendants who do not seem to have had a very savoury reputation. Evidence of finds from the legionary baths at Caerleon and the lead curses at Bath suggests that women used both military and civilian bath-houses in Britain.[28] It might, therefore, be presumed that Romano-British bath-houses were staffed by female bath attendants, as were the baths in Rome. The list of items stolen while their owners were taking the waters at Bath certainly indicates that one would have been well advised to use the services of such women – bath-house theft was an acknowledged problem throughout the Empire.

Peacock has put forward a theory, based on anthropological parallels, that women were involved in the production of black-burnished ware pottery.[29] Regrettably, the only fragment of evidence which seemed to name a female potter – a piece of a mortarium from Brockley Hill bearing the name Catia Maria – has been dismissed by Kay Hartley as graffiti referring to the owner of the mortarium rather than a potter's stamp of a female potter or pottery owner.[30] It was hoped that some of the fingerprints, which are occasionally to be found on pots, might prove to be female, but none has so far done so. Analysis of pottery stamps has revealed dynasties of potters and daughters being involved as well as sons is not entirely out of the question, although it would be useful to have some conclusive proof.

A town's population included people who worked in various materials. A few of these in Roman Britain are known by name, but all are men, such as Lucius Aebutius Thales the shoemaker, Bonosius the blacksmith, Verctissa the cooper, and Cabriabanus the tiler.[31] The complete silence from the female workforce may give an erroneous impression of town life. The number of craftsmen who have left their names is minute compared with the thousands who must have existed, so the lack of inscriptions for female workers may not be so surprising; after all, only ten per cent of all inscriptions from Roman Britain refer to women at all. However, even if the women of Britain did not leave any epigraphic evidence of their involvement in trade or industry they would have had difficulty avoiding work, as many would have lived above the shop, or more accurately, behind it.

Shops and workshops in towns and *vici* were mostly built to a strip plan with open fronts facing on to the road, which could be closed by doors or shutters after hours. The front half or two-thirds of the premises would be used for selling or manufacturing or storing items with the living quarters confined to the rear portion. Some of these establishments were owner-occupied while others were bought as investments by local businesspeople and rented out or run by slaves. It is often presumed that the women of the families of the owner-occupiers or tenants would have played a part in selling or making the stock, but it is also likely that freedwomen and widows carried out business on their own behalf, as did the women of Pompeii, Rome and Ostia mentioned previously. Certainly, in the fort *vici* there may well have been a high proportion of working women. Some will have been the unacknowledged wives and daughters of the soldiers – unacknowledged, that is, by the army until the Severan Edict of AD 197. Others will have been the mothers and sisters of serving soldiers who had accompanied them on their tour of duty: a soldier was responsible for the unmarried females in his family if he was the eldest son and his father had died. The government in Rome tried hard to ensure that soldiers were exempt from this responsibility, but failed, and many soldiers were accompanied by several sisters as well as their mothers.[32] An auxiliary's take-home pay was not over-generous and extra sources of income would have been sought to support this extended family. There would also have been the widows of soldiers and veterans; the army had no pension rights for dependants and, although we have some documentary evidence for a deceased soldier's fellows having a whip-round for widows, many will have had to fend for themselves.

All these groups of people are well attested in inscriptions and must have had some means of keeping body and soul together. These women may have turned to crafts or agriculture or have offered their services to the population of the fort or the surrounding countryside as laundresses, publicans, entertainers, clothes menders, etc. Carol van Driel Murray has recently compared the occupations of the women attached to the Dutch army in Indonesia with those of women attached to the Roman army.[33] This comparison, however, can only offer suggestions rather than solid proof.

In Britain the wattle-and-daub or wood structures of those *vicus* buildings which have been excavated have failed to provide any graffiti of the sort found on the walls of the buildings at Pompeii or Ostia and remarkably little evidence for industry other than a few hearths and fragments of moulds or slag. We can only guess at the occupation of the woman found buried in the floor of an inn at Housesteads; none of the others have left even the smallest clue.[34]

To return to the saints and sinners – one profession which must have been practised in Britain was prostitution. No building has been confidently identified as a brothel in Britain, although there are hopes of a building at Wroxeter judging from the suitability of its architecture and its prime position next to the baths. In Italy prostitutes were often of Syrian or Egyptian origin and were identifiable by their hairstyles, short tunics and brightly-coloured cloaks.[35] Some were independent operators who rented rooms in inns while others were employed by pimps and madams. Hadrian tried to stop the development of large brothels by banning the sale of a male or female slave to either a pimp or a gladiatorial trainer, but he does not seem to have been successful.[36] At all levels of operation, prostitutes had to be registered with the authorities and from the reign of Caligula they had to pay a tax equal to the sum they might reasonably expect to earn from a single client on any one day.[37] This tax was payable even after retirement. Prostitution was, therefore, a financial fact of life in the Roman Empire and provided a consistent income for the authorities who appear to have encouraged the setting up of brothels all over the Empire as a consequence, despite imperial disapproval.

The evidence for priestesses in Britain is not confined to the altar at Corbridge. Figurines of priestesses sacrificing are also known, for example, at South Shields.[38] It is also to be expected that cults, such as that of Isis, which appealed to women in particular, would have had women as priestesses as well as female musicians, etc. Many of the latter would have been slaves. Some female slaves are known by name from the province but none gives any indication as to how she was employed. The writing tablet from London, for example, in which Rufus urges Epillicus to 'turn that slave girl into cash' gives no clue as to her skills.[39] If we follow the Italian pattern then we might presume that the majority of female slaves in Britain were employed in domestic work and the quality of their lives will have depended on the number of other slaves occupied in the same household as well as the character of their owner.

There are some objects in Britain which may give some indication as to occupations, although it is impossible to tell if the objects were used to earn a living or in a domestic setting. A bronze statuette of a girl playing a *tibia* from Silchester is a case in point.[40] Does this depict a professional musician or an amateur who played for her own pleasure? If the former, would she have been employed as an entertainer or was she attached to a temple in a religious capacity? Equally, a weaving tablet from South Shields may have been a piece of professional equipment or for domestic use only, an argument which can be extended to spindle-whorls, needles and the like.[41]

In the country the lives of many women may have been only slightly affected by the Roman invasion of Britain. These are the women who lived in the self-sufficient farmsteads. Artefact analysis from these sites suggests that the settlement sites may have only been occupied by women, children and the elderly who were responsible for growing, gathering and hunting food while the men lived and worked elsewhere.[42] This is based on anthropological parallels and is very suspect, but whether this is acceptable evidence or not it is likely that the women living on those sites would have been fully involved in agricultural and craft activities. Recent work has shown that the settlement sites were a source of small metal objects, particularly enamelled artefacts, and glass bracelets. None of these requires complex equipment to manufacture but equally none has been found signed with a maker's mark, either male or female.[43]

In this volume there are papers about women in industry in other periods of Britain's history and from the evidence of those other times we can postulate the involvement of women in all sorts of industries in Roman Britain. There were no laws barring women from working but, regrettably, there is remarkably little evidence for them having done so. However, there is also little evidence for *men* doing much work in Roman Britain either. From metalworking debris, pottery kilns, mines, quarries, etc, we know that Roman Britain was a hive of industry, but identifying the individual workers is difficult. It has been presumed that all the workers were men, but there is no satisfactory reason for that presumption. Tombstones and other inscriptions tend to record the well-to-do with a bias towards the military families; Romano-British architecture does not lend itself to the survival of graffiti; few civilian writing tablets have been found: the ordinary workers have left little trace, whatever their gender.

This has been an attempt to put Roman Britain in its context. There is little evidence for women in industry, but what evidence there is tends to reflect a similar paucity of evidence as elsewhere in the Empire. This in itself reflects the limited evidence for industrial workers as a whole.

ENDNOTES

1   CIL VII.1335.4 (see Huebner, A., 1863).

2   RIB 1129 (see Collingwood, R. G. and Wright, R. P., 1965).

3   See D'Avino, M., 1967, pp17–18, 50.

4   Ibid, p18.

5   Ibid, pp29–30; 30–31.

6   Ibid, pp31–2; for Ascellina see ibid, pp55–9.

7   Ibid, p21.

8   Ibid, pp19, 34, 37.

9   Ostia Museum Inv. 1170; 1340.

10 Vegetable seller: ibid 198; poultry seller: ibid 134; shoemaker: ibid 1418.

11 CIL VI.9683 (see Huebner, A., 1863); ILC V.685b (see Diehl, E., 1925–31); CIL XIV.2850; CIL VI.9801.

12 CIL VIII.24678 (see Huebner, A., 1863).

13 Pomponius Sextus Digest XXIV.1.31 (see Krueger, P. and Watson, A., 1985); see also Treggiari, S., 1976, pp82–4.

14 Plautus, Mostellaria, pp157ff (see Nixon, P., 1924).

15 CIL VI.9727; see also Treggiari, S., 1976, pp78–80.

16 Tacitus, Germania XX (see Hutton, M. and Warmington, E. H., 1970).

17 Soranus, Gynaecol.II.19 (see Temkin, O., 1956).

18 CIL VI.4352 (see Huebner, A., 1863); see also Treggiari, S., 1976, pp88–90.

19 CIL VI.9723; CIL VI.9723 (see Huebner, A., 1863); see also Treggiari, S., 1976, p87.

20 Soranus, Gynaecol. I. 3–4 (see Temkin, O., 1956).

21 Metz: Esperandieu 1911, IV, no. 4363; Juvenile, Satires II.141 (see Ramsey, G.G., 1979); Martial, Epigrams XI.IX; XI.IXXX (see Kerr, W.C.A., 1919); see also Treggiari, S., 1976, p86.

22 Papinian, Digest 37.15.11 (see Krueger, P. and Watson, A., 1985).

23 Bradley, K., 1985.

24 RIB 162 (see Collingwood, R. G. and Wright, R. P., 1965).

25 Justinian, Digest 49.15.6 (see Krueger, P. and Watson, A., 1985).

25 Peterborough Museum; Toynbee, J. M. C., 1962, no. 56; see Treggiari, S., 1976, pp90–91 for other entertainers in the Roman Empire.

26 McWhirr, A., Viner, L. and Wells, C., 1982.

27 Wenham, L., 1968, pp150–52.

28 Zienkiewicz, J.D., 1986, p18; Cunliffe, B., 1988.

29 Peacock, D. P. B., 1982, p86.

30 JRS LIX (1969) p237.

31 Lucius Aebutius Thales: Britannia IV (1973) p332; Bonosius: Britannia III (1972) p359: Verctissa: JRS LI (1961) p196; Cabriabanus: Britannia II (1971) p297.

32 Eg RIB 934 (see Collingwood, R. C. and Wright, R. P., 1964): Greca, sister of Crotilo Germanus and Vindicianus; RIB 1483: Ursa, sister of Lurio; RIB 936: Aicetuos, mother of Lattio; RIB 1250: Aurelia Lupula, mother of Dionysius Fortunatus.

33 Van Driel Murray, C. (1995).

34 Birley, E., Charlton, J. and Hedley, P., 1933, pp82–96.

35 Horace, Satires 1.2.36 (see Fairclough, H. B., 1978); Ovid, Fasti 4.134 (see Frazer, J. G., 1931); Ovid, Ars Amatoria 1.31ff (see Mozley, J. H., 1969).

36 Scriptores Historiae Augustae: Hadrian 18.8 (see Magie, D., 1922).

37 Suetonius, Gaius Caligula 40 (see Graves, R., 1957).

38 Allason-Jones, L. and Miket, R., 1984, no. 3.392.

39 Antiquaries Journal XXXIII (1953) p207.

40 Reading Museum: Toynbee, J. M. C., 1962, no. 52.

41 Allason-Jones, L. and Miket, R., 1984, no. 2.49.

42 Allason-Jones, L., 1989.

43 Allason-Jones, L., 1991, pp1–5.

ABBREVIATIONS

CIL   A. Huebner, Corpus Inscriptionum Latinarum, Berlin: 1863

ILC   E. Diehl, Inscriptiones Latinae Christianae veteres (3 vols), Berlin, 1925–31

JRS   Journal of Roman Studies, London.

RIB   R.G. Collingwood and R.P. Wright, The Roman inscriptions of Britain, Oxford, 1965.

GRANNY'S OLD BONES:
WOMEN BONEWORKERS IN ROMAN BRITAIN

Nina Crummy

Epigraphic evidence for women's occupations in Roman Britain is extremely scarce.[1] Pathological studies undertaken on women buried in Roman inhumation cemeteries are perhaps even less informative.[2] Archaeology cannot fill this gaping void, for the remains of craft activities recovered from excavations are totally genderless. Fortunate would be the site director who found a pile of smithing slag and a sign stating 'Shop of Marcella, worker in iron'.

To provide hard evidence of female boneworkers in Roman Britain is therefore impossible. This leaves the evidence of circumstance, provided by some historical facts, some archaeological facts, and rather a lot of imagination.

FIG. I
A group of bone hairpin roughs from Winchester, Hampshire (Winchester Museums Service)

Are you sitting comfortably? Then I'll begin …

Once upon a time there was a great empire which stretched from the rising to the setting sun, from the dark fir-forests of the north to the hot deserts of the south. A city called Rome lay at the centre, a city ruled by men, with laws composed and imposed by men. Children grew up in the power, the *potestas*, of their father, and girls escaped patriarchal dominance only by submitting to the hand, *manus*, of their husband. The only power permitted to women lay through domestic routes, food, clothing and children.

The attitude of male Romans to their female co-citizens found literary expression through the poet Juvenal who, bemoaning attempts by some brave women to redress the balance, wrote in *Satire VI*:

> And what about female athletes, with their purple
>
> Tracksuits, and wrestling in mud? Not to mention our lady-fencers –
>
> We've all seen *them*, stabbing the stump with a foil,
>
> Shield well advanced, going through the proper motions:
>
> Just the right training needed to blow a matronly horn
>
> At the Floral Festival?

He goes on:

> In the old days poverty
>
> Kept Latin women chaste: hard work, too little sleep,
>
> These were the things that saved their humble homes from corruption –

What would Juvenal think of an organisation such as WHAM? He would probably spit out that pithy piece of prejudice written by his crony, Martial:

> Wives should obey their husbands; only then
>
> Can women share equality with men (*Epigrams* 8, 12).

But, as when a pebble is dropped into the waters of a still lake the ripples grow weaker and weaker as they spread outwards, so on the edges of the great Roman Empire things were just a little different.

In a small island province in the far north-west corner of the Empire, customs had been different before the coming of the legions and the imposition of Roman law. One woman, Boudicca, leading an army of over 100,000 men, women and children, rose up in revolt against the invaders. She left a valuable clue to the status of women in her land in her speech to her army before their defeat by the iron might of Rome.

> We British are used to woman commanders in war. But now I am fighting for my kingdom and wealth. I am fighting as an ordinary person for my lost freedom, my bruised body, and my outraged daughters. The Roman division which dared to fight is annihilated. The others cower in their camps, or watch for a chance to escape. They will never face even the din and roar of all our thousands, much less the shock of our onslaught. Consider how many of you are fighting – and why! Then you will win this battle, or perish. That is what I, a woman, plan to do! Let the men live in slavery if they will (Tacitus, *Annals* 14).

The end to that story is well known: Boudicca fell, and for four hundred years the land of the Britons lay under the Roman yoke. No doubt men of land and property chose to co-operate with their conquerors in order to retain a vestige of power. They followed the Roman way of life, and so they came to treat the women in their families in the Roman way.

But there was more than one layer of Celtic society. Down an economic notch or two, or three, or more, daily survival was more important than status, and any contribution to its achievement would surely be respected, whether made by male or female, child or adult.

There was also, no doubt, more than one social and economic layer of craftworkers. Goldsmiths and gem-cutters would have been people with sufficient funds in hard Roman coin to permit them to purchase materials and employ assistants. The products of many Romano-British potters travelled over a far wider area than the local market.[3] Talent alone would not achieve this; staff and transport would also be needed.

To work in bone (or antler, or horn) needed no staff, no premises, few tools, and raw materials could be obtained for little, or even for free.

It is clear from excavation that the Romano-British diet included a good proportion of meat, from a range of animals. Bones would always be available, at different points of the meat-preparation process, and possibly from associated processors such as tanners.

Butchers would remove non-meat-bearing parts from carcasses. Metapodials, for example, have very little flesh on them, and were probably removed at an early stage. They are straight and strong, ideal bones for a number of bone artefacts. The butcher may have then supplied a boneworker direct or, if he removed the metapodials in one with the hide, may have passed them on to a tanner. A boneworker may then have taken them off a tanner's hands.

This presupposes an established and organised boneworker, with the means of carrying away from butchery or tannery a large quantity of raw materials. But since meat was part of the diet, anyone eating meat could obtain bones to work, or discard them for someone else to use.

Who then is our boneworker? Down that far in the economic chain we are looking not for a *petit bourgeois*, satisfying the demands of customers who live in a world of conspicuous consumption, but for a person who knows how to satisfy the small demands of small consumers.

Let us then imagine a small family in AD 61: a woman, her daughter, and her granddaughter. They were with Boudicca's army when it sacked Verulamiun, Londinium and Camulodunum, and in the last battle both her husband and her son-in-law were killed.

They are a family of little wealth but great resourcefulness and considerable talent. The woman saw as soon as the Romans came to the island that there was a penny or two to be made from them. She saw how the soldiers' women fixed their hair into fancy styles using long pins of bone or horn.[4] She saw how the soldiers themselves loved to gamble, playing for high stakes with bone dice shaken in bone cups, pushing bone counters around a board for hours at a stretch.[5] She saw their bone-handled swords[6] and their ornate parade uniform buckles[7] and how they would use a bone spoon to eat an egg, then turn the same spoon round in their fingers and use the pointed shaft to winkle the flesh out of snails.[8] She saw their children play with model swords[9] and, most importantly, she saw bones thrown on to dungheaps waiting for an enterprising woman to snatch them away.

So when the crushing of the Boudiccan revolt left both her and her daughter widowed and responsible for a child, they camped near a Roman

FIG. 2
A red deer antler
comb from
Winchester, Hampshire
(Winchester Museum Service)

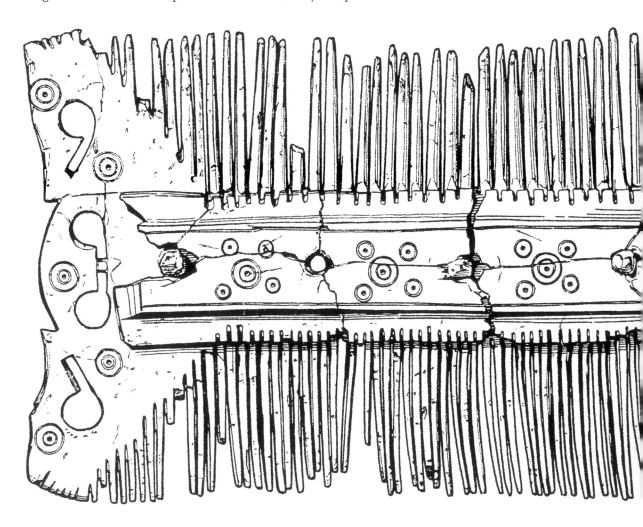

town and began to scavenge for bones. Together they found out how a straight hollow leg bone provides the tube from which a sword handle can be made, how lengths of shattered bone and horn can be made into dice, hairpins or spoons, and how people with just a little money will pay just a little of that little to have a new pin, or replace lost dice.

The only tools they needed they already had or could find to hand: a small hammer or stones to smash the bones into handy-sized fragments, a knife to trim the fragments into shape, sand or stones to smooth away any small rough patches on the surface, and rags and oil to make it shine.[10]

At first their products were rather poor,[11] but as they got more proficient they found the people of the town willing to part with money for a few small pieces. Then they heard that their fellow native Britons were beginning to ape Roman ways, so they travelled from village to village, even going over the sea to other provinces, getting their raw materials from local

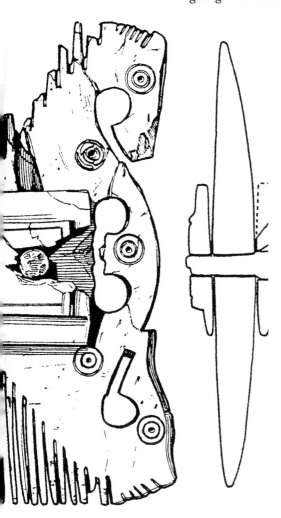

butchers and tanners, turning out spoons, in particular, by the dozen, and often leaving evidence of their visit behind in the form of waste and discarded blanks or blundered pieces. In Britain they reached Winchester, Hampshire, Woodcutts Common, Dorset,[13] Settle, Yorkshire, and Borness in Kircudbrightshire. On the continent they left evidence of their passing at Augst, Switzerland,[14] and Sainte Colombe-les-Vienne, France.

When the granddaughter was older the family came back to Britain, and invested in a pole-lathe which they needed to make counters[16] and other round or circular objects.[17] The girl married, and when the first great-grandchild arrived her husband's mother moved in with them too, all four generations in a small rectangular construction of wattle and daub on the outskirts of a Roman town. Even nearly forty years after the Roman conquest, and twenty after Boudicca's defeat, they are still pure-bred Britons, for no Roman has seen any economic advantage in marrying into this family. Daily survival for them is a struggle, with each individual contributing according to his or her ability.

The great-grandchildren go each day with their father's mother into the countryside, fishing in small streams, foraging for birds' eggs, fungi, fruit, herbs and seeds, anything edible to fill their stomachs. On a good day they may gather enough to be able to sell some on to their neighbours or at market, on a bad day they cannot find enough to feed themselves.

The others work away on a heap of bones and horns, churning out a range of small Romano-British necessities, selling some in the local markets, sometimes loading others into packs and going off to peddle them around the countryside.

That is how it might have been. It is fact that bones and horns were freely available; dig on any Roman site to find that out. It is fact that spoon blanks and other fragments from bone and hornworking have been found in Gaul, Germania and Britannia. It is fact that even when found within a Roman town this debris has never been identified as a primary deposit, it is always in dump, backfill, or general topsoil build-up, the product of clearance from elsewhere.[18] The family is pure fancy, but there is no good reason why women could not have worked bone. Only a good eye, a strong wrist and a strong arm would be necessary, and many women have those.

That story dealt with boneworking in the early Roman period, antlerworking in the late Roman period is not that different.

Many generations on, in the mid-fourth-century, in the north-western provinces of the Empire, composite combs of antler became very fashionable among both men and women. Late Roman combs are part of a centuries-long tradition that was to reach its peak in the middle and late Saxon periods, when itinerant craftworkers travelled to markets.[19]

Red deer conveniently shed their antlers each season, leaving them in the woods for anyone to collect, anyone who knew that antlers could be turned into all sorts of saleable items. It seems likely that antlers were harvested by people who stored them until a travelling craftworker visited at market time and turned them into combs or anything else that was required, or that a craftworker might over-winter somewhere, and manufacture a store of items for sale during a summer on the road. Combs of this type reached Britain in about AD 360, perhaps when the first enterprising itinerant craftworker crossed the sea to test the markets of Britain.

Comb-making was a more complex matter than the trimming of a fragment of bone into a spoon in that it involved cutting out different components, assembling, and finishing. It was a craft with all the signs of developing into art, but it need not have been a male preserve. The antlers were cut into lengths and the outer solid part removed. These pieces provided the various components of a comb, endplates, toothplates, connecting plates, which were then fixed together with iron rivets.[20] The end and connecting plates provided fields for decoration, in some cases quite elaborate, in others quite minimalistic.[21] The variations might reflect the ability of the maker, but are more likely to reflect the price commanded by the item.

As with boneworking, there is no reason not to postulate a female presence in antler comb-making, whether it was a home-based or a travelling industry. A woman could collect antlers, cut them into pieces, assemble the combs and decorate them. She could travel to markets, make combs on site or sell ready-made pieces. She could operate alone, with her family or in a business partnership. There is no proof that this happened, but there is no proof that it did not happen.

Interpretation of the evidence is the final part of the archaeological process, but interpretation must usually stay within firm limits dictated by the recovered evidence. It is a rare experience to be able to put forward theories so free that they should be called stories. However, nearly everything in this paper is true, only the sex and sales techniques of the manufacturers are uncertain.

ENDNOTES

1   Allason-Jones, L., this volume.

2   Pinter-Bellows, S., this volume.

3   Going, C. J., 1987, figs 56–9.

4   Crummy, N., 1983, figs 17, 18.

5   Liversidge, J., 1973, figs 133, 134.

6   Crummy, N., 1983, fig. 153.

7   Ibid, fig. 144, 4176.

8   Crummy, N., 1992b, fig. 6.11, 122.

9   Greep, S., 1981.

10   Crummy, N., 1981, p283.

11   Crummy, N., 1992a, fig. 5.2, 256.

12   Crummy, N. et al, forthcoming.

13   Pitt-Rivers, A., 1887, p145.

14   Ibid, p130.

15   Schmid, E., 1968, Abb 1, 6; Drack, W. and Fellmann, R., 1988, Abb 157.

16   Crummy, N., 1983, p91.

17   Crummy, N., 1981, p283.

18   Crummy, N., forthcoming.

19   Ambrosiani, K., 1981.

20   Galloway, P. and Newcomer, M., 1981; Ambrosiani, K., 1981, pp103–27.

21   Galloway, P. and Newcomer, M., 1981, pp84–89; Crummy, N., forthcoming.

PORTRAYING WORKING WOMEN
THE APPROACH TAKEN AT VERULAMIUM MUSEUM

Vivienne Holgate

In 1991 Verulamium Museum, St Albans, opened its newly-displayed galleries to the public. The museum had been built over fifty years before to house the material recovered by Mortimer Wheeler and his wife Tessa from their excavations of Verulamium, the third largest city in Roman Britain. Tessa, in fact, was instrumental in persuading the city fathers to provide the money for the much-needed museum but was to die before seeing her work come to fruition. The museum is a fitting tribute to her work and is dedicated to her memory. Since its opening though, with the exception of the addition of a side gallery in the early 1960s, the displays had changed little.

This paper will outline the approach taken in designing the new galleries and the way in which women are portrayed both living and working in and around the Roman city. Reconstruction illustrations and full-sized figures in room settings are used to convey the working lives of these women; these illustrations and the research undertaken on the appearance of the female figures will be discussed. Finally, the way in which women from this period are depicted at other museums in Britain will be reviewed briefly.

DESIGNING THE NEW GALLERIES AT VERULAMIUM MUSEUM

The design brief did not set out to make a feature of displaying working women but it was acknowledged that they must have played an integral role in the economic life of the city. It was thus considered essential from the outset that there should be an equal representation of men, women and children. In general, women are shown performing stereotypical tasks in domestic situations such as food production, food preparation and looking after children. Under Roman rule it is known that women worked as maids, cooks, laundresses, spinners, weavers, midwives, wet-nurses, bath attendants, agricultural workers, craftswomen and prostitutes; needless to say, many must have assisted husbands, fathers and sons in other lines of work.[1] Evidence from the rest of the Roman Empire indicates that women were employed in a far greater range of professions and industries than there is evidence for in Britain. The only two career women in Britain known by name are Verecunda, the actress and girlfriend of Lucius, a gladiator at Leicester, and Diodora, the priestess at Corbridge who dedicated an altar associated with the cult of Hercales of Tyre.[2]

Archaeological investigations in and around Verulamium provide information on a number of industries and trades that took place. The major industries were pottery production at Sulloniacis (Brockley Hill), Radlett and Bricket Wood (?Lugdunum) and tile production at Old Parkbury, Netherwylde and Park Street. Other forms of employment included small-scale metalworking, farming, shopkeeping and market trading, baking, spinning, weaving and dyeing, and work at baths, temples and the theatre. The discovery of a child's footprint in a tile from Gorhambury villa possibly indicates that tile manufacture was a family affair. It is thus possible, despite the lack of tangible evidence, that women worked in some or all of these industries and trades at Verulamium.

FIG. I
Preliminary sketch of labourers working the land which was totally male dominated. *Andy Martin*

Since a large proportion of annual visits to the museum are made by schoolchildren, the general themes followed in the displays were tailor-made for the 'Invaders and Settlers' core subject of the history National Curriculum. There were a number of constraints which influenced the new layout: for example, the large mosaics already on display had to remain in their original positions because of their size and weight. It was also felt that the general feel of the old displays could be retained by reusing the drawers beneath the cases, some of which are now accessible to the public and provide 'visible storage'. They have been one of the successes of the new displays.

An introductory area, entitled 'The Rise and Fall of Verulamium', outlines the history of the city from the late Iron Age to its decline in the fifth century using objects and reconstruction paintings. The visitor then enters what is referred to as 'the rotunda', where some of the 'choice' objects are on display. From there it is possible to reach four 'discovery' areas, so called because there are various hands-on features allowing visitors to 'discover' more about the city for themselves. These areas include 'rites and recreation', 'food and farming', 'merchants and markets' and 'making a living'. The side gallery, themed 'at home in Verulamium', has a range of contrasting walk-through reconstructed rooms comprising two from the house of a wealthy merchant and his family and two from the home of a carpenter and his wife. Where appropriate, original wall paintings have been incorporated, together with objects relating to activities which may have taken place in such rooms. The contents and features of the rooms are all based on the archaeological evidence recovered from excavations at Verulamium. The final section deals with the people of Verulamium through their burials.

Of the reconstruction paintings and illustrations, some were specially commissioned for the new displays, while extensive use was also made of paintings produced by Alan Sorrell in the 1960s. Of the former, three that were used in the introductory section are worthy of note. First, that of Boudicca, who razed Verulamium to the ground around AD 60–61. Second, a bronzesmith and his assistant in their workshop, where women play a cameo role in the street in front of the workshop. The final painting in this section, which shows the demise of the city in the fourth century, depicts large administrative buildings in ruin in the background and women carrying out domestic chores in the foreground, for example grinding corn, carrying pails of water and looking after children.

In the 'food and farming' discovery area, a large illustration showing people at work was used as a backdrop to demonstrate the way various agricultural tools, such as rakes, billhooks and scythes, were used. The initial sketch was totally male-dominated (fig.1). However, it is known that women and children would have helped out, particularly at harvest time, as exemplified by the reference to Ruth gleaning in the fields in the Old Testament. Women and children were thus deliberately included in the final version as this was considered to be a more accurate picture of rural life (fig.2).

CREATING THE COSTUMED FIGURES

Life-sized costumed figures of men, women and a child were used in the section on life at home. The clothing and general appearance of the wealthy woman was based on Regina, whose tombstone is displayed at Arbeia Roman fort, South Shields. She was chosen as a model since she came from the tribe of the Catuvellauni, the native tribe inhabiting the Verulamium region. On her tombstone she is described as the freedwoman and wife of Barates of Palmyra, a Catuvellaunian by tribe. Barates was a flagmaker or standard bearer who presumably had done quite well for himself to erect such a fine tombstone to his wife. Interestingly, the fact that Regina is described as a freedwoman indicates that she was a slave at some point in her life.[3] The tombstone shows Regina with her right hand on a casket and her left hand in her lap holding what looks like a spindle. The basket on the floor presumably holds the already-spun balls of wool. She wears the classic costume of the north-western Empire, comprising a Gallic coat over a long-sleeved dress. Her hair is dressed in an elaborate style of the late second century and she wears earrings, bracelets and beads appropriate for the period. The small child shown in the same setting wears a simple belted tunic with sewn-in sleeves.

FIG. 2
Final illustration of labourers working the land which includes men, women and children.
Andy Martin

It is still not known to what extent cloth was woven either at home or in workshops in Roman Britain. Regina is using a spindle, but she is clearly a woman of some means to have such a memorial erected in her honour. It is possible that wool was spun whenever time permitted; perhaps it was picked up and put down in the same way that we knit today. The spun thread could then be woven up by someone skilled at weaving. The range in the quality of the fabric might also suggest that the rough cloths with faults were woven at home and the finer, well-made and, consequently, more expensive textiles were produced in a workshop. This may well be the case; evidence for three types of cloth were found in a burial recently excavated at the William Old site, King Harry Lane, Verulamium, some pieces of which included mistakes indicative of home weaving.[4]

In the new displays, the area on craftworking includes illustrations of women weavers using a warp-weighted loom and a vertical loom where the cloth is stretched across two beams. The absence of loom weights from the Roman city, as opposed to the number which has been found at the nearby pre-Roman site of Prae Wood, might indicate that either they were not used to a great extent and that the second type of loom was preferred, or they have yet to be discovered by excavation. The quantity of spindles from all over the city implies that spinning was undertaken in households rather than workshops. Dyeing on a commercial scale was undertaken during the Roman period and at Verulamium several features excavated in the late 1980s have been interpreted as dye vats.[5] It is quite possible that women, as well as men, would have worked in such an industry.

Considerable effort was taken to produce as authentic a costume as possible for the wealthy woman. Through the British Wool Marketing Board, a local weaver was contacted who was willing both to spin and dye the yarn using, where possible, natural dyes such as madder and nettle and to weave a garment to our exact requirements. The Gallic coat was woven in one piece with the fringing and method of stitching copied from the piece of cloth found in the child's tomb which is on display at the museum. The fragment of cloth is particularly interesting: its selvedge, stitching and perfectly made 'buttonhole' (although it is not known what specific function this performed) are clearly visible.[6] The woollen costumes on all the figures were made up of cloth by the same weaver. Flax seeds recovered from excavations at Verulamium may indicate that linen was produced in the area. This, together with the fact that wool worn next to the skin can be uncomfortable, led to the decision to clothe the wealthy woman in a linen under dress. It is just possible, in fact, to see the hemline of a dress beneath the tunic worn by Regina.

The ground plan of a workshop excavated near the theatre at Verulamium and which fronted on to Watling Street[7] was used as the model for the reconstruction of a carpenter's workshop and living quarters. The carpenter works in the front of the shop, while his wife prepares a meal in the room behind (fig 3). The actual building was destroyed in the fire of AD 155, which gutted Verulamium. Tools found in the workshop, some of which are displayed in an adjoining case, indicate that it had been used as a carpenter's shop. As was usual in houses of this type, the main workshop occupied the front room while the back room was used as a kitchen and general living room for the family. The woman in her kitchen wears the traditional clothes of a native Celtic woman living in the early Roman period: a long tunic, belted at the waist, over a plain dress. She stands over her table, which is piled with ingredients for the meal. The room setting incorporates the hearth, pottery and metalwork that were found during excavations of the kitchen area. The pottery vessels displayed on a shelf above the hearth are, in fact, the actual pots from the kitchen and are arranged in the positions

FIG. 3
The reconstructed kitchen at Verulamium Museum.
Copyright St Albans Museum

in which they were found. The range of foodstuffs includes ingredients known to have been available in Verulamium. The fact that a weaving tablet was excavated from the living quarters suggests that such weaving was a domestic activity. Osiers (willow rods) and rushes are known to have grown along the river Ver and it is not impossible that women working from home were involved in making baskets and matting from these raw materials.

PORTRAYING ROMAN WORKING WOMEN AT OTHER MUSEUMS IN BRITAIN

Further examples of three-dimensional figures used in reconstructions, although they are not necessarily depicted at work, include the high-status woman and her child with their female attendant at the Corinium Museum, Cirencester, and a mother and child at the Roman baths at Bath. At the Corinium Museum, effort has been made to represent accurately the costume and furniture of the period, whereas at Bath less attention has been paid to the authenticity of the figures' clothing as emphasis has been placed on creating a dramatic setting at the entrance to the museum displays. As at Verulamium Museum, Ipswich Museum has produced room settings which show the traditionally perceived division of labour: a woman working in a kitchen and a man in his workshop. The Museum of London avoided the issue of portraying women merely as housewives by not including any figures in their reconstruction of a kitchen in their pre-1996 displays. Interestingly, Corinium Museum includes the figure of a man in its kitchen scene!

At Chesterholm Museum, the reconstruction of a kitchen of a *vicus* building dating to the late third century from Vindolanda fort evokes the bleakness of life for a woman living at one end of the Empire's outposts. Here 'Materna', the woman, cooks a meal and looks after her children. In a taped commentary, Materna describes her life, her family and domestic arrangements. It is assumed that Materna spins and weaves her own cloth, as her loom is propped up on the wall behind her. In another scene from the museum, 'Lepidina' dictates a letter to her scribe, who is represented as a man. This scene is based on the contents of one of two wooden writing tablets which were sent to Lepidina by her friend Claudia Severa. The tablets are written by two different scribes suggesting that, if Severa did indeed write part of the letters, they were not entirely written in her hand.[8]

A different approach has been taken at Colchester Museum, where full-sized, two-dimensional figures are used both in street scenes and for displaying various hands-on features. Although costumes used are more in keeping with classical Italy than a north-western province, the figures provide a low cost and effective method of portraying full-sized characters.

With such a paucity of information, it is not surprising that attempts to depict working women in museum displays are confined very much to the stereotypical roles: the housewife toiling in the kitchen and the wealthy woman sitting in the ubiquitous wicker chair with her feet up. We are perhaps still blinkered in our perception of the role of women in society and should be more adventurous in showing women in other roles. There is thus clearly the opportunity in future displays to explore further the role of women in the workplace.

ACKNOWLEDGEMENT

I am grateful to Ros Niblett who kindly read and commented on a draft of this paper.

ENDNOTES

1   Allason-Jones, L., 1989, pp80–81.

2   Ibid, pp80, 157.

3   Ibid, fig. 6, p24.

4   Ros Niblett, personal communication.

5   Niblett, R., 1995, p90.

6   Wild, J. P., 1968.

7   Frere, S. S., 1972.

8   Bowman, A. K., 1994, p88.

CHAPTER 3

APPRENTICES, WIVES AND WIDOWS

WORKING WOMEN IN MEDIEVAL LONDON
Judith Stevenson

It is hard to draw the line between what constitutes industry and technology as we think of it today and the wide range of working activities in which women were generally involved in the medieval period. When does a woman's work at home, such as spinning and weaving to produce homespun clothes or tailoring clothes from bought cloth, become an industry? Is it when enough excess produce is sold outside the family and associates to warrant the title of a business? Women were expected to clothe their families, launder, prepare food and stock up for the winter months, bake, brew, garden, tend livestock, rear children, perhaps sell produce on the streets as vendors or hucksters, as well as assist in the work of their husbands! They were also expected to administer family medicine, some to act as midwives and if wealthy or cloistered, manage lands, tenants, finance and accounts. None of these industrious activities, however, will be addressed here, instead we will turn to look at the 'paid' employment of women in industry during the medieval period and specifically to those centred in London.

London's source material is abundant and has been utilised by numerous historical researchers past and present who have made the information widely available. Legal documents, City of London records, particularly those of the Mayor's Court recording various disputes, petitions to the Chancellor, wills and testaments, provide much of the source material. The content of this paper, however, relies entirely on secondary sources of information, the compilations and publications of other researchers.

As a child, a girl could receive a basic, mostly vernacular education, with little or no Latin, probably in a school, or if wealthy from a home tutor, a nunnery school or in the household of another wealthy family.[1] Most girls would help their parents at home and at work and often learn the basics of a trade through assisting their parents. The range of lifestyles thereafter included working as a servant, from about the age of twelve years,[2] apprenticing to a trade from the age of about fourteen years or more,[3] and subsequently remaining single or marrying from around nineteen years, unless from a fairly wealthy family, where marriage was often enforced earlier or the alternative of joining a nunnery was also available.[4]

Young women could be apprenticed to a wide range of trades in London, from the cutlers to the silk industry.[5] Although, in the early-medieval period, apprenticeship started from about the age of fourteen, this gradually rose towards the end of the fifteenth century. By the early fourteenth century the period of indenture in the City of London was set at a minimum of seven years.[6] Apprentices were always required to provide a sponsor and had to be enrolled with the Chamberlain of London by their mistresses or masters within a year and a day of starting an indenture.

Having completed an apprenticeship to a trade, women were not admitted into the guilds to which their male counterparts could belong. They could generally become members only as wives, widows or daughters of guild members. A woman who had completed her apprenticeship with a tailor, for example, would become a dressmaker and not be able to enter the tailors' guild.[7] No female guilds existed in London, whereas in Paris women silkworkers worked in a recognised craft established by ordinances and administrators by the thirteenth century.[8] The women silkworkers of London were nevertheless a strong enough force to petition the Mayor of London and parliament several times during the late fourteenth and fifteenth centuries to protect their livelihoods from foreign competitors.[9] Most working women had no public voice or political power to protect their livelihoods except through the mouths of their husbands as guild members, if it happened that both spouses were in the same or allied trades, which was often the case.

A woman was able to work as a sole trader in her own right. As a 'femme sole', registered with the Mayor of London, she was entitled to trade and take on male and female apprentices as well as being answerable for all her own financial dealings and debts incurred. Both single and married women could hold this status through registration, while a married woman who worked with her husband in his trade rather than in her own was known as a 'femme couverte' and held no legal or independent rights.

Women with a skill or business were highly marriageable, particularly to men within or allied to the same industry. For such a woman a marriage-cum-work partnership also benefited her business or career as a 'femme sole' and, as noted above, could provide an outlet for voicing grievances and the like, through her husband's political and fraternal powers, that she was denied in her own right.

Many such marriage partnerships are found in the records, such as that of Alice Claver, a fifteenth-century silk woman, apprenticed for perhaps between seven and fifteen years, who married Richard Claver, a mercer, but continued to work in her craft, probably as a 'femme sole'. It was from the Mercers that silk women bought the materials for their work: the raw silk, ready-made silk threads and gold and silver threads for weaving into ribbons, laces and other fineries. The Clavers lived in the parish of St Lawrence Jewry near the Guildhall, an area inhabited by a high concentration of mercers, which provided a secure community and working environment. Alice outlived her husband and son and continued working in the silk industry as a respected and highly skilled tradesperson, supplying the royal household on several occasions with accessories such as the silk and gold thread laces, tassels, buttons and tufts to ornament the coronation attire of Richard III in 1483.[10] On her death in 1489 she employed four servants, some of whom may have previously been apprenticed to her, one named apprentice and probably many pieceworkers.[11]

Not all women wanted or needed the advantages that marriage could provide. In particular, the London silk women were strong enough to survive quite successfully without husbands. Soper Lane in Cheapside housed a 'community' of single and widowed silk women, who as well as producing threads and 'narrow wares', sold their goods at market stalls and in shops, along with related items like pins, velvet, gloves and other accessories.[12] A good income and relative independence could be had in this industry, which attracted many women as workers, pieceworkers and apprentices from as far afield as Bristol and Yorkshire[13] as well as from in and around London itself.

It was more usual, however, for a woman to work in the industry of her husband as a '*femme couverte*'. Women may be found as '...butchers, chandlers, ironmongers, net makers, shoemakers, glovers, girdlers, haberdashers, purse-makers, cap-makers, skinners, bookbinders, gilders, painters, silk-weavers and embroiderers, spicers, smiths and goldsmiths among many other trades...'[14] Wives and daughters were therefore accustomed to assist their menfolk in their trade, so much so that it was common throughout the later-medieval period to find widows carrying on their husband's trade after his death. This is indicated in the husband's will, where both the tools of his trade and his apprentices are frequently left to his wife to continue the business.[15]

Of all medieval women, widows are often the most visible for, being without a husband and beyond the responsibility of a father, they were allowed to act independently and were no longer subsumed within the persona of their husbands as 'one flesh' or, to use the phraseology of the medieval lawyers, they were no longer femmes couvertes'.

So begins Caroline Barron's introduction to the book *Medieval London Widows*.[16] Any London widow was given a third to a half of her husband's portable goods, lands and tenements and, as long as she remained single, the right to continue to live in their home,[17] to become a freewoman if the husband had been a freeman of the City, and to continue her husband's business.[18]

It is from the wills and testaments of the widows (married women were not entitled to make wills) as well as those of their deceased husbands, that we gain some further insight into the industries in which women were active.[19] Matilda Penne, a skinner and shopkeeper, took over the business of preparing and selling furs for between twelve and thirteen years after her husband William died in 1379-80, at their shop and home on Wood Street near Cheapside. With no children but several apprentices and servants, she was highly successful and well respected in her trade, with a richly furnished home and enough material and financial possessions to divide between forty-three people at her death in 1392-3 as outlined in her will.[20]

Twenty-five tanners' widows, identified by Derek Keene,[21] were part of a large and coherent tanning industry within the City of London and its suburbs between 1280 and 1370. Four of these women also inherited stalls, tables or plots of land in Tanners' Seld, located on Cheapside opposite St Mary-le-Bow, the main trading outlet for the hides supplied by the tanners.[22] Other widows, such as Johanna Hill and Johanna Sturdy, who both continued their husbands' bell-founding trades in London – bells carrying their individual maker's mark are still in existence today[23] – and Katherine (wife of Walter de Bury), blacksmith at the Tower of London are outlined in Jane Geddes's paper on the heavy metal industries.[24]

This introduction to medieval women working in industry and technology has already expanded into the realm of another paper in this chapter, that of the textile and silk working industries.[25] However, it has omitted several trades in which women have traditionally played an active if not a primary role, that of brewing – brewsters – innkeeping, and to a lesser extent of baking bread – baxters or bakeresses. Without mentioning all the trades in which women were active in the medieval period, or the physical work involved in those trades outlined, the extremely broad range of industry in which women were participating, often equally with men, has it is hoped, been emphasised.

Finally, some mention should be made of the representation of medieval women in museum displays. It was noted by Siân Jones in 1991 that: 'In the Museum of London, there is hardly a woman in sight until you come to the sixteenth century and there you find the most fascinating objects: wire constructions found in the Thames used to support head-dresses ...'[26] This humorous observation may well encapsulate the normal situation in museum displays albeit with differing factual parameters for each museum.

In the last five years a few museums have gently tried to redress the balance, one such instance being the Museum of Archaeology in Southampton. In the 'Medieval Southampton' exhibition, the curators have incorporated images of women wherever possible in equal numbers to those of men, and through the inclusion of a female merchant in the section on Southampton's merchant community, aimed to show that some women had economic power and played a significant part in Southampton's trading activities during the medieval period.[27] Despite criticism that some of the images are misinterpreted by the public; that other images incorporate stereotyped juxtapositioning of male and female characters, and that a major part of the display consists of a tableau of a woman working in a kitchen, to include women in the gallery at all is praiseworthy. Sadly, such attempts are few.

Many members of the public probably associate the medieval period with the development of trade and industry into organised guilds and an increasing control over production and the workforce, but they are rarely made aware of the female role in these industries. It is hoped that museums, which frequently portray these activities through objects, text, visual imagery and other interpretative media, will in future aim to include the female contribution to the economic labour force of medieval life.

ENDNOTES

1   Power, E., 1975, p80.

2   Hanawalt, B., 1993, p179; Goldberg, P. J. P., 1986, p23.

3   Hanawalt, B., 1993, p179.

4   Power, E., 1975, pp39–41, 89–90.

5   Dale, M. K., 1932–4, p325; Lacey, K., 1987, p187; Power, E., 1975, pp58–9, 61.

6   Hanawalt, B., 1993, p135.

7   Ibid, p143.

8   Lacey, K., 1987, p187; Dale, M. K., 1932–4, p324.

9   Dale, M. K., 1932–4, p324–5.

10   Sutton, A., 1994, p137.

11   Ibid, pp129–42.

12   Lacey, K., 1987, p191.

13   Ibid, p193; Dale, M. K., 1932–4, p325.

14   Power, E., 1975, pp59–60.

15   Ibid, pp55–6.

16   Barron, C. B., 1994a, pxiii.

17   Ibid, pxiv.

18   Power, E., 1975, p60.

19   Barron, C. B., 1994a, pxiii.

20   Veale, E., 1994, pp47–54.

21   Keene, D., 1994.

22   Ibid, pp11, 20.

23   Barron, C., 1994b, pp99–112.

24   Geddes, J., this volume.

25   Pritchard, F., this volume.

26   Jones, S., 1991, p24.

27   Ibid, pp25–6.

MEDIEVAL WOMEN IN THE HEAVY METAL INDUSTRIES

Jane Geddes

This brief account of medieval women in the metal industries grew out of a rather different study, namely decorative ironwork in the Middle Ages. Efforts to tie in surviving artefacts with documentary records proved frustrating, but there was more information about the smiths themselves, particularly those living in towns. The search was fairly limited in scope, picking up mainly the 'easy' sources of the printed guild records and various printed wills from the major medieval cities. After surveying the evidence about the blacksmithing craft as a whole, it was clear that about ten per cent of the material concerned women and they merited a closer look. Women's activities in the iron industry could be compared with their equally strenuous work in the bronze foundries.

This paper consists of three sections: first the documentary evidence; then an examination of the formidable woman who served as the logo for this conference; and last, how this information could be used in a museum context.

The documentary evidence located so far is rather patchy, with nothing before the fourteenth century. The date range of the records corresponds with what Caroline Barron has called the 'Golden Age' for women's self-determination through paid work.[1] The records, from the fourteenth to fifteenth centuries, cover the period of population decline following the Black Death when women were drawn into responsible and paid areas of the labour force as never before. This situation continued until the period of population and economic expansion in the sixteenth century, when women were to some extent forced back into the home and out of the marketplace. The records clearly show women working in a tight family environment, sharing tasks and responsibilities with their fathers, husbands and sons and in return sharing the benefits of guild membership with their spouses. The peak example of a woman's responsibility is shown by Katherine, the mother of Andrew of Bury, the king's smith at the Tower. When Andrew and nearly all the other royal smiths were sent abroad on the Crécy campaign in 1346, Katherine was paid a wage equal to her son's (8d per day) to 'keep up the King's forge at the Tower and carry on the work at the forge'. She was clearly a very experienced smith because she had been married to Walter of Bury, previously the king's smith for nine years. She was probably the same

Katherine 'the smith wife' who was paid for steeling and battering the masons' tools at Westminster in 1348.[2]

Women could also be responsible for apprentices in the same way as male masters of the craft. In 1364 Agnes the cutler's wife promised to train Jusema as a cutler in London, to feed her, clothe her and not to beat her with a stick or knife.[3] Katherine, the daughter of a cutler in Lothbury, inherited from him all the tools of his trade and the remaining terms of his

FIG. 1
Henri Bles,
Ironworking scene,
early sixteenth century.
Graz. Photograph
© Courtauld Institute

apprentices Robert and John, in 1340. It is interesting that this inheritance came directly to Katherine and not to her husband, who was also a cutler.[4] Although the guilds did not specifically enrol female members, wives and daughters were automatically assumed to become members when their husbands or fathers joined. It was taken so much for granted that female family members would help the master that special concessions had to be made for a bachelor. Thus, in York, a founder from Lombardy was trying to run his business with one statutory apprentice and no wife. Eventually the founders' guild made a special concession allowing him to employ another apprentice because he lacked the usual female assistance.[5] Women also joined in guild activities. They came to the guild feasts but presumably consumed less than men: the London cutlers in 1370 charged 2s for a brother and 1s for his wife.[6] For the blacksmiths it was 6d for a man and 4d for his wife, in 1434.[7] Finally, the lorimers' fraternity (makers of horse bits and spurs) arranged for an equal number of masses to be sung at the death of any brother or sister, provided they had paid their subscription.[8]

Documentary information about the actual work performed by women is very scarce, but there is one set of accounts from a forge at Byrkeknott, Durham, between 1408 and 1409, which mentions women's conditions.[9] The male workers were paid at a constant piece rate. John Gylles the smytheman smelted the ore and was regularly paid 6d per bloom (that is the unworked iron extracted from the hearth, in this case weighing 195lb). He earned between 1s/6d and 5s depending on the output. Over the same period his wife earned between 2½d and 1s/8d per week. Her tasks were described as follows: helping to break up rock, blowing or working at the bellows, divers labours and helping her husband. It is not clear what working the bellows entailed because they were driven by a waterwheel. However they kept on breaking down, so presumably Mrs Gylles spent her time trying to adjust them. This seems likely because in January 1408 she was paid 12d for work on the bellows, at a time when no iron was produced. Once the bellows were working more reliably she moved on to assist her husband with production, and at this stage earned a regular piece rate: she was paid 1d for every 1s he earned. She was generally better paid when breaking rock or working on the bellows, but this work was irregular. The wife of Thomas Whenfell, the foreman, also worked occasionally on the bloom hearth and was always paid more than Mrs Gylles for the same task. Mrs Whenfell was allowed to work on the string hearth, working up the raw bloom to a purer state, where she was paid between 6d and 9d per week.

Although there is no visual evidence of this activity in England, there are a series of landscape paintings by the Flemish artist Henri Bles who depicts the situation just as it was at Byrkeknott, but in fact drawn from life near Liège/Dinant, between 1500 and 1550.[10] The reproductions are far from clear, but they show the general run of activities in a busy late-medieval bloomery. The first comes from the Uffizi: at the bottom-right are three pits which would be bell-shaped underground, with winches for hauling up the miners and ore. The extreme bottom-right figure is a woman breaking up the ironstone like John Gylle's wife. She appears to have a child behind her. The woman in the centre-foreground is possibly bailing the mine. In the centre is a blast furnace, fed by bellows driven by a waterwheel. Just visible to the right of the furnace, disappearing into the background, is a woman climbing up to the top of the furnace with a basket of charcoal and ore to feed the fire. The molten iron is trickling out to the right, to consolidate into a sow. A woman is helping the group of founders to carry a sow to the weight scale. The sow is then taken by a horse-drawn waggon to the forge.

The left side of the picture shows the processes required to turn the brittle cast iron into malleable wrought iron. It had to be reheated in an open finery hearth, to oxidise the iron. The person here is wearing a long skirt but it might be a man with an apron. A woman with child behind is riding towards the hearth area. After the iron was heated and oxidised in the finery, it was consolidated by heavy hammering with a power hammer at the chafery (in the background). In front of the third hearth (on the far left) there appears to be another woman, operating the chafery. She is heating the iron up between the sessions with the power hammer.

Another version of the picture by Bles is in Graz, Lichtenstein. At the bottom-right is a woman breaking up ironstone. In the centre foreground a woman works with the drainage of the mine, while another woman helps to carry the sow to the balance. On the left (fig. 1) one woman is working face on to the sweltering finery hearth, while another helps a man with hammering. She holds the iron with tongs. In the background the power hammer is lit up by the chafery hearth which is also being tended by a woman.

Further evidence of women working at the hot and heavy end of industry comes from the stained glass window at York Minster, donated by Sir John Tunnoc, a goldsmith and bell-founder of York in 1328[11] (fig.2). The entire window is framed by golden bells, and shows a bronze bell being cast. The furnace is in the middle and the molten bronze trickles down to a bell mould on the right. The figure on the right is a woman operating hand bellows and the one on the left, also a woman but poorly restored, is apparently operating foot bellows. On an adjacent window women are shown turning a new bell on a lathe, to smooth out the interior so that it will strike the correct tone. Casting a large bell was a highly skilled task, described in the early twelfth century by the medieval monk Theophilus.[12] Sir John saved his soul, but apparently his womenfolk did the work.

Tunnoc's female associates are not personally identified, but documentary evidence both in York and elsewhere shows that they performed a significant role in the industry. Heather Swanson[13] has recorded some: Margaret Soureby, the widow of a York founder, who took over his business and bequeathed all the utensils 'of my craft of foundercraft' to Thomas Burton 'of my household' in 1415; and the Shrewsbury woman, in the early fourteenth century, who continued to work as a potter (ie maker of copper pots) long after her husband Peter the Potter died.[14] Caroline Barron has identified the career of two notable London widows, Johanna Hill and Johanna Sturdy, who successfully carried on their husbands' foundry

FIG. 2
York Minster, Window nxxiv
Women casting a bell,
c. 1325. Photograph
courtesy of National
Monuments Record/
RCHME © Crown Copyright

businesses in the fifteenth century.[15] Twenty-three bells made by Richard Hill, Johanna's husband, still survive, identifiable by his distinctive stamp. For Johanna there survives from 1441 both a contract with the parishioners at Faversham to replace any of the five bells she had made if they proved defective, and seven bells identified by her mark.[16] Johanna Hill bequeathed her business to her daughter, Johanna, and son-in-law, Henry Jordan. It was then taken over by John Sturdy, who produced bells with his own mark but used the old letters of Richard Hill. John Sturdy was dead by 1459 and his widow Johanna took over the business, marking fourteen surviving bells with her own stamp, and replacing one of the Faversham bells made by Johanna Hill when it proved defective in 1459. George Elphick has published further documentary information about women founders in the Middle Ages,[17] including Agnes le Belyetere of Worcester, between 1274 and 1275 and Christina la Belytere of Gloucester, between 1303 and 1304.

Bell-founders can frequently be identified by the stamps on their bells, and in the case of widowed founders, the stamp can be distinguished by a lozenge motif over the husband's mark. This makes the study of bell-founders more precise than that of smiths, most of whose works (apart from armour and some knives and weapons) remain anonymous.

Next comes an explanation of the hearty woman who served as the logo of the conference. This selective illustration, far from extolling female accomplishments, is in fact a strongly anti-Semitic and sexist piece of propaganda. The story originates in Passion plays performed in the thirteenth century. According to these texts, the Jews asked around for someone to provide the nails for Christ's crucifixion. The earliest version just says that a certain ribald person made them, but this later hardened into a ruthless Jewess.[18] When the Jews asked the smith himself, he was rendered miraculously crippled and unable to perform the job, whereon his wife scolded him and volunteered for the job. The robust verse in the Northern Passion tells the story best:[19]

> **Forth then came the smith's wife**
> **A fell woman and full of strife,**
> **By the Jews there they stood,**
> **She spake her husband little good;**
> **Sir, she said, and loud 'gan cry,**
> **Since when had you such malady?**
> **Yester even when day was gone,**
> **Evil on thy hands had thou none.**
> **But since sickness is sent to thee,**
> **These men shall not unserved be.**
> **They shall have nails before they go**
> **And soon myself shall them make.**
> **She blew the bellows fairly fast**
> **And made the iron hot at the last.**
> **The Jews helped her for to smithe**
> **So that the nails were made full tight.**
> **Her husband saw and stood full still**
> **He dared not say that she did ill.**

The earliest depiction of this scene is on the central tympanum of the west front of Strasbourg Cathedral, carved after 1277.[20] The scene shows Christ bent over carrying the cross and a woman clasping three nails in front of it. A rather timid version is found in the Queen Mary Psalter.[21] It shows a daintily-dressed woman holding a hammer, tongs and nail at a small anvil, with her husband and Jews watching. The version in the Holkham Bible picture book (fig.3) provides a detailed rendering of the hearth with an elaborate set of bellows operated by hand. The energetic smith's wife is wearing a thick apron like her husband and stands with one hand raised holding her hammer. Her husband points pathetically at his enormously swollen hand, covered in boils.[22]

Jehan Fouquet painted the scene in the Book of Hours of Etienne Chevalier, dated around 1461.[23] The smith's wife in a white apron stands

FIG. 3
Detail of an Illustration from the Holkham Bible, BL Add ms 47682, f.o.31. Photograph courtesy of the British Library

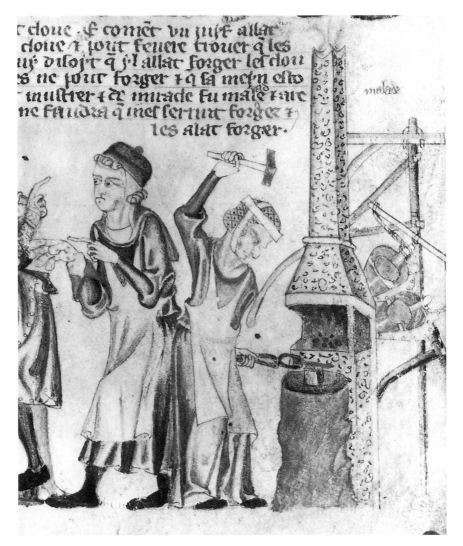

over a hexagonal anvil placed on a tree trunk. She swings the hammer and grips the tongs. Finally she appears in the *Mystère de la Passion d'Eustache Marchadé*, also from the fifteenth century.[24] In this text she is named as Hédroit. She stands by the forge with her skirts drawn under her arm while she holds a nail in her bare hand and strikes it with a hammer.

Finally, concerning the application of this information to a museum context, obviously it is not possible to distinguish artefacts made by men or women unless they are identified and as we have seen there was so much team work anyway. However, the activities of the Wealden Iron Research Group have brought medieval iron technology to life. Using considerable archaeological expertise and local knowledge, they have spent much time recreating the activities of the medieval bloom smiths in the Weald. They have studied the remains of old iron ore deposits and hearths. They have experimented in many different ways how to make charcoal, how to make a furnace with the local clay, how to make bellows, how to pump bellows by hand for days on end, and how to forge the miraculous products. This type of experimental work could usefully be replicated in an open-air museum and provide many people with the arduous experience of medieval iron production.[25]

ENDNOTES

Parts of this article are substantially derived from Geddes 1983 and 1991.

1 Barron, C. B., 1989, p25.

2 Colvin, H., 1963, pp222–4. Salzman; L. F., 1952, rev. edn, 1967, p337.

3 Thomas, A. H. and Jones, P. E., 1926, p274.

4 Sharpe, R. R., 1871, pp63, 67.

5 Sellers, E., 1912, p93.

6 Welch, C., 1916, pp249–59.

7 Coote, H. C., and Tyssen, J. R. D., 1871, pp32–5.

8 Sharpe, R. R., 1899–1912, pp165–7.

9 Lapsley, G. T., 1899, pp509–29.

10 Schubert, H. R., 1957, pp156–60. Schubert's frontispiece is an illustration of the Uffizi painting. Dasnoy, A., 1952, pp619–26. Bles made five very similar paintings of foundry scenes, which are at the National Museum, Prague; Landesmuseum Johanneum, Graz; Collection of the Prince of Lichtenstein, Vaduz; National Museum, Budapest; Uffizi, Florence. These are illustrated by Dasnoy.

11 O'Connor, D. E., and Haselock, J., 1977, pp350–55; Tylecote, R. F., 1976, p71.

12 Theophilus, introduction by Hawthorne, J. G. and Smith, C. S., 1979, pp165–79.

13 Swanson, H., 1989, pp74–5.

14 York Minster Library, Dean and Chapter Prob. Reg. 1, fo. 175v, Swanson, op. cit.

15 I am grateful to Caroline Barron for letting me see a pre-publication copy of Barron, C. and Sutton, A., 1994, pp99–111.

16 Barron, op. cit., 105.

17 Elphick, G., 1970, p113; Barron, op. cit., p111.

18 Foster, F. A., 1916, orig. series, no. 147, pp164–5.

19 Foster, F. A., 1913, orig. series, no. 145, pp168–73. The Harleian text is B. L. Harley MS 4198, fo. 76.

20 Klein Ehrminger, M., 1970, p24.

21 Warner, G., 1912, pp28, 256. The manuscript is B. l. Royal MS 2 B VII, fo. 252b.

22 Hassall, W. O., 1954, p28, fo. 31b. The manuscript is B. L. Add MS 47682.

23 Trenchard Cox, 1931, pl.xxiv, p71.

24 Cohen, G., 1928, vol. 1, pl.33. The manuscript is Arras Bib. MS 675.

25 *The Bulletin of the Wealden Iron Research Group* (WIRGS) records their activities and experiments. H. Cleere and D. Crossley, *The Iron Industry of the Weald*, Leicester, 1985, acknowledge the enormous contribution of WIRGS to our understanding of the Wealdon iron industry.

THE TEXTILE INDUSTRY AD 500–1500

Frances Pritchard

This paper is chiefly confined to England between the sixth and fifteenth centuries, although some information is drawn from continental sources. Within this timespan of one thousand years, the later centuries offer a sharp contrast to the early period, for while the evidence for Anglo-Saxon England is extremely patchy, it points to textile production being a wholly female domain engaged in by women of every class, whether slave or aristocrat. By the eleventh century the gender division began to diminish and men became involved in certain processes. The rise of guilds in the twelfth century shifted the emphasis in weaving, dyeing and finishing cloth on to men and these activities became strictly regulated, especially within towns. However, the role of women in textile output was not eclipsed. Certain skills such as spinning and braidmaking, for which little equipment or space was needed, remained their sole preserve, while in other fields, for example weaving and embroidery, they worked on a similar footing to men except in respect of their legal status.

Archaeology and written documents are the principal sources for the Anglo-Saxon period. Textile production was important, but the extent to which it was organised is difficult to judge. The celebrated passage in a letter from Charlemagne to Offa in 796 complaining about the short length of cloaks supplied from England and requesting that cloaks of the accustomed length be sent in future implies that a marketing network existed and that a ruler could intervene to regulate production.[1]

Based on her study of Old English, Christine Fell has argued that 'in the early stages of their culture Anglo-Saxons distinguished male and female roles as those of the warrior or hunter and of the clothmaker'.[2] The ordinary word for woman in Old English, 'wif', and its compound 'wifman' appear to be linked with weaving. Moreover, many words associated with the production of textiles, for example spinster, seamster, webster and dyster, terminate in the Old English form '-stere', which usually represented a feminine occupational suffix, although already by the eleventh century the terms were occasionally applied to men.[3] Gravegoods, including spindles, woolcombs, weaving swords and needlecases, likewise indicate that it was women who practised spinning, weaving and sewing in the Anglo-Saxon period.

Until around the eleventh century the warp-weighted loom appears to have been the most common form of loom in north-west Europe. Archaeological evidence, including the distribution of loomweights and the position of post holes, reveals that these looms were often over two metres wide. Hence weaving was frequently a communal pursuit involving two women working side by side.[4] It should also be borne in mind that much of the work was carried out by slaves on large estates and slave trading, as well as slave raiding, helped to diffuse textile skills throughout northern Europe. Female slaves usually possessed specialised skills and in this capacity they were sometimes listed among bequests in wills. Thus, Wynflaed, a wealthy widow owning land in south and south-west England, bequeathed two female slaves, a '*crencestre*' and a '*semestre*', to her granddaughter in the tenth century.[5]

Anglo-Saxon England was especially renowned for its gold embroidery, which attracted the admiration of many commentators including William of Poitiers, chaplain to William the Conqueror, who reported that 'the women of the English nation are very skilled with the needle and in weaving with gold'.[6] While much of this work may have been carried out in religious houses, like Barking Abbey where scraps of waste from the making of gold thread were recovered during rescue excavations in the 1980s, workshops also existed on secular estates. The Domesday Book mentions two examples, Leofgyd, a widow with an estate at Knook, Wiltshire, who made gold embroideries for the king and queen and Aelfgyd, an unmarried girl living in Oakley, Buckinghamshire, who taught gold embroidery to the daughter of Godric, a sherriff.[7] There is little to indicate that these workshops were very large, although many hours of labour would have been needed to accomplish epic works of the size of the Bayeux Tapestry. This is also the general impression that one gains of most workshops in the high medieval period. Four women, for example, took three and three-quarter years to embroider an altar frontal for the high altar in Westminster Abbey during the reign of Henry III.[8] However, a few professional workshops supplying London merchants and the court may have been larger and it has been estimated that the embroidery workshops of the Setter family in the City of London in the late thirteenth century employed as many as twenty workers.[9]

The organisation of many textile trades underwent a radical change during the twelfth century as growing urbanisation brought about the formation of guilds. This resulted in the greater involvement of men, although women were not usually excluded and, indeed, they continued to dominate certain crafts such as spinning and bleaching linen which were not regulated by guilds or confraternities at this period and which were essentially rural activities. The establishment of guilds brought about a system of apprenticeship whereby an apprentice was bound by an indenture to serve his or her master or mistress for a period of approximately seven years, during which time the apprentice was instructed in the relevant craft. The precise length of apprenticeship varied between different crafts and in different places; girls apprenticed as seamstresses to hosemakers in Paris in the early fourteenth century were only required to serve a term of two years[10] and female yarn finishers, goldbeaters and goldspinners in Cologne served apprenticeships of four years.[11] There were also restrictions in Paris forbidding women to undertake certain types of tapestry weaving and finishing processes as they were considered to be too physically demanding, while in Cologne in 1378 felt hatmakers forbade all female help.[12] Similar restrictions do not, however, appear to have applied in England. Sometimes mistakes occurred, for example in 1417 William Tikhyll, a saddler, complained that a woman from Buckinghamshire had apprenticed his daughter, Agnes, to a wiredrawer for a term of fourteen years but in reality she was just taught cardmaking.[13]

What proportion of girls went through this system of training is difficult to calculate. Jeremy Goldberg has stated that 'female apprentices, though found, appear to be rare outside London'.[14] Nevertheless, many fourteenth- and fifteenth-century documents refer to women licensed to trade in a wide variety of textile-related crafts including weaving, dyeing, fulling and shearing cloth. Single women were able to work independently. Married women frequently worked alongside their husbands or could elect to trade as *feme sole*. When widowed, wives could if they so wished take over and carry on their late husband's craft. For example, Alice Byngley pursued her late husband's craft of shearman until her death in 1464 when she bequeathed the tools of her trade to her manservant.[15] However, in some trades and towns, such as dyeing in York, widows were only allowed to trade for a year after their husband's death unless their servant was admitted to the franchise.[16] Not surprisingly, specialised skills were often concentrated within families, among the best known being families of London embroiderers such as the Setters who lived near Cheapside in the late thirteenth and fourteenth centuries, and the Heyrouns, who had business links with the Setters.[17]

One group of textile workers active in London was exceptional, namely the silkwomen who made and sold narrow wares including braids, cords, fringes, tassels and hairnets of silk thread which they also twisted and plied before use.[18] By 1368 they were sufficiently influential to petition the mayor and aldermen against a Lombard merchant who was cornering the market in all raw and coloured silks and so pushing up prices. They also petitioned parliament on several occasions during the second half of the fifteenth century, resulting in enactments protecting their work from foreign competition.

It can, therefore, be seen that women held a different position in regard to the production of textiles in 1500 as opposed to AD 500. No longer were all textile workers women and frequently slaves. Some remained at the margins of the labour force working as spinsters subject to cheating by employers and middlemen.[19] Others worked as part of husband-and-wife teams. A number were respected as independent, highly skilled operators, such as Christina of Enfield and Catherine of Lincoln, both embroiderers who worked at the court of Edward I.[20] But the sixteenth century was to see the role of women undermined as changing economic conditions led to increasing competition from men and growing exploitation.

ENDNOTES

1   Stenton, F. M., 1943, p220.

2   Fell, C., 1984, p40.

3   Ibid, p41.

4   Hoffmann, M., 1964.

5   Owen, G. R., 1979, p222; Fell, C., 1984, p41.

6   Budny, M. and Tweddle, D., 1984, p90.

7   Fell, C., 1984, p42.

8   King, D., 1987, p160; Staniland, K., 1991, p12.

9   Fitch, M., 1976, p295.

10 Dixon, E., 1895, p221.

11 Wensky, M., 1982, pp632, 636.

12 Howell, M. C., 1986b, p115.

13 Dale, M. K., 1928, p24.

14 Goldberg, P. J. P., 1992a, p14, n19.

15 Goldberg, P. J. P., 1992b, p121.

16 Ibid, p122.

17 Fitch, M., 1976; Staniland, K., 1991, p12.

18 Dale, M. K., 1932–34, pp329–31; Lacey, K., 1987 p188.

19 Goldberg, 1992b, p119.

20 Lachaud, F., 1993, pp37–9.

WOMEN, WORK AND THE INDUSTRIAL LABOUR MARKET 1500–1800

Katrina Honeyman

The purpose of this paper is to provide a general overview of women's contribution to industrial activity, 1500–1800, and to draw out the main themes of recent academic enquiry into women's work in the early modern period. It should be emphasised that this research is still at an early stage, records are sparse and great ingenuity is required to assemble an accurate picture.[1] Broadly, progress has followed two paths: the first consisting of detailed studies of small groups of women, which ultimately will enable us to reach general conclusions, but as yet, it is difficult to know how typical or how unusual these groups are;[2] while the second comprises research which attempts to provide a wider framework, incorporating economic, social and ideological change in order to analyse the meaning and significance of women's role in industry and work.[3]

Until the last ten years or so, historians were less concerned with the *extent* or even the *status* of women's work before industrialisation, than to find that they had been active at all.[4] This tendency reflected the early stage of the field of enquiry. During the last few years, however, research has turned on attempts to explain why women became concentrated in the secondary labour market; and why women had less attractive opportunities than men.[5] A very recent tendency in the literature is to emphasise the extraordinary qualities of the large numbers of working women who earned a living for themselves and often dependants, despite the barriers put in their way.[6]

Historians, therefore, combine efforts to identify what women did, with how women came to occupy particular employment positions, and the extent to which they had choice over what they did. Historians now look more closely at the relationship between men and women at work, and the processes by which jobs became gendered (associated with men or with women but rarely both); and at the same time structured in a hierarchy which placed men in more skilled, more specialised and more highly-paid work, while women became *associated with* lower-status, irregular, casual, flexible and poorly rewarded occupations.[7] This clearly has less to do with the respective *quality* of the work men and women did, than the way in which this work became perceived.

By 1800 this categorisation of employment by gender was well established and became more deeply embedded in the context of industrial capitalism, for which a hierarchy of labour seemed to be important. However, historians, especially of the early-modern period, believe that there was a time when women engaged in rewarding occupations,[8] and when men and women co-operated in the same or similar tasks. The late Middle Ages is often identified as the high point for women, before economic and social changes in the early-modern period altered the nature and quality of work available and influenced the gender distribution of that labour.[9] There is doubt, however, that a 'golden age' existed even then.[10]

The first theme of recent research is the identification of the work that women did. Women's importance in industrial activity and economic life in the years between 1500 and 1800 is undisputed. Women may have been marginalised politically and socially, but they were not *excluded* from work, consumption, thrift or accumulation.[11] Yet because the work in which women engaged did not always fall into formal or clearly recognised occupations, the historical record of this work is incomplete. What is clear, however, is that the work of women was elastic and flexible. Women's manufacturing activities expanded or contracted or otherwise changed according to the requirements of the business; the state of the economy; marital status (widows, for example, might sustain their husband's business after his death); or domestic or other commitments. In other words, whether the industrial activity was located in the household or in the workshop, women participated as and when required, thus they *held everything together*; though as Mary Prior says, '[i]t was important to good order that this was never recognised'.[12] It is also clear that the work that women did was *different* from men's and more protean. Even where women and men were engaged in the same trades, they did not perform the same tasks. Further, the various functions were not allocated on an equal basis. Within the household economy and in the workshop, women performed *adaptable* functions and they were almost always perceived as assistants, rather than equal partners.[13]

Such research as has been carried out so far, confirms that women's work was more variable than men's across time and space. It took different forms in the countryside and in the towns; in different regions and localities; at different stages of economic cycles; or according to individual family circumstances. In urban centres, women engaged in a range of trades, especially those where regulatory influence was weak, which was often the case in textile production; or where occupations were linked to traditional production undertaken on an informal domestic basis. In addition, women *participated* in a range of 'male' trades (tailoring, victualling) either as general assistants or, in the case of a husband's death, they might take control. In this context, women were not accorded the same privileges as men within the guild, and, in the event of remarriage, would be required to cease trading. This marginality in trade is confirmed by the evidence of death certificates, where a woman who continued to run her deceased husband's business is described merely as 'widow'. The majority of women, however, were not associated with a skilled trade at all and worked in a range of menial activities, typically domestic service or in the clothing trades.

Although much work recently has explored the particular dynamic of rural industry and the interaction of town and countryside, earlier research focused on the identification of women's work in the urban context. The earliest and best-known study of the subject of women's work is that by Alice Clark,[14] whose research remains the most complete description, though its accuracy is sometimes doubted.[15] Clark found women engaged in a wide variety of trades: especially textile spinning, which was monopolised by women until the late eighteenth century; and silk and linen production. Any skilled work to which women had access was primarily located in silk, millinery and upholstery. Women were also to be found in printing and bookbinding; metalworking and retailing or sometimes shopkeeping, to which girls might become apprenticed, but more commonly, women were located in the lower levels of peddling and hawking.[16] Clark also found that women were more likely to be prominent in trades that could be domestically-based than those that required a separation from the home. Thus women could and did become pewterers and smiths; but they were more constrained in becoming carpenters and masons.[17]

Clark successfully identified plenty of occupations for women, but seemed to be satisfied to find that women were economically active. She engaged in little qualitative analysis which may have illuminated contemporary perceptions of the status and value of women's work. Clark's vision of a seventeenth-century 'Golden Age' which was readily adopted by feminist historians until recently, has failed to be confirmed by robust historical enquiry. Earle's analysis of employment opportunities for women in mid-seventeenth-century London, for example, indicates a narrow choice of jobs which were structurally similar to those suggested by the Census of 1851.[18] Women worked, casually and seasonally, in domestic service, making and mending clothes, charring and laundry work and nursing.[19] Earle found few cases of husbands and wives working together[20] and few widows continuing their husbands' trades for more than a short time.[21] He concludes that while most women worked for a living, they had limited choice; they were barred from sharing in men's work and were forced to seize opportunities wherever they could.[22]

Prior's work on Oxford suggests a more positive interpretation; possibly because Oxford offered greater employment opportunities for women because of a more liberal environment or a different economic structure.[23] Yet while Prior confirms that women had less than equal access to skilled work, she makes two qualifications. In the first place widows successfully continued their husbands' businesses, particularly when economic circumstances required this (that is, women tended to be particularly active in times of general economic crisis, or when family survival was in doubt) and they continued to take on apprentices. These women, however, were not typical, and in the 280 years between 1520 and 1800, only 140 widows took apprentices.[24] The second peculiar feature of the Oxford case was that women actively probed the weak points in the institutional structure of crafts and marketing, and seized opportunities whenever developments created the possibility of an entry into new trades. These entries, however, were overwhelmingly in inferior positions. Those in mantua making (a loose outer gown), provide an illustration. The appearance of this fashionable item threatened the male monopoly on clothesmaking and tailoring – because the mantua was not tailored and could be made up and sold ready-made outside the regulation of the guilds. As it passed into the hands of women, it became identified as an inferior trade.[25]

Roberts's work on the sixteenth century confirms the difficulty of finding women behind the male-dominated public face of work. His findings also suggest that women's participation in work did not follow a linear or progressive trend but rather that women adapted to the cyclical rhythms of the urban economy and their own lives. Always they struggled to 'reconcile the ideal of the household with the wayward but necessary improvisations of working women'.[26] Roberts's analysis also indicated that while women were often located in such submerged casual trades as herb wives, oyster wives and several other kinds of wives, they might also engage in skilled work – but on an informal basis – particularly in the family economy.[27] Thus although female apprentices to skilled trades were rare, daughters often acquired skills informally through their fathers and held responsible positions within his workshop.[28] Wright's work on Salisbury confirms that women played only a small part in formal craftwork;[29] and because of a range of difficulties comparatively few women took over their spouses' businesses.[30] Thus most women participated in the large and submerged world of casual and seasonal unemployment.[31]

Most recent work on urban women's trades has shown that women did not enjoy equality of opportunity, but that they revealed remarkable determination and tenacity in creating and exploiting opportunities. They created new niches for themselves, especially in retailing activities and in the clothing trades, often superseding the constraints imposed by the more powerful groups in society. Recent work has also indicated that women made a vital contribution to industrial production processes, but were often considered to be ancillary and flexible labourers. Thus whether or not the work women did was less skilful and less specialised than men's, that is how it was perceived. Historical analysis needs to confront the distinction between the real nature of what women did and what was perceived to be the case.

In the rural areas, where work for women was even more fluid, variable and seasonal than in the towns, gender distinctions in employment were less apparent. Female labour in rural manufacturing is now acknowledged to have been vital to eighteenth-century industrial expansion. In contrast to the suggestion of constraints on women's economic contribution in the pre-capitalist town presented by historians, the approach taken by researchers on rural industrial manufacture emphasises the decisive contribution of women to industrial change, particularly in the context of proto-industry.[32] Proto-industrial activity in the seventeenth and eighteenth century depended on, and increased opportunities for, home-based female employment; and seemed to be associated with a reasonable co-operative partnership between men and women in the household, where childcare, chores and decision-making appeared to be allocated on an equitable and non-gendered basis.[33] There is little evidence, however, that the status or prestige of women's jobs were enhanced within this structure.[34] Possibly the reverse was the case as it was the cheapness and flexibility of women's labour that encouraged the expansion of a proto-industrial manufacturing sector.

It was women who provided the bulk of the labour for spinning, lacemaking, handknitting, glovemaking, button-making, straw plaiting, silk manufacture, metalworking and pottery – industries that were dispersed throughout the rural regions in the seventeenth and eighteenth centuries.[35] Women were vital to the production of these new consumer goods; and were also vital to their consumption as they assumed a more important role in household-level decision-making.[36] Thus women enjoyed a high profile in rural manufacturing and were influential as producers and consumers in the area of the economy that was dynamic and provided the locus of subsequent industrial change.[37] Thus they were carriers of innovation, not simply in technical terms, but also in product innovation, marketing, distribution networks and divisions of labour.[38] Women in the countryside, more than in the towns, were concentrated in creative innovative activities and were instrumental in the high-productivity industries of the eighteenth century.[39] Despite their objective value, there is little evidence that women enjoyed any improvement in status or reward.[40]

Having represented the state of current knowledge on women's participation in pre-capitalist industry, we now explore the second theme of historical research in this area. This has been concerned with identifying the forces that influenced women's employment opportunities and historians in this category have been intent on developing a framework within which women operated. Women's access to work was influenced by contemporary perceptions of women's role and of their ability to engage in productive activity, by the availability of 'suitable' work for women; by labour supply characteristics; by the organisational structure of business, and by their life-cycle. The identification of women's work with flexibility has already been noted. The work women did accommodated irregular requirements for supplies of labour, and fluctuating economic circumstances. This flexibility was essential to the efficient running of industrial activity, but at the same time it confirmed women's marginal position in the labour force.

There was nothing 'natural' about this flexibility. It was the outcome of social and economic constraints, and particularly the imposition of barriers to training and therefore to skilled work. Apprenticeship patterns, for instance, reveal that girls and boys did not share equal access to formal training;[41] and while boys were guaranteed employment in a skilled trade following a period of apprenticeship; for girls, apprenticeship, where it existed, rarely led to recognised status as a skilled tradesperson.[42] Training for girls was more likely to be informal, broadly-based and typically confined to a narrow range of domestic activities.[43] Thus, girls' training was more likely viewed as a good general preparation for marriage.[44]

Women's choice was also influenced by life-cycle and occupational opportunities might change at each new stage of life. This tendency also served to confirm women's flexibility and adaptability as well as their non-specialist job status. The specialist status of men's work, by contrast, was reinforced by their commitment to a single, or a small number of jobs during their working life. Although life-cycle variations did not apply to the large number of women who were not married,[45] evidence suggests that widows as well as spinsters were typically located in the same range of occupational categories as their married sisters. They were similarly constrained by domestic forces, and had little impact on the overall structure of women's employment.[46]

Women's experience of work was also influenced by the organisational structure of business. The family economy or the family production unit, which was widespread at the beginning of the early-modern period, appeared to offer the best chance for women to engage in skilled work on roughly equal terms with men;[47] and its decline during the early-modern period as the market economy developed is believed to have reduced opportunities for high-status work for women.[48] Within the expanding formal market economy, some high-status work for women did exist but there were big locational variations. Typically, women entered market production through the family economy and they were therefore most active in sectors that grew out of tasks relating to their roles in the traditional household economy: namely textile and clothing production, food production and retail sales.[49] Sometimes, women acquired lesser and usually temporary roles in the male-dominated trades by virtue of their late husband's trade.[50]

During the early-modern period, however, women's position in the labour market became disadvantaged, not only by the decline of the family unit of production,[51] and a strengthening domestic ideology, but more overtly by the regulation of work. This operated to exclude women in indirect and direct ways. Indirectly, women were disadvantaged in the labour market by the impact of regulation on craftwork production and training.[52] The new rules introduced in various provincial centres during the early-modern period created difficulties in accommodating work in the formal economy with domestic responsibilities.[53] More directly, women in many early-modern towns became excluded from skilled work as male members of guilds practised exclusionary tactics as their trade and the position of their guild became threatened by growing competition from rural manufacture, by fluctuations in the demand for labour and other economic changes.[54] The male response to this threat was to exclude women specifically to reduce the quantity of available labour and therefore to protect and enhance their own position.[55] This suggests the operation of patriarchal forces in the determination of labour market positions and occupational choice, even if these forces were activated by trade-specific or short-term economic crises.[56]

In these ways the undermining of women's role in economic production became an essential element in the redefining and reasserting of the patriarchal order, and was supported by contemporary social forces that reaffirmed women's domestic and familial responsibilities and priorities. The exclusion of women from an increasing number of crafts and trades, and the debasement of women's work in general, confirmed the growing social ideology of women's natural inability to attain skills. The subsequent predominance of women in less skilled areas of work was apparent proof that these tasks were all that women were fit to do.[57] Thus the attempts by guilds to raise their prestige by controlling competition for work through restricting numbers (of women) had a greater impact on the perceived status and value of work, than on what the work actually entailed. Women were not always excluded from particular trades, but their work became downgraded by the fact that it was women that did it and because men had successfully gained a monopoly of skill.

An example of this process is provided by the textile trades, the most important sector of pre-industrial manufacture. In 1500, women were to be found in prestigious textile crafts. By 1650, these same crafts were no longer prestigious and the more predominantly female the trade, the lower its social standing and monetary reward.[58] Individual processes became taken over by men, typically in the context of innovation of process or product. In the silk industry, where women workers had far outnumbered men at the beginning of the early-modern period, the introduction of new weaving techniques changed the skill differential between men and women. As a result of seventeenth-century Huguenot immigration and imported machines, women became confined to subsidiary roles in silk weaving and ribbon weaving while men worked the broad looms which women were considered too weak to operate. Thus, as the supply of labour came to exceed demand, work was divided into specialised and non-specialised components, and men created a relatively high-status occupation for themselves and prevented women from gaining access to it.[59]

The conclusions to be drawn from the findings of recent historical enquiry may be grouped into four main themes. First, despite the real value of work that women did in urban and rural industry, their choice of work did become more limited, especially in the towns, during the early-modern era. Second, women had never enjoyed equal status in guilds or skilled work and they now became more or less excluded from guild membership. They enjoyed less than equal opportunities when it came to training and apprenticeship. Third, the process by which this came to take place must be seen in the context of economic change (the decline of the family economy, the growth of market economic structures and growing competition) and profound social changes that placed greater emphasis on women's responsibility for the home and the family. Finally, despite the enormous constraints faced by women, the flexibility of women's work and their range of adaptive skills and general knowledge meant that they continued to insert themselves into any opportunity, however slight, which emerged. They were also welcomed into men's activities whenever economic circumstances required it; that is when men could not cope without them.

So recent work shows us that we must not lose sight of the processes that restricted women's choice of work and pushed them towards domestically-oriented trades; or the forces that initiated and then confirmed women's subordinate position at work. Nor should we minimise the significance of the exceptional women who carved out for themselves a successful position in skilled work and trade. Neither should we forget that these women were exceptions. We must not underestimate the strength of women's struggle to continue to engage in paid employment against all the odds. Women may have dominated lower-status occupations, but that they continued to work at all in such large numbers is a tribute to their determination and inventiveness.

ENDNOTES

1 Prior, M., 1985, pxv.

2 Clark, A., This book provides a classic example of this approach, and its enduring popularity, especially among feminist historians, is reflected in its frequent reprinting, most recently in 1992. Mary Prior's edited volume, *Women in English Society*, is another instance. A number of the papers presented at the WHAM conference, 1994, also followed this approach.

3 Judith Bennett has published extensively in this area: see Bennett, J., 1992. Also influential are Cahn, S., 1987; and Howell, M. C., 1986b.

4 Prior, M., 1985, p.93.

5 For a survey of the literature that has focused on this issue, see Honeyman, K. and Goodman, J., 1991, pp608–28.

6 See especially Berg, M., 1993; Prior, M., 1985.

7 See summary in Honeyman, K. and Goodman, J., 1991. It was the *perception* of women's work as of lower value than men's that was significant as Bennett, J., 1992, p152, makes clear.

8 See, for example, Hufton, O., 1983; and citations in Bennett, J., 1988, pp270–80.

9 Cahn, S., 1987, Introduction and chs 2 and 3.

10 Particularly doubtful is Bennett, J., 1992, p159, who identifies, for example, guild restrictions in every century from 1300–1700. Barbara Hanawalt likewise reveals doubt in her Introduction to *Women and Work in Pre-industrial Europe*, Hanawalt, 1986b.

11 Humphries, J., 1994.

12 Prior, M., 1985, p96.

13 There are, of course, recorded exceptions to this, some of whom were identified at the WHAM conference 1994, but women acting as, and being perceived as equal partners were very unusual.

14 Clark, A., 1982.

15 Criticisms have been levelled from several quarters. See especially Bennett, J., 1992, pp149, 151–8; Hanawalt, B., 1986b, Introduction; Howell, M., 1986b, pp30–32.

16 Clark, A., 1982.

17 Ibid, p294.

18 Earle, P., 1989, pp341–2, though he adds that a larger proportion of women probably worked in the earlier period.

19 Ibid, pp339–44.

20 Which Clark, A., 1982, pp292–3, had identified.

21 Earle, P., pp338–9.

22 Ibid.

23 Prior, M., 1985, pp99–100, 102.

24 Ibid, p106–7; Roberts, M., 1985, p143, confirms the small number of female 'masters' but argues that there were many signs that a woman may have been involved in training a girl, although this was rarely formally acknowledged.

25 Prior, M., 1985, p110.

26 Roberts, M., 1990, p95.

27 Roberts, M., 1990, p94; also supported by Cahn, S., 1987, ch.2.

28 Roberts, M., 1990, p91.

29 Wright, S., 1985, pp100, 116.

30 Ibid, pp111–5.

31 Ibid, pp100, 116.

32 See the various contributions of Berg, but especially Berg, M., 1993. See also Hudson, P., 1994; Hudson, P. and Lee, W. B., 1990, Introduction; and Kriedte, P., Medick, H., and Schlumbohm, J., 1991, esp ch.2.

33 Hill, B., 1989b, p46; Kriedte et al, op. cit., ch.2.

34 Hudson, P. and Lee, W. B., 1990, p13.

35 Berg, M., 1985, p137.

36 De Vries, J., 1993, pp85–132, cited in Pat Hudson's contribution to the Women's Committee session at the 1994 Conference of the Economic History Society.

37 Berg, M., 1985, p70.

38 Berg, M., 1994.

39 Ibid.

40 Hudson, P. and Lee, W. B., 1990, p13.

41 According to Hill, B., 1989b, pp88–9, only ten per cent of apprentices in the eighteenth century were female, and because most of these were recruited through the parish apprenticeship scheme, they were unlikely to gain access to highly skilled work.

42 Berg, M., 1988, p72; Bennett, J., 1992, p160.

43 Roberts, M., 1990, p91, has emphasised the less formal nature of women's 'training'; while Keith Snell's research, confirmed in Hill, B., 1989b, pp88–9, indicates that by the eighteenth century, fifty per cent of female apprentices were to housewifery trades and a further twenty-five per cent to clothing occupations.

44 While boys underwent systematic industrial training and entered a guild. Lown, J., PhD thesis, University of Essex, 1984, p100.

45 Berg, M., 1991, p2, shows that celibacy peaked in the 1670s and 1680s, when the age of first marriage also peaked at thirty. See also Sharpe, P., 1991, p63; Hill, B., 1989a, pp129–47.

46 Earle, P., 1989, p339. Although the range of occupations was the same, the proportions varied, so that spinsters, for example, were more heavily represented than married women in domestic service.

45 The notion that there was equality of opportunity within the family economy has recently been challenged in particular by Bennett, M., 1992, p155, who believes the family economy was 'shot through with sexual inequality'.

48 Howell, M., 1986a, p215.

49 Ibid, p215; Howell, M., 1986a, pp43, 178–83.

50 Howell, M., 1986a, pp201–2, 215. A critique of Alice Clark's description of the family economy is contained in Howell, M., 1986b, pp30–32.

51 Howell, M., 1986a, p216.

52 Roberts, M., 1990, p90, also refers to the 'resolutely male' public image of the crafts.

53 Howell, M., 1986a, p215.

54 Honeyman, K., and Goodman, J., 1991, pp610–14.

55 Howell, M., 1986b, p183, shows how men battled to strengthen the traditional order and to restore the patriarchal structure which women might have overturned had they not been forced to depart from positions in market production.

56 Honeyman, K., and Goodman, J., 1991.

57 Cahn, S., 1987, p51.

58 Ibid, p53.

59 Berg, M., 1988, pp72, 77–9.

WOMEN PEWTERERS OF LONDON 1500–1800

Rosemary Weinstein

'… though women were seldom carpenters or masons, they figure as pewterers and smiths', states Alice Clark in her *Working Life of Women in the Seventeenth Century*,[1] discussing the involvement of women in the crafts and guilds, and cites the few entries from the Pewterers' Company records to support her case. This paper attempts to extend Clark's survey of women in the pewter trade. Although documentary evidence remains scant, curators now have the advantage of studying the increasing numbers of extant items identified as made by women pewterers. This, in turn, leads to further questions of interpretation.

In 1451–2 the earliest extant accounts of the Pewterers' Company record that '*sustren*' (sisters) as well as '*brethren*' paid their quarterage (dues) that year, and hence were admitted to the craft of pewterer, as well as to the social and religious life of the fellowship connected with the guild.[2] These 'free sisters' were probably widows of freemen of the Company, having by marriage acquired freedom themselves, and hence the right to conduct a business in the pewter trade.

Regarded as her late husband's partner, a widow was entitled to continue his business, taking over his leases, stock and apprentices (fig. 1). That she was expected to continue in the business has been suggested by her right to occupy the family property for life (or until remarriage) rather than the mere forty days, as was customary outside London.[3] A list of the livery and yeomanry of the Pewterers' Company in 1670 which separately enumerates eleven 'widows',[4] all presumably continuing to run their late husband's business and use his 'touch' (touch mark or maker's mark) as free of the Company, shows the practice continuing. A dish, with the touch mark of Mary Langley (in fact an adaptation of her husband Adam's restruck touch of around 1670, after the Great Fire of London)[5] also bears advertising devices known as 'hallmarks' after the Goldsmiths' fashion, and which incorporate his initials 'AL'. Adam, a Warden of the Pewterers' Company in 1680, was dead by 1682. Mary was thus assuring customers that his business continued as usual. The status of 'free sister' might be lost if widows married out of the Company. In 1678, for example, one Mrs Sicily Moore, formerly the wife of Edward Fish, pewterer, 'since married to one Moore, a fforeigner, now also dead, desired to be admitted into the freedom

FIG. I
Apprenticeship Indenture.
This indenture binds
Richard Henson of
Yelverstoft,
Northamptonshire, as
apprentice to Mary Priest,
citizen and pewterer of
London for seven years
from 14 October 1680.
Guildhall MS, 22,185
The Pewterers' Company

of this company'. The court of the Company agreed, on payment of the usual fines, but only on condition that she did not take on an apprentice. Some widows insisted that their new husbands join their Company, so that they might retain privileges inherited from their late husbands. By the nineteenth century, the trade directories reveal the numerous women pewterers operating throughout London. The classic case is that of Susannah Cocks, widow of Samuel Cocks, a supposedly prolific pewterer of Shoe Lane, Holborn. Samuel died in 1819 before he struck the 'touch' bearing his name. This touch mark was struck by Susannah in 1820. All the substantial output, previously believed to be his, can therefore be attributed to Susannah's workshop.[6] In addition to retailing pewterware, some women hired it out. In 1702, 1704 and 1705 Elizabeth Baxter and Prudence Ryland supplied the Clothworkers' Company in this way for their dinners.[7]

While the position of a woman as titular head, successfully running a pewter business is thus not in doubt, the crucial question of her role in the manufacturing side remains unclear. The York Pewterers' Ordinances of 1599 state that:

> If any master of the said craft having an apprentice shall fortune to die before
> the end of the term of the said apprentice, the same apprentice shall not be set
> over to any other to serve forth his term with but only to his mistress or dame,
> if he be an able workman, or if she keep an able workman to instruct or teach

him. And if he be neither an able workman, nor she have an able workman to
teach him, then he be set over to some master of the said occupation ... By
consent of the searchers or of my Lord Mayor.[8]

That Company did not expect the mistress or dame to teach the apprentice herself, it appears.

The increasing difficulties for women working in the craft guilds from the beginning of the sixteenth century have been discussed elsewhere.[9] This affected women countrywide and was not solely a London guild situation. It was now less easy for women to become apprenticed to a craft (and hence to gain the freedom of the company in their own right). Various reasons have been given for this, including population growth and the threat to men's jobs, and Protestant codes of conduct relating to women in the home.

The position was serious in the pewter trade. Owing to the increasing demand for pewter from the early sixteenth century, large numbers of apprentices were taken on, until the qualified journeymen resulting could not find enough work for themselves. They petitioned the Pewterers' Company regarding their plight in 1521.[10] The Company limited apprentice numbers as a result, and in 1534, guaranteed employment to all those who became freemen.[11] Other guilds were affected with varying degrees of severity: the Weavers and Bakers prohibited women working entirely (at least officially), while the Pinners restricted involvement in the craft to the wives and daughters of freemen.[12] This, in the main, appears to have been the course taken by the Pewterers' Company. In 1591, one Andrew Bowyar was fined five shillings for his second offence in employing a woman engraver 'contrary to the ordynaunce of the house'. The next offence would be a costly three pounds.[13] Clearly some women could, and did, perform specialised skills in the craft.

Of the mere seven women granted the freedom of the Company between 1680 and 1760, four had permission to strike their own touches, and did so. These were always of a conventional form, like that of a male pewterer; the lozenge formation, an heraldic device representing widowhood, is not found on pewter (unless used by a man!) – though familiar on the work of women goldsmiths, for example. Under normal working practice we would assume that pieces with women's touch marks were made by the women concerned – at least prior to 1747 when the touch of the vendor alone was officially allowed,[14] as also happened in the Goldsmiths' Company.

In 1691 Elizabeth Witter was granted permission to strike her touch (fig.2), Ann Tidmarsh hers in 1728 (fig.3), Mary Willey hers in 1760 (fig.4).

More pewter made by Martha Fly survives, however, than any other woman pewterer although she had no formal permission to strike her touch (fig.5). Martha was probably the widow of William Fly (touch mark 1679–80) and hence gained her freedom through him. Martha's pieces date to the 1680s. Elizabeth Boyden is even more elusive, not having permission to strike her touch, and having no known husband. She may have been the sister of Richard Boyden of Cambridge. Her fine 'wrigglework' plate, dating from between 1720 and 1730, is in the collections of the Pewterers' Company (fig.6). Mary Redshaw added the date of her own freedom (1733) to her father's touch but left his name unaltered on it. Perhaps she had no brother to carry on the family business, so Mary was trained instead.[15]

FIG. 2–5
Fig 2: Elizabeth Witter,
Fig 3: Ann Tidmarsh,
Fig 4: Mary Willey,
Fig 5: Martha Fly

All the above, except Mary Willey and Elizabeth Boyden, as far as is known, came from established pewtering families, and gained their freedom by patrimony through their fathers, not by servitude; they paid the usual fine of 9s/2d to do so. None was recorded as having a formal apprenticeship – indeed only two girls are so mentioned, and the nature of their apprenticeship is unclear.[16] The high cost of apprenticeship (between £20 and £40), comparable to that of the Goldsmiths' Company, would have been a major deterrent to most families as far as daughters were concerned – even had it been encouraged by the Company. Such training as might be received was within the family workshop. The high cost of setting up shop (£500) would have been a further obstacle;[17] the maintenance of a going family concern perhaps the only option available to her.

There is much further investigation to be done. Future correct interpretation could lead, not only to a better understanding of women's work in the trade, presently rather camouflaged, but also to a better understanding of the marking system of pewter in general and the fundamental distinction between manufacturer and retailer.

FIG. 6
Pewter Dish
Collection of the
Pewterers' Company

ACKNOWLEDGEMENT

The author wishes to thank the late Dr A. S. Law, past president of the Pewter Society, Dr R. F. Homer, Archivist to the Pewterers' Company, Peter Hooper and Charles Hull, past master of the Pewterers' Company, for information and advice during work on this paper.

ENDNOTES

1   Clark, A., 1919, p294.

2   Welch, C., 1902 (vol. I), pp16–18.

3   Barron, C. M., 1994a, pxvii.

4   Guildhall Library, MS 70.95.

5   Cotterell, H. H., 1929, p253 (Cott. 2828) and Peter Hooper, personal communication.

6   Guildhall Library MSS 7090/11 and 12. Court Minute Books of the Pewterers' Company, and the late Dr A. S. Law, personal communication.

7   Homer, R., 1977, pp24–30.

8   'Ordinances of the Pewterers' Company of York, 1599', cited in *The Reliquary*, 5, 1891, p76.

9   Barron, C. M., (in notes 3) op. cit., xxxiv.

10   Guildhall Library MS 22.204, and *Journal of the Pewter Society*, 5, Spring, 1985, pp13–14.

11   Ibid., and *Journal of the Pewter Society*, 6, Spring, 1987, pp22–3.

12   Cited in Rappaport, S., 1989, pp38, 39.

13   Welch, C., 1902, (vol.1), p6.

14   Ibid, (vol.II), p193.

15   Cotterell, H. M., 1929, nos 1703a, 3879, 4739, 5163 and 5246, and Dr R. Homer, personal communication. Only six other women were made free, by patrimony: Katherine Wetwood in 1633, Mary, Elinor and Elizabeth Witter in 1712, and Mary and Elizabeth Cleeve (1743): Welch, C., 1902, (vol II), pp92, 179, 191

16   Only two girl apprentices are recorded: one, Lucy Sellars, in 1713–14, the other Charity Pearson, 1664. Guildhall Library MS 70.90.

17   Hatcher J., and Barker, T. C., 1974, pp247–51.

CAN OCCUPATIONS BE SUGGESTED USING HUMAN SKELETAL REMAINS?

Stephanie Pinter-Bellows

The ability to identify occupations and habitual activities in skeletal populations has raised interest and debate in recent years. It has long been acknowledged by anthropologists and anatomists that specific individuals can be affected by habitual movement in their occupations or leisure pursuits. One of the earliest studies comes from 1888 and described the changes in an individual shoemaker to chest, hip and thumbs from working with leather.[1] Despite the popular belief that stresses to the bone can be associated with usage, evident in terminology often associated with overuse syndromes, such as 'tennis elbow', occupations and leisure pursuits do not produce stresses that leave unique fingerprints which can be observed and recognised on the bones. The elbow extension and hooking of the wrist which cause 'tennis elbow', for example, also present themselves in participants of ice hockey and gymnastics.[2]

Bone has an elegant simplicity in dealing with changes to it – the healing of fracture, the alteration of bone in size and shape during growth, the combating of infection, the enlarging of muscle attachments – it reacts to all circumstances with just two responses: either bone is added or taken away. However this system leads to difficulties in distinguishing lesions which resulted from a specific occupation, or habitual activity from those which resulted from a direct traumatic incident, age degeneration, or developmental defect. Some lesions may be a mixture of genetic disposition for a particular response.[3] So it can also be difficult associating lesions with occupations. Even in the modern clinical situation the relationships between many occupations and lesions are not clearly understood, with investigations providing conflicting evidence for relating particular skeletal features to specific activities.[4]

There have also been cautions that the correlation of specific physical stressors with skeletal characteristics can be virtually impossible for prehistoric groups and may not be possible even for people for which historical records and ethnographic analogy are available.[5] Even broad distinctions between subsistence patterns could not be made in a study which reviewed the published evidence for osteoarthrosis in hunter-gatherers and agriculturalists.[6]

OSTEOARTHRITIS

Osteoarthritis is the most frequently found pathology in skeletal material and so it has been used most often in attempts to link stresses to occupations. Osteoarthritis is a disorder characterised by deterioration and abrasion of articular cartilage and formation of new bone at the joint surfaces (Fig. 1). Palaeopathologists have an advantage over clinicians in studying osteoarthritis in that they can examine the entire skeleton, examining joints which do not normally come under scrutiny and observing osteoarthritis at sites rarely mentioned in textbooks of rheumatology. An example of this is osteoarthritis affecting the odontoid peg of the second cervical vertebra. It is not an unusual location to find osteoarthritis in skeletal material but it is rarely, if ever, referred to clinically.[7] The reason for this, beside the difficulty in examining this joint clinically or radiologically, is that patients do not complain of discomfort at this location. Correlating discomfort with gross osteoarthritic change in modern populations, in order to understand how incapacitated individuals in the past were, has been a very difficult objective. There has not been much success in associating the severity of osteoarthritis and the clinical

FIG. 1
Osteoarthritis of the facet joint with eburnation of a cervical vertebra, some marginal osteophytes and pitting are also shown. (specimens photographed in this paper are courtesy of The Paleopathology Group, Bristol University)

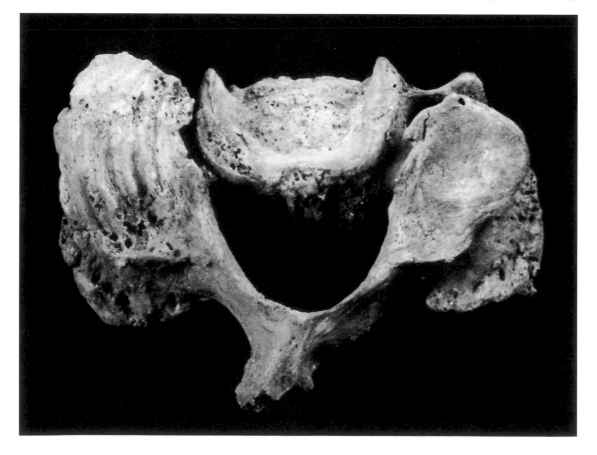

manifestation: some individuals complain vociferously when radiologically their lesions appear to be relatively minimal; while others with gross changes appear to be troubled only to a slight degree.[8] This is due in large part to the problems in recognising and therefore diagnosing osteoarthritis from radiographs.[9] Nevertheless, in a comparison of prevalence rates per thousand of osteoarthritis in modern populations with rates of modern-day attendance to general practitioners for osteoarthritis, it was found that the former was at least ten times the latter.[10] It would appear, then, that in the past more people had osteoarthritis than were bothered by it, but it is impossible to know how much pain was felt by any particular individual.

Several factors can lead to degenerative changes in the joints. The major factor is simply biological ageing with its concurrent decrease in bone vascularisation and ability of the bone to repair itself.[11] Repeated minor trauma or 'wear and tear' on the joints gradually produces the degenerative changes in the articular cartilage and subsequent bone reaction. There is no sharp borderline between ageing phenomena and incipient degenerative arthritis.[12] Genetic factors may be important in the causation of osteoarthritis.[13] Anthropometric studies indicate a correlation between physical type and degenerative joint disease.[14]

Since mechanical factors are important in the production of the pathological changes,[15] many researchers have looked for evidence which links occupations directly with patterns of osteoarthritis. A few clinical studies have found some connection: one, that miners had a higher prevalence of osteoarthritis in the hips and knees than non-miners,[16] and another that different patterns of osteoarthritis in the hands were related to tasks carried out in a cotton mill.[17] Other clinical studies have been unable to demonstrate any relationship between occupation and osteoarthritis.[18] When attempting to interpret patterns of osteoarthritis, aside from considering repetitive stereotyped tasks, age, sex, heredity, anatomy, size, posture, mobility, and trauma must all be considered.[19]

One of the recent studies to compare patterns of osteoarthritis with occupation is Waldron's study of the Spitalfields skeletal sample.[20] Weaving was the occupation of the largest number of known individuals. Modern weavers operating handlooms report that they get aches and pains in the hip, knee, wrist and fingers. Therefore it was expected that osteoarthritis in the hip and knee and in both wrists and fingers would be found if the weaver's occupation was, in fact, determining the location of the osteoarthritis. However, osteoarthritis occurred on both hips of only one weaver and in one hip of another. A further weaver had osteoarthritis in the wrist and it occurred in the hands of three elderly weavers. None had the disease in the knees.

When a case-control study was undertaken, in which all cases of osteoarthritis of the hands in males within the named sample were compared with a control group of randomly chosen adult males without osteoarthritis of the hands from the same sample, fewer weavers were found among the cases than in the controls. Nor does manual work itself seem to have been important, for when the occupations were categorised into manual and non-manual classes, the ratios were identical in both cases and controls. Age, however, seems to be related to the appearance of arthritis in the hands in this sample as there is a significant difference in the mean age of the two groups. The mean age of the cases was 71.6 years and of the controls, 57.8 years.

When analyses were carried out to determine whether there was any relationship between occupation and osteoarthritis of the shoulder or the spine, or for osteoarthritis at any site, none gave any support to the hypothesis that weaving as an occupation was related to the development of osteoarthritis in this sample. When a comparison was made for those in manual and non-manual occupations, there was still no evidence that being in a manual occupation predisposed those towards the development of osteoarthritis. In fact the only statistically significant result was for a significant difference in the number of non-manual workers with osteoarthritis of the spine. This finding appears at variance with the generally held view that the likelihood of developing osteoarthritis is directly related to the physical effort involved in work.[21] It remains to be seen whether there is an as yet unidentified factor which predisposed these non-manual workers to develop osteoarthritis of the spine and which may have an occupational component.[22]

Concluding his study, Waldron made only one tentative link between an occupation and a disease. This occurred with Thomas Mecham and his wife, Ann. Mecham was a victualler and both he and his wife died of dropsy, according to their death certificates. Waldron speculated that if what they really had was ascites of the abdomen, perhaps this was induced by alcohol which might have been liberally available to them because of Mecham's trade.[23] Sadly, this disease affects only the soft tissue and so cannot be identified from skeletal material.

CHANGES IN THE MUSCULOSKELETAL SYSTEM

Habitual occupational activity has been considered a contributor to changes in the musculoskeletal system, and some clinical work supports this view.[24] Inferences as to levels of activity have been made from comparisons of long bone dimensions and diaphyseal structures.[25] At this time it appears that only the asymmetry of the maximum length of the humerus is congenital in origin and is connected with side dominance.[26] Under high levels of mechanical loading, new bone may be added to counteract the resulting strains.[27] Dynamic loading (in which there is repetition) produces more cortical remodelling than static loading.[28] These occurrences may lead to change in the shape or size of the diaphyseal cross-section. Additionally, it appears that the response of bone to particular forces is quite specific, with remodelling occurring primarily in those areas of the bone which are under greater stress. Research has suggested that asymmetry decreases with age,[29] so again the age of the individuals to be studied is important.

In a study of asymmetries, long bone dimensions of the humerus were compared for skeletal samples from the *Mary Rose* and those from males excavated from the cemetery of the medieval Norwich church of St Margaret *in combusto ubi sepeliunter suspensi*.[30] The males from the Norwich sample were found to be more asymmetric than those from the *Mary Rose*, and as it is generally known what the men from the *Mary Rose* were doing, this asymmetry was interpreted as a lower level of activity. While all the asymmetries showed a right-sided dominance and the group from the *Mary Rose* showed more symmetry, the *Mary Rose* sample demonstrated an increase over the Norwich sample in many dimensions, particularly those of the left shoulder. It was suggested that these results might represent the presence of professional archers in the *Mary Rose* group.[31]

A broader study attempted to examine changes in habitual physical activities associated with the shift to maize agriculture in the prehistoric South-eastern United States by comparing long bone dimensions and diaphyseal structures.[32] In general, the agriculturalists were found to have thicker and stronger long bone diaphyses than the hunter-gatherers. This was interpreted as the agriculturalists having engaged in more strenuous activities. Differing patterns of changes were found for males and females. Males showed their largest increases in strength in the legs, while females showed fewer changes in both arms and legs. The more widespread increases in females suggested to the author an increase in a variety of chores; while males, showing fewer differences, might have been less affected by the introduction of maize.[33] However, there is unfortunately no real knowledge of the activities involved.

Osteoarchological reports often note morphological variants such as the hypertrophy (build-up) of areas of muscle insertion on bones. The size of these areas relate to muscle use and strength and by inference to occupations and habitual activities. A problem with this type of research is that there are very few actions for which the exact muscles involved have been studied. The majority of the researched actions and those used in sports as correct or incorrect movement can make the difference in winning and in injuries; throwing has been one of the more studied motions. Throwing is a complex series of movements which

> involves angular displacement of the forearm as a result of medial rotation of the arm at the shoulder, shoulder and arm hyperextension, and abrupt shifts from forearm supination to pronation (from turning your hand palm up to palm down). There are variations in these biomechanics depending upon individual anatomical differences, the style of training, and the nature of the missile itself. Starting and terminal follow-through positions involve the entire body, and these postures are relevant to successful performance, varying with the nature of the missile.[34]

In prehistoric samples of males 'known' to have used missile weapons such as spears[35] a suite of variants including the hypertrophy of the supinator crest on the ulna, the deepening of the ulna fossa and the ridging of the insertion of the anconeus muscle have been observed. Similar changes have been seen in modern individuals, of both sexes, who regularly engage in occupational or athletic activities involving similar patterns of arm movements.

However, the entire suite of changes must be seen in order to suggest that individuals whose activities are unknown were throwing missiles. A hypertrophic development of the supinator crest of the ulna is observed in many populations for which throwing is not thought to be a major activity.[36] The supinator muscle has its origin on the lateral epicondyle of the humerus and the adjacent portion of the ulna along the supinator crest. It inserts on the lateral surface of the upper third of the radius. It acts alone in slow, unresisted supination or in fast supination when the elbow is extended. It requires the assistance of biceps in supination during rapid movement with the elbow flexed. Certainly habitual throwing actions would involve the musculature of pronation and the morphology of hand bones, especially of the phalanges (fingers), which are modified by forceful grasping actions.[37] A twisting movement with the elbow extended and precision grip is also required for the use of an axe to cut trees, use of a hoe or rice flail,[38] perhaps in lifting and paddling certain boats,[39] some crafts, and even in the operation of a jack-hammer.[40]

Of recent interest are the osseous sites of tendon and ligament attachments, entheses and syndesmoses respectively; these can have alterations occur in the fibres. Disruption of the fibre bundles that are anchored to the underlying bone can cause hyperostotic (bone growth) (Fig. 2) or

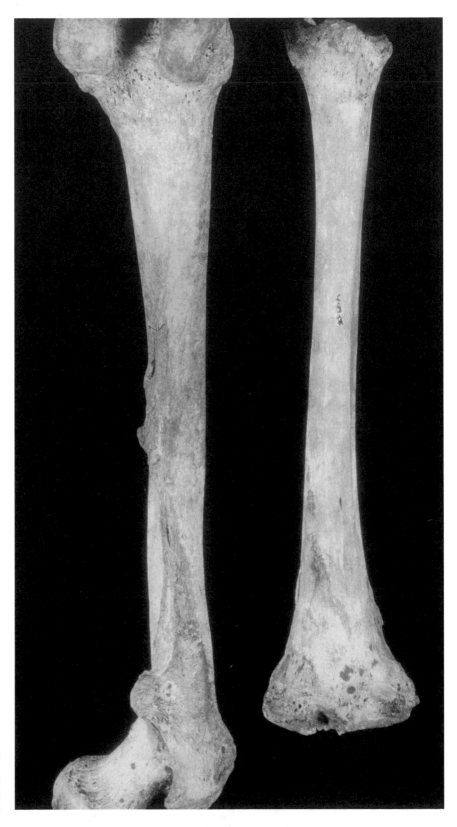

FIG. 2
Enthesophytes of the
linea aspera of the femur
and the popliteal line
on the tibia

osteolytic changes (bone loss) to that bone. Tendons attach the muscles to the bone; ligaments attach near particular joint surfaces and limit movement. As with osteoarthritis, the literature makes it clear, especially for enthesopathies (pathologies of bone growth or loss at the sites of tendon attachment), that they are often degenerative in nature and are 'common in older individuals'.[41] When enthesophytes are not thought to be metabolic or inflammatory in origin, the age of the individual becomes important. The changes concerned may be accelerated by trauma or chronic stress,[42] and, therefore, activity. If the individual in which the lesion occurs is young and robust and direct trauma or disease are not suggested as the causative agent, occupations and habitual activities can start to be explored. Not all the changes to entheses and syndesmoses which are thought to be a consequence of occupation will be pathological, some may be morphological; the former may be due to work-related trauma, while the latter appear to be related to loading stresses.[43]

The relationship between these changes and specific occupations is, however, another matter. As with enlarged areas of muscle insertion, an enthesis or syndesmosis cannot be interpreted in isolation. Stress at one site means nothing without examining related areas of the body to try and assess what repeated movement might have caused it. Nor is there information on how often a particular group of movements might cause such changes; it will certainly depend on force, style, physical type and genetics, among variables. The absence of change at a particular site should not be used to preclude particular movements or activities. Using data from a study[44] of two archaeological samples which tentatively interpreted certain enthesopathies as belonging to the same pattern as that which might be found in an archer, another group of investigators partially eliminated overuse as an explanation for greater size and degenerative changes because enthesopathies 'typical' of hunters were not present.[45]

A VARIETY OF OTHER STRESS INDICATORS

Schmorl's nodes are represented in the superior and inferior surface of the vertebra centra as a small cavity which occurs when the disc located between the vertebrae ruptures. The bubble of escaped material may then press against the body of the adjacent vertebra, which gradually yields to the pressure, forming a small cavity in its body. Schmorl's nodes provide evidence of torsional and compressional injuries that have occurred as a result of the sudden application of loading stresses if they are not degenerative or related to various diseases.[46] A possible example of this can be seen in three young adult skeletons found in close association with a cannon on the *Mary Rose*. All exhibited a great deal of stress to the thoracic and lumbar areas, including Schmorl's nodes. Those cannons weighed up to two tons and were operated entirely by hand by a gun crew, being hauled in and out of the gun port on a wooden carriage. The ball shot used was also very heavy and had to be fetched in baskets from the Orlop deck below.[47]

Spondylolysis is a relatively common abnormality;[48] it is also frequently found in skeletons from archaeological contexts. It seems there may be a genetic propensity for a weakness between the arch and the centre of the vertebrae; then due to the stresses and strains of daily life, these vertebrae may fracture between infancy and early adult life.[49] In most instances the defect does not create symptoms. In a comparison of skeletal material from Romano-British and Anglo-Saxon sites in the south of England with that from Christ Church, Spitalfields, used for burial between 1729 and 1869, Spitalfields was found to have a lower frequency of spondylolysis than the other groups. The likely explanation seems to be a lifestyle that was much less arduous or physically demanding as compared with earlier populations in Britain. As the early populations have a prevalence of spondylolysis that compares closely with modern data, the Spitalfields group may have experienced a way of life that involved less trauma to their spines than the population today.[50]

Os acromiale results from an inhibition of fusion of the acromion element to the rest of the scapula. The non-fusion appears to have a genetic component but in samples where it is found in a high frequency it is probably caused by long-term shearing stresses starting at an early age on the acromion.[51] In one case os acromiale may be related to long-term use of the longbow from an early age by the professional archers on the *Mary Rose*.[52]

Finally, a suite of variants are suggested which may be associated with habitual kneeling. These include the development of accessory facets on the dorsal surfaces of metatarsals and pedal phalanges from hyperdorsiflexion of the toes[53] and more controversial, osteochondritis imprints and flattening of the femoral condylar surfaces.[54] Unlike the other stress indicators discussed, this group of variants has been studied only in skeletal material; and while there is enthnographic and pictorial evidence for this posture, it is still only a closely reasoned supposition. Therefore, it should not be cited as proof that this activity occurred at other archaeological sites, but instead the skeletal material from other sites and the reason for believing that this habitual posture was practised should be taken as providing supporting evidence.

CONCLUSIONS

As yet no occupations have been unequivocally identified in skeletal material. There is, however, a small group of activities and stresses for which a consensus is forming; and many others for which continued comparisons between assemblages will advance our knowledge. It is essential that during this period of investigation we do not abuse the speculations which are put forward for peer review by treating them as proven facts.

The study of skeletal samples is faced with problems associated with the nature of the material and the lack of controls. Perhaps with our current state of knowledge a rigorous approach should be observed. Merbs[55] first suggested and Stirland[56] had advocated criteria for investigating occupational stress in skeletal samples which include: a limited number of specialised, but known, activities; good skeletal preservation and recovery; a relatively narrow timespan; and both cultural and genetic isolation.[57] Only a very few skeletal samples, perhaps four, have met this standard: the indigenous Sadlermiut in Canada;[58] the crew of the *Mary Rose*, Henry VIII's flagship excavated off the coast of Portsmouth;[59] the identified individuals from Christ Church, Spitalfields;[60] and the *voyageurs* from the Seafort burial site, unfortunately an extremely small sample, near a fur trading post in Canada.[61]

The bulk of the studies carried out so far have been on male rather than female skeletal samples; this is because it has often been easier to find a limited number of specialised, but known, activities involving males. This need not always be the case; carefully thought out hypotheses can be tested. If, despite the problems, some habitual activities can be identified in skeletal material it will be an important contribution to archaeology and the study of past lifeways.

ENDNOTES

1   Lane, W. A., 1888.

2   Krejci, V. and Koch, P., 1979, p46.

3   Frederickson, B. E. et al, 1984.

4   Kellgren, J. H. and Lawrence, J. S., 1958; Lockshin, M. D. et al, 1969.

5   Jurmain, R., 1991.

6   Cohen, M. N., 1989.

7   Waldron, H. A., 1993.

8   Doyle, D., 1986.

9   Rogers, J. et al, 1990.

10   Waldron, H. A., 1993, p73.

11   Hadler, N. M. et al, 1980.

12   Ortner, D. J. and Putschar, W., 1981, p419.

13   Lawrence, J. S. et al, 1962.

14   Seltzer, C. C., 1943.

15   Nuki, G., 1980.

16   Kellgren, J. H. and Lawrence, J. S., 1958.

17   Hadler, N. M., 1977; Hadler, N. M. et al, 1978.

18   Lindberg, L. and Danielsson, L. G., 1984; Sairanen, E. et al, 1981.

19   Anderson, J. A. D., 1984; Ortner, D. J., 1968.

20   Waldron, H. A., 1993.

21   Tainter, J. A., 1980.

22   Waldron, H. A., 1993, pp74, 75.

23   Ibid, p75.

24   Bird, H., 1990.

25   Bridges, P. S., 1989; Stirland, A., 1993.

26   Pande, B. S. and Singh, I., 1971; Schultz, A. H., 1937.

27   Lanyon, L. E. et al, 1982.

28   Lanyon, L. E. and Rubin, C. T., 1984.

29   Stirland, A., 1993, p113.

30   Ibid.

31   Ibid, p112.

32   Bridges, P. S., 1989.

33   Ibid, pp391–2.

34   Kennedy, K. A. R., 1983, p873.

35   Ibid, p872.

36   Angel, J. L. et al, 1987; Owsley, D. W. et al, 1987; Rathbun, T., 1987.

37   Kennedy, K. A. R., 1983, p874.

38   Rathbun, T., 1987, p248.

39   Lai, P. and Lovell, N., 1992, p229.

40   Kelly, J. O. and Angel, J. L., 1987, pp207–8.

41   Resnick, D. and Niwayama, G., 1981, p1297.

42   Ibid, p1300.

43   Stirland, A., 1991, p45.

44   Dutour, O., 1985.

45   Hershkovitz, I. et al, 1993, p186.

46   Resnick, D. and Niwayama, G., 1981, p1404.

47   Stirland, A., 1991.

48   Resnick, D. and Niwayama, G., 1988.

49   Frederickson, B. E. et al, 1984.

50   Waldron, H. A., 1991, p64.

51   Stirland, A., 1989.

52   Ibid.

53   Molleson, T., 1989; Ubelaker, D. H., 1979.

54   Lai, P. and Lovell, N., 1992; Trinkaus, E., 1975; Ubelaker, D. H., 1979.

55   Merbs, C., 1983.

56   Stirland, A., 1991, 1993.

57   Merbs, C., 1983, pp4–5.

58   Ibid.

59   Stirland, A., 1987, 1991, 1993.

60   Molleson, T. et al, 1993.

61   Lai, P. and Lovell, N., 1992.

CHAPTER 4

FROM THE PIT TO THE OFFICE – Nineteenth to the Twentieth Century

FORGE MILL NEEDLE MUSEUM AND WOMEN IN THE NEEDLE INDUSTRY

Sue Werner and Su Jones

INTRODUCTION

In the nineteenth century Redditch rose to pre-eminence on the basis of a needlemaking industry. Millions of needles were exported all round the world. Forge Mill alone could clean and polish three million needles a week. This paper introduces you to the history of needlemaking, Forge Mill Needle Museum, its permanent exhibitions and their limitations. It shows the ways in which we have attempted to redress the gender imbalance through some of our temporary exhibitions and our educational and outreach work.

NEEDLES AND NAILS

Redditch, like many other industrial Midlands towns, was built on the development of small metalworking. With Birmingham twelve miles north and the edge of the Black Country to the north west, you could expect to find parallels in employment practices between women workers in the needle industry and other women metalworkers in the region. Women employed as chainmakers, bucketmakers and nailmakers at the end of the nineteenth century are presented as hard, economically independent and unusual for being so. In appearance and manners, their drinking and smoking habits, these women were considered oddities, and this was attributed largely to their unnatural independence through work.

Women have always been employed in needle production, although most accounts of the industry are based on histories written by Redditch needlemasters in the nineteenth century. They tend to focus on the early processes of manufacture, the drama and dangers and conflicts of the pointers, rather than aspects of work in which most women were employed, such as spitting and packing. Some refer to the 'manual dexterity' and 'nimbleness' of women.

The manufacture of needles is complex, involving as many as thirty different stages of production. Originally a cottage industry, soon these many processes were being undertaken in the factory, small workshop and at home. Furthermore, there was overlap between the processes done in these different places. As Maxine Berg comments: 'It is particularly difficult to gain a clear idea of the sexual division of labour in trades which displayed

FIG. 1
Women sticking
pins at Abel
Morrall's factory
at the turn of
the century

such varied industrial structures...'[1] In this way needlemaking is significantly different from, for example, nailmaking. Maxine Berg suggests that in the Black Country women were involved in heavy work because there was no other work open to them. This was not the case in Redditch, nor in the Birmingham trades: 'In the nineteenth century women were still employed over a wide range of processes in the Birmingham trades, but these were, by and large, concentrated in the newer, lighter or more unskilled branches.'[2]

At the moment evidence of the role of women in the needle industry in previous centuries is sparse. There is still so much research to be done, thus we rely to a great extent on nineteenth-century needlemasters' accounts, men who were keen to bask in the glory of their good works, altruism and civilising influence. Men such as local historian and needlemaster, William Avery, who wrote: 'It has always seemed to be a great mistaken notion in Redditch that women were ordained to work in a factory instead of attending to their home duties.'[3] were unlikely to give detailed information about women involved in heavy physical labour in their own industry.

Charles Dickens visited a Redditch factory in 1852 and wrote in some detail, not to say awe, about the numerous processes involved in needle production, commenting on the skill and strength of the women needle workers: '... a woman ... who sat before the little anvil, filing with precision between rows of heads, so that they are separated easily, and then by another movement, cleaning away all the extraneous bits and sharp edges, delivering her spitfuls of needles complete in form'; and 'It is altogether an affair of tact; and fine must be the touch, and long the experience required to do such sorting with accuracy.'[4]

Dickens's account does recognise that women were involved in aspects of needlemaking, although the general picture reflects women as spitters, stickers and packers (fig 1), working in the cleaner and lighter side of the industry. He does acknowledge women were filing needles and comments on their 'strong wrists'. But all of this is overshadowed by the heavy, dirty and lung-destroying work that is presented as 'men's work'.

To support the segregation of work practice the mythology of women being more nimble-fingered has arisen. Thus women were considered more suited to spit, stick and pack needles. The same mythology can be found in the electronics industry today.

The alarmed reaction of late-nineteenth-century writers about women nailmakers has provided us with evidence of women's involvement in that industry. Our task is to try to discover the true extent of women's role in the history of the needle industry and the effect of gender and class bias in contemporary accounts.

FORGE MILL

Forge Mill was established as a museum of needlemaking in 1983. It was originally a museum trust, but is now owned by Redditch Borough Council. It is housed in eighteenth- and nineteenth-century buildings on either side of a working waterwheel. The earlier building is the Scouring Mill, which contains water-powered machinery which was used for scouring (cleaning and polishing) needles right up to the 1950s, still driven by the waterwheel. The other building was put to a number of uses until, at the time of Redditch's development as a New Town, a group of local enthusiasts started plans for a needle museum, appalled at the devastation being wreaked on the town and its past. By the time the museum opened, few people were still employed in the needle industry.

THE PERMANENT EXHIBITIONS

The bottom floor of the east wing illustrates the main stages in the needle manufacturing process, based on nineteenth-century descriptions. Imaginative use of limited space has been made by the designers. Scenes

THE WORKSHOPS OF THE WORLD.

STAMPING AND·EYEING.

are evoked with manikins, paintings, machines and tools of the period. Text panels describe the stages illustrated and give supporting information. Integrated with exhibits are three handsets with recordings of local (male) workers describing their respective jobs.

The processes illustrated are: men drawing the wire to size; men cutting the wire to length; the straightener rubbing the wire; the pointer grinding points on the wires; the kick stamper marking eyes on the wire; and the fly press operators (female) drilling eyes (fig.2); a woman and child threading the wires on to spits at home; the hardener dipping a tray of heated needles into a vat of fish oil; a woman rubbing straight a needle made crooked in hardening. Except where specified, the illustrations and/or manikins are male.

Visitors are then directed to the Scouring Mill, with its heavy water-driven machinery. We have tried to create the sense of a worker having just stepped out. An audio tape and photographs explain how the machinery was used to scour, wash and dry needles. A video in the east wing shows a scourer at work.

The top floor of the east wing contains static displays showing the great variety of needles manufactured locally, from surgical to bookbinding, from gramophone to packing, from smocking to gloving; needles for sewing up tennis balls and needles for sewing on space-shuttle panels.

What is not illustrated, nor brought out in the exhibits, is all the things that happened to the needles after this: they were sorted, checked, stuck in paper, labelled and packaged. These tasks were mostly carried out by

FIG. 2
Men kickstamping eyes in needles. Women drilling eyes using flypresses.
The Working Man: Weekly Record of Social and Industrial Progress, vol. 1 No. 9, Sat. 3 March, 1866

women and young people. Little time is spent on this in nineteenth-century accounts (with the exception of Dickens), nor is there much indication of the level of outwork and the extent to which women worked with their men to achieve their outwork targets. There are considerable gaps in our knowledge which we are only slowly and in a piecemeal fashion beginning to address.

THE BEGINNINGS OF AN ORAL HISTORY PROJECT

The invitation to the 1994 WHAM conference was the catalyst to start recording local women talking about their experiences of needlemaking, from the mid-twentieth century until the 1980s when the industry was in serious decline. We have started on a small scale, talking to three women, now in their sixties and seventies, whose testimonies are included in this paper. The women, all from Redditch, spent an afternoon in the museum, talking informally to colleagues. One was Margaret Hemming, who works part-time in the museum and has worked in needlemaking in the past. She agreed to invite two friends to join her. With their help we are beginning to build up a picture of the later days of the local needle industry. Early in their working lives they could swop from company to company and to different jobs, so they have, between them, quite wide experience. For us at the museum, it is a small beginning in updating our understanding of the industry and the role women have played in the second part of the twentieth century.

PEGGY BURROWS

Peggy originates from Kent. She started working at Victoria Works for ENTACO (English Needle and Fishing Tackle Company) in 1945. She worked on a conveyor belt, putting needles into packets and stapling them. It was piecework and she earned '£2 and a few coppers' for a forty-eight hour week. She worked from 8.00am until 12 noon with a ten-minute break and from 1.30pm until 5.00pm with another ten-minute break. There were six weeks of holidays per year.

She says the work was very repetitive and that she often ate on the job, although they were not supposed to. They were especially in trouble if they were caught eating apples or oranges, because of their acidity. Prospective employees had to do the 'hand test': their hands were checked to see that their palms were dry. Sweat carried acid which stains the needles. Even those employed in the offices were checked as they would be handling samples. Peggy says that there were pads of material impregnated with chalk which they rubbed their hands on, to dry them, before they started work.

As she remembers, if the company needed to complete an order in a hurry, everybody did overtime, but at the normal piece rate.

Peggy left ENTACO in 1952, having worked there for seven years. Some women had been there forty or fifty years. There was no age limit in those days and no pension. She recalls one woman at Abel Morrall's who went on until she was over eighty, as a glassblower (making glass pinheads).

After doing other work, Peggy joined British Needles in 1963. There she did much more varied work, furnishing sewing needles, packaging and stapling a variety of needles and also papering (sticking needles on to acid-

free paper), and despatching. For this work she earned £5 a week, as she had in 1952 when she left ENTACO, the only difference being that now it was for a thirty-five- rather than a forty-eight-hour week, that is 'part-time'.

She describes how they were all women, except for one man whose job was to set up the machine and the men who did the beginning processes (that is, the initial manufacturing). Peggy says there were old, antiquated machines, run off belts, on a spindle, driven by a motor at one

FIG. 3
Peggy Burrows at work on Anderson's new machine

end of the shop – 'very crude' she calls them; 'I think they must have come out of the ark!' A man called Anderson at Needle Industries invented the machine that did the sticking and Peggy is photographed on her brand-new machine (fig.3). These machines were a big improvement; each one had its own motor, rather than all the workers working off the same belt and also, previously, it had been necessary to stick a lot of needles by hand.

Women never worked the night shift, so when a woman came to work in the morning, she had to waste valuable time sorting her machine out if the night-shift worker had left it in a state.

I used to have a man who worked my machine and he hadn't got a clue. Every morning I went and the machine was in such a disgrace – one day I marched into the office and I told 'em that they was having no more – if this man was not taken off I was going. Mr Burton said to sit down and get calm. He said, 'There's no need for you to be like this' and I said, 'Well there's nobody else to speak for me, so I've come in.'

He came and looked at the machine and then he took him off it, because, you see, I'd got to get the machine all clean before I could start my piecework job. I was losing money.

And then I said to him, 'What about a rise?' And I got a farthing a gross and that was as far as he would move. All the women got it and they seemed happy enough.

Eventually, after many years of pinsticking, Peggy became a supervisor. She says that while men and women started at the bottom, men had more opportunities for promotion. In 1988 she was made redundant after the Coates Viyella takeover.

IRIS DODD
Iris started work with British Needles in 1950 on the heading machines, making sure all the needles were lined up the right way. Using an evening tool, like a small palette knife, she lined up the needles in a big tin. She had her evening tool specially made for her because her hands were so small. Five years later she moved on to doing gilding, which was done after the needles had been plated. This was a relatively short-lived 'novelty' which, she says, was phased out because it was too expensive.

Iris left work in the late 1950s when she got married, and returned in the mid-1970s, going back to heading needles, using the same machines as when she first started out. She recalls that in those days if you had children, outwork was the norm. If you were experienced you could return to work very easily after children and the experienced were often asked to help out to meet big orders.

Later on, Iris was asked to work in the plating mill — which she loved although it was a heavy job, using dangerous chemicals. You had to wear wellingtons and rubber overalls and gloves. Work arrived to be plated. It was washed in hot suds, put into trays, then into baskets and then lowered into vats. The baskets had to be continually shaken with big forks to stop the needles sticking. Iris describes it as 'heavy work'. Afterwards the needles were dried in barrels with sawdust, evened out in trays and checked. She says the work just 'fizzled out as the bottom fell out of the market' and she went on to make epidural needles at Morrall's until she eventually took voluntary redundancy.

MARGARET HEMMING

Margaret began at Morrall's in April 1974 in the Inspection Hypodermic Department. She inspected epidural needles for point damage. The needles were stainless steel so there was no need for workers to go through the hand test. Workers loaded needles into a gig; they were coated with silicone and then baked. This gives the needles a smooth surface, so they can pierce skin more easily. Then the needles were given a tip protector. After this they were packaged and moved on to another firm where drip tubing was attached.

Margaret was given a three-month training period. She says that 'most of the girls took to it' and that there was a low failure rate. She wore a hat and overalls. Her take home pay was £14.

She says the women often pricked their own fingers which made it very hard for them to 'work the needles' as they were bleeding and covered in plasters! Iris and Peggy told how sewing needles were so fine that fragments often snapped off, pierced the skin and got carried into the bloodstream, only to be revealed in X-rays! Before starting work seating areas were all carefully checked and all the cushions were shaken.

FUTURE PLANS

Even these brief accounts take us forward. We find that most of the processes remained broadly the same throughout the industry's history. Nowadays many of the heavy jobs, previously done by men, have been fully automated, whereas women are still employed sorting needles by touch, as they have for generations. Yet we still have many questions about gender-based divisions of labour and their expectations. From Iris's description it is clear that women were involved in heavy manual work, even small women.

We shall proceed with this project, and we hope to have material for a temporary exhibition in the not too distant future. In the longer term, our permanent exhibitions are beginning to look very shabby. Lacking resources to update other displays, we have focused on using the mill's ground-floor area to hold textile exhibitions and to display the work of local textile artists. The museum complex has been developed as a meeting place for women, with classes and talks and as a workplace for craft groups. By the time we have funds to revamp the permanent displays, we hope to have sufficient evidence to give a more balanced picture of the role of women in the industry.

ACKNOWLEDGEMENTS
With special thanks to Peggy Burrows, Iris Dodd and Margaret Hemming for sharing their work experiences with us and to Tony Jeffs for his support.

ENDNOTES

1   Berg, M., 1985, pp310–1

2   Ibid, p311

3   Avery, W., 1887, p xxiv

4   Dickens, C., 1852, pp544 5

'EQUAL TO HALF A MAN': WOMEN IN THE COALMINING INDUSTRY

Rosemary Preece

For the past 150 years coalmining in Britain has been almost exclusively male. It is true that there were women working right into the 1970s on the colliery surface, but statistically their numbers were tiny, only 6.25 per cent of surface workers even at their peak.[1] There were certainly women working on the colliery surface in canteens and in offices, but as far as deep mining is concerned women had no real part to play in the industry, as opposed to the community, after the mid-nineteenth century.

In 1842 an Act was passed banning children under ten and women (note the juxtaposition) from working underground in coal-mines throughout Britain. As with many laws, there was some evasion, so it is not possible to say, and indeed would be quite wrong to imagine, that all women left the pits at that time. But that was the beginning of the end, and it is at that point that this paper can truly begin.

It seems probable that women have always worked in coal-mines, from the days when the properties of coal were first discovered. Outcrop working with coal at or very close to the surface and shallow bell pit workings were often family concerns, with the extended family involved in the day-to-day extraction. The extent of women's involvement is, however, quite speculative, as records are scant. Where women are mentioned, it is difficult to assess whether references are to regular employment. Often evidence of women working only appears when accidents occur.[2] In some areas, for example the north-east coalfield, where women had worked in the eighteenth century, the practice had died out by the nineteenth,[3] and there is little doubt that by the time of the 1842 Act, the employment of women in mining was in decline. By the 1840s women underground workers were concentrated mainly in specific regions: west Lancashire, south Wales, east Scotland and parts of Yorkshire. In the 1830s investigations began into the employment of children in factories, although the reports which ensued showed that there were worse jobs for many children than labour in a factory. Coalmining was cited, with many other industries, as a case for investigation. Anthony Ashley Cooper, the Tory MP better known as the Earl of Shaftesbury, took up the coalmining issue in 1840 by requesting an enquiry into working conditions for boys and girls. Although this was later extended to include 'young persons' (between thirteen and eighteen) it seems initially to have been the sub-commissioners' own decision to add the condition of adult female workers to the Children's Employment Commission report.

Until the publication of this report, conditions in Victorian coal-mines had been concealed from public scrutiny. Although by 1800 Britain was producing eighty per cent of the world's coal, most people had little or no idea of how it got from the coal seam to their fire grate. Many mining areas were geographically remote and mining communities were viewed as wild and savage. Shift work divided miners from the local community, and they were often seen only when coming home in their pit dirt. Additionally, the underground work meant that working conditions were hidden from all but other miners.

What type of job did women do underground? The essentials of providing a coal supply require hewing the coal from the seam, wedged like jam in a sandwich between layers of rock; moving the hewed coal from the coalface to the shaft; conveying it up the shaft and distributing it from the colliery surface. This latter task, which later was to become so important for women surface workers, would also come to include sorting and cleaning the coal.

Underground hewing was almost exclusively a male job. There are a few records of women hewers, but primarily it was a job to which youths aspired and towards which they trained. Women and older children were used to move the coal from the coalface. They would load the coal into tubs, corves or baskets and push or pull them to the shaft side. There were very wide variations to this work depending on the size of the pit, thickness of the coal seam and degree of mechanisation. Some pits used wheeled tubs or baskets on bogeys, the woman at the front with a harness round her waist and a chain between her legs, a second woman or child pushing with their heads and hands from behind. A similar system involved sleds on runners, particularly in thin seams. In Scotland women bearers carried the coal on their backs in huge baskets.

For very thin seams, as low as sixteen or eighteen inches, young children were considered vital. When legislation grew imminent many colliery agents protested that ten was too old to start a child in thin seam working. If they did not grow accustomed to the constricted spaces at eight or nine, they would never be able to learn the work.[4] Descriptions of mines in the Yorkshire coalfield describe the entrance to the workings off the main roadways as like crawling into a rabbit hole.

This, then, was the type of work which the sub-commissioners saw and reported on when they visited the coalfields in 1840. Their report caused a public outcry when the newspapers showed its findings. This might be considered surprising in the light of conditions in other Victorian industries.

Was coalmining so much worse than mill work, the sweatshops of the clothing industry, the match industry or even the hidden long hours and drudgery of domestic service? There were major differences. One was that for the first time in a report of this type there were illustrations. There could be no doubt about the degradation of a woman hauling a tub harnessed like a beast or a boy and girl being lifted to the surface, clinging together, when the sketches were there for all to see. And it was this morality issue that caused the outcry. Not the working as beasts of burden, although this was condemned for 'the weaker sex' but the morality of men and women working together semi-naked underground. Time and again this was referred to, the torn clothing, the isolated workplaces, work which made women unfit for their proper role as wives and mothers.[5] When the legislation was enacted, the very first section of the Mines and Collieries Bill excluded women entirely from underground work.

As far as Yorkshire is concerned that is the point at which women and coalmining parted company. There is some evidence for women continuing to work underground in some of the more remote areas. At the National Coal Mining Museum's Caphouse Colliery there is an oral record of a woman underground worker. Traced through the Census, she appears to have worked underground after 1843. But on the whole, after their evidence given in 1842, these girls and women vanish into obscurity. Even surface workers, recorded from the 1870s by the mines inspectorate, show (for Yorkshire) twenty-nine women in 1874 and only two by 1890.[6]

FIG. 1
Women surface workers, Lancashire. (National Coal Mining Museum Collection)

It is hard to find an explanation for the fact that women did not move on to surface work in west Yorkshire as they did in Lancashire. Many of the images of women remaining in the coalfields are from Lancashire, partly due to its accessibility and partly due to the work of A. J. Munby, a Victorian barrister who devoted a great deal of his life to recording the life and work of working women in that coalfield (fig.1).[7]

Even at their peak women formed only a small part of the colliery workforce.

But in particular areas they could assume great significance. In 1886 in west Lancashire 21.58 per cent of the surface workforce was female (only 4.29 per cent nationally).[8] In Lancashire this employment remained high and increased throughout the nineteenth century, whereas many other areas saw a notable decline. The type of job on the surface was often heavy manual work and varied from pit to pit depending on the degree of mechanisation. Moving tubs of coal from the pit brow (shaft side), unloading into waggons, pushing the empties back to the cage and operating tipplers to tip coal on to screens were typical. Screens sorted the coal into sizes and women were frequently employed to rake out the coal and pick out dirt from picking belts, conveyor belts which carried coal and dirt to be sorted manually. Women were almost exclusively employed on screening and sorting by the start of the twentieth century.

For the vast majority of women in coalmining the 1842 report is the first and last record we have of their daily working lives. From then on they vanish into the household. Wives, mothers and daughters have only the spoken voice to reveal their testimony. This applies particularly in Yorkshire, and one can only speculate as to what happened when a source of employment for hundreds of women vanished at the stroke of a pen. For one thing is quite clear from their testimony: these women were not there for their interest in coalmining or an affinity for working life underground. It was work at the local pit or no bread on the table. For underground women workers and mothers of child labourers there was a common thread – if there was other work they would do it. From the bearers of coal in Scotland to the hurriers of Yorkshire there was no more arduous work.

There is a little more to be said when speaking of the remaining coalmining women, the surface workers who predominated in Lancashire and Scotland. Many of them appear to have made the transition from underground to surface work within their own area, displacing men from positions on the surface. This seems to have been one of the factors which earned the hostility of the strengthening miners' unions, and in fact the coalmining women were never to gain support from the men's unions either through working men's or officials' organisations. Many unions took up the battle for a breadwinner's wage to enable a man to keep his wife and family. In these negotiations a woman's wage was seen as eroding the male wage earner's bargaining position.

There were periodic challenges to the surface workers, petitions to parliament and changes proposed to the Coal Mines Acts. The women weathered these through lobbying of their own, often supported, not entirely surprisingly, by the coal owners from their own pits. Hostility to their work was usually expressed for its inappropriateness, requiring 'unfeminine' strength and leading to 'moral degradation'. In fact, as the nineteenth century progressed and women were more often employed in screening and sorting than physical moving of coal, this was a far less valid criticism.

Be that as it may, women continued to work during the twentieth century. The last 'pit brow lass' finished work in the Whitehaven area in 1972.[9]

One might be forgiven for believing that to be the end of the story, if one did not go on to consider the hidden army of women who made up half the coalmining communities. The women who provided husbands, lovers and sons for the coal industry and who washed their bodies when

they were brought home from the pit. The unseen women who got up at four in the morning to provide a warm drink and breakfast for the wage earner, not by switching on the oven but by stirring into life the coal fire which had been banked all night. The same women who would be there when he got back from the shift to fall asleep over his dinner, to fill the tin bath and to hang the coal-dust-caked clothes by the fire. And to do the same again for sons on different shifts.

These women are only seen as glimpses, their lives wound around coalmining, involved but apart. Women's faces during strikes and lockouts, from the evictions of the 1890s and beyond to the strikes of the 1980s. Women standing at the pithead, waiting for news after roof falls and explosions, the solitary shawled figures unrecorded. Women appearing at local galas and celebrations, as Coal Queens or to applaud the erection of new housing estates. Women were even used as incentives for safer working practices (fig.2).

FIG. 2 Safety poster (courtesy of British Coal/National Mining Museum)

These voiceless women, unheard for 150 years, are like so many working men and women. In a museum context it is difficult to show their story. Museums are about objects, but for women and coalmining there are few objects which have any relevance to their lives. In looking at Yorkshire women's voices the Mining Museum first considered the women who had worked in deep mines and the children who like them were prohibited from underground working. The exhibition 'Out of the Pit' designed in 1992 to commemorate this 150-year ban ironically coincided with its lifting. Today women can once again work underground, but with few jobs remaining for men or women in the industry, this is a hollow triumph.

In many ways the 1842 legislation has been the easiest of women's issues to tackle at the museum and it was dealt with on several levels. Interpretation panels using illustrative material from the 1842 reports gave a brief historical background to the events (fig.3). Quotes from the reports made by young children were read by children from the local school in a village which had figured in the original reports. Spoken voice was again used to convey the comments on the living conditions of local mining families. Child visitors to the exhibition were invited to compare their diet, weight and physical attributes to those of mine workers in 1842, using a coal sack scales and tape measure. A final attempt to convey some idea of the labour involved allowed visitors to try to pull a replica coal-filled corve using a human harness based on contemporary illustrations.

FIG. 3
Out of the Pit exhibition

Questions designed to stimulate discussion around the role of women and their choices at that period were initially used in the exhibition. Finding that the gallery did not prove the ideal place for discussions of this type meant that many were incorporated into a series of information sheets, 'Victorian Workers', for use in schools. These posed questions such as 'Why do women work today? Are the reasons the same as those in the past?' 'Are we shocked today by the idea of women working underground? If so, why?' and 'Have the attitudes of men towards women changed?' which were intended to provoke discussion, and used primary source material from the 1842 report.

The silent years which follow are proving much more difficult in exhibition terms. The museum has few oral-history recordings and few autobiographical accounts from women. With more staff time these could be augmented, but in a museum devoted entirely to a male-dominated industry this is not without contention. Women have been assigned a peripheral or complementary role, as providers of sons and meals, washers of clothes at home, cleaners and secretaries at work. A divided society where images of women have remained curiously old-fashioned. Sociological research carried out around Featherstone in Yorkshire during the 1950s showed a divided society split along lines of work and gender. The miner returning from work expected to find 'a meal prepared, a room clean and tidy, a seat comfortable and warm, and a wife ready to give him what he wants'.[10] He looked for entertainment outside the home, preferably with his 'mates', male friends. The wife's position: to keep the household in good order by judicious use of the housekeeping money given to her by her husband each week.

Recent research carried out in the same area shows that social attitudes are beginning to change, particularly among younger people.[11] Perhaps the biggest element of change is the diversity of jobs, no longer the closed and incomprehensible world of the miner for men and no jobs for women, but a widening of opportunity for women, albeit often in low-paid, part-time jobs as the opportunities for men's work in the pit diminish. Despite these findings it is still quite usual to hear miners express the opinion that women should stay at home; that it is pointless to educate a woman who will just become pregnant; that mining is not a suitable job for women; that if women stayed at home there would be no unemployment.

Just over 150 years ago women worked alongside men in the coal-mines of Britain. They were considered at that time to be 'equal to half a man'. When the museum considers images of women within the coalfield, for an exhibition showing how women have been seen in mining communities, it will include the comment of a modern-day miner: 'What, as much as half?'

ENDNOTES

1 John, A. V., 1984.

2 Pinchbeck, I., 1930.

3 Church, R., 1986.

4 Children's Employment Commission, 1842.

5 Hansard, 1842, col. 1335.

6 John, A. V., 1984.

7 Hudson, D., 1972.

8 John, A. V., 1984.

9 Ibid.

10 Dennis, N. et al, 1969.

11 Warwick, D. and Littlejohn, G., 1992.

SITTING, KNITTING AND SERVING: THE PORTRAYAL OF WOMEN IN INDUSTRIAL MUSEUMS

Andrea Taziker

In the past two years I have visited and assessed at least eighty-five industrial museums around the country and I have lost count of the number of working-class cottage interiors I have seen with women sitting by the fire knitting, almost without exception accompanied by a stuffed cat. In most circumstances the woman is sitting in a comfortable chair by the black grate in the kitchen. Bedrooms seem scarce, although I have seen the occasional living room and quite a few 'back privvies' – or 'outside lavs' as they are known at home in Lancashire. The rooms are very tidy, very clean and contain some of the trappings of domesticated industrial living, though many are strangely empty, but they are sterile of the real histories of the women who lived and worked there.

I have looked in vain for the woman boiling water to fill the tin bath for the miner returning from the pit, for the endless struggle to bear and keep alive large families in cramped, overcrowded conditions on near starvation rations.

I reflect on the lives of the women in my own past – my great-grandmother was a tailoress who walked a round trip of twelve miles a day to her work, in winter with a candle in a jar to enable her to see the way. She went on to bear ten children, of whom five survived into adulthood, in a two-bedroomed terrace. She never learned to write and my family still has the death certificates of her children with her mark of X. My grandmother had to turn down a grammar school scholarship to work in the mill as the family could not afford for her to go. She worked until she was seventy in a hard job in the laundry. My other grandmother made nuts and bolts, my great-aunt was a carder in the mill, and our next-door neighbour was a pit-brow lass. Where, I ask myself, were the lives of these women? Women who worked long, hard hours in the home but equally worked hard in paid occupations. Where was the portrayal of the harsh realities of their history?

Industrial museums have a tendency to be machine-oriented, with emphasis on process, technology and historical development. However, as J. G. Jenkins pointed out in his book on interpreting Welsh Heritage, 'The industry of Wales is not just a history of machines and technological processes, but a history of a people and of communities that were concerned with making a living.'[1]

Many museums have attempted to show the human side of industry. However, this generally means the lives of the male 'worker' and the only way the participation of women is illustrated in these lives is through the ubiquitous collections of household material that most industrial museums have, in some cases with the additions of a back yard – with privvy – and occasionally an entire building such as a miner's cottage.

These tableaux of the interior design of the industrial period can be said to represent the 'woman's collections'. Here would be the artefacts the women bought, made, used, the women's tools and implements. In the interpretation of such collections the female role is often a ghost to the over-emphasised reality of the 'male worker' who lived there. For example, at the Scottish Maritime Museum at Irvine there is a preserved tenement dwelling described in the Ayreshire Tourist Guide as showing 'the living conditions of the shipyard workers of the early twentieth Century'.[2] Hamilton Cottage at the Bo'ness and Kinneal Railway – soon to be the Scottish Railway Museum – is described in the 1993 leaflet as reflecting 'a working man's home life of the 1920s …' Such collections do not seem to be taken seriously. Many seem to have what might be called a dribbling collection policy where people just bring old things along to the museum that their grandmothers used. This appears to be the case with Hamilton Cottage, where there seems to be little academic rigour and they are presented as tableaux with very little or, in most cases, no interpretation. Apparently the visitor is supposed to know about the tableaux as a sort of playground for the memory. Strict dating chronology seems flexible, artefacts and furnishings from different periods and of different costs being shown together, for example, at Wanlockhead Lead Mining Museum there is the interior of a 1740s cottage and an improved 1890s cottage. Both have the same chairs, which actually look as though they belong in the twentieth century. William Morris wallpaper is also used in the 1890s interior – according to the guide, because it was 'of the period'. It is doubtful whether a lead miner in the wilds of Scotland in 1890 would have aspired to such interior design! Here, too, we have the woman sitting by the fire – in this case a shop dummy dressed in Victorian mourning dress (fig.1).

Interpretation of such collections is sparse. There are very few labels or information boards. What there is tends to be room plans or hand-held boards which concentrate on furnishings, date, type, usage. At the very tidy tableaux at the Workers Cottage Interior (1840) at Quarry Bank Mill, Styal, there were no labels, no interpretation; it was just there to be seen. The 'traditional' miner's cottage scene of indeterminate date from the Welsh Miners' Museum at Afon, Argoed, has the music of brass bands and choirs

FIG. 1
Improved 19th century
cottage interior
(Wanlockhead Lead
Mining Museum)

playing in the background but again no interpretation. The Weaver's Cottage, that is the kitchen, at the Scottish Museum of Woollen Textiles, Walkerburn, had a floor plan with labels but everything had been moved around and a number of artefacts were missing.

If there are any women interpreters in such cottage interiors they are usually sitting by the fire, knitting, embroidering, making rope-bottom shoes, baking biscuits and cakes. For example in the Black Country Museum, when I visited, the lady in the Crooked House was reading and the lady in the terraced house, French knitting. Such interpreters have extensive knowledge of the history and usage of the furnishings and fittings but give the impression by the mere act of their interpretation, in a subtle and unconscious way, of a life of relative leisure. They do not reflect the hard, backbreaking work that it took to simply keep a family alive, fed and clothed. This view is perpetuated by publicity material and by the images in the guidebooks and pamphlets. In a pamphlet on the Black Country Museum, we are told 'faithfully restored homes are brought to life by local characters dressed in period costume – when you wander in you might catch them sewing or preparing a meal … enjoying a cosy chat by the kitchen range'[4] … in the Guidebook we have pictures of women sitting knitting on page eleven and slicing bread on page twelve.[5] In the guide at

Morwellham Quay women are shown sitting knitting by the fire and in very expensive clothing standing outside shopping and chatting.[6]

Good interpretation can however be bought in the form of guidebooks and specialised leaflets and pamphlets in the museum shops. They are often taken home as a glossy souvenir of the visit. An example of this is to be found in the 'Brief Guide to Beamish': 'in 1913 there were few occupations available to middle-class women. A single woman without private means could find herself in financial difficulties'; and 'in pit villages women married young and bore large numbers of children at home. They thus had little opportunity for paid work, keeping the home, washing, cleaning, baking and feeding the family was a full time and onerous task.'[7] However, much research points to both a lack of the buying of guidebooks and of reading them on site.

Women, despite this being the place where they lived and worked, are barely ever mentioned as people and are always on the periphery, their role negated by the over-emphasised role of the male worker. Even when sometimes the collection is formed by or around a particular woman she is not necessarily mentioned. For example, the description of the Manager's House at Abbeydale Hamlet consists of four sentences in the Guidebook.[8] It was set in the 1890s and in an article in the *Industrial Archaeology Review* 1989, one of the reasons given for this is that the lady 'who lived in it as a child was living when restoration took place and she described in considerable detail how it was set up when she lived there' and that, 'she donated some of the actual furniture that had belonged to her family'.[9] No mention is made of this in the Guidebook or the on-site interpretation.

One of the household jobs of working-class women illustrated in industrial museums is that of 'washday' – obviously regarded as the most important task in the home. At Beamish there is a working display of washing with a dolly at periodic intervals at the Pit Cottages. At Woodhorn Colliery Museum there is a kitchen interior and backyard with dolly tub and tin bath and there are background sounds of women talking about washday. The publicity leaflet states 'you can eavesdrop on the miner's wife in her 1930s kitchen ...'[10] but this is the only mention of women in this part of the museum. Similarly, at Summerlee Heritage Trust the only section in the entire museum dealing with the part played by women in industry is an exhibition of 'washing'. The information board states: 'whilst men laboured at the ironworks or pits, women faced the constant struggle to look after their families'. At Beamish there is a leaflet on 'washday'[11] and in the 'Big Pit Guidebook' there are old black-and-white photographs of women washing[12] – the only mention they get.

But what of the world of work outside the work of the home for women? Of the seven coal-mining museums that I have visited around the country five have kitchen interiors. In four of these this was the only mention in the museum of the role of women in the coal industry. Little mention is made of the work of women down the coal-mines prior to the 1842 Act. At most museums this Act features prominently, but mainly with reference to children. The Scottish Mining Museum has a section on community life

FIG. 2
Model women in pit-workers kitchen. (National Coal Mining Museum for England)

based on a miner, Wullie Drysdale, with the usual cottage interior. In the museum's information sheets it mentions the 1842 Act in the context of Wullie's grandmother, who 'nursed a sense of grievance at the sudden loss of wages when she was excluded from the pit bottom', but admitted that 'her home was better kept afterwards …'. In the section on Wullie's wife, Agnes, it suggests that 'men see themselves as the providers and the women's place as being firmly in the home'.[13] The Welsh Miners' Museum has the usual etchings of women barrow-pushers and models of the same but makes little direct reference to women. This pattern is repeated elsewhere. However, at the Yorkshire Mining Museum (now the National Coal Mining Museum for England) there is an excellent display entitled 'Out of the Pit'. Dealing with the 1842 Act, it explains the underlying moral issues behind the Act and the impact of the loss of essential wages. Accompanying this there is a series of very good information sheets on 'Victorian Workers',[14] useful for school project work. This, however, is only a temporary exhibition housed away from the main museum displays above the blacksmith's shop. Next to it is an area being developed as the 'Homelife Exhibition'. When I visited, the kitchen was taking shape with its most indispensable feature ... yes ... the woman sitting knitting! (fig.2).

The pit surface work of women is often merely commented on or stated rather than interpreted. At Chatterly Whitfield Mining Museum they were part of the questionable tableaux in the Salt Hall. In the Salford Mining Museum there are a number of large black-and-white photographs with 'pit- brow wenches' but no interpretation. At Wigan Pier there are models next to the stairs but no interpretation apart from a mention in the 'Heritage Trail' leaflet that they preferred to work on the pit top rather than the mills because it was a healthier occupation.[15]

In the textile industry museums that I have visited, women present the cottage industry sections, for example, at Styal, the handcarding and spinning. The women workers in the mill industry are often in the background. At Helmshore Textile Museum greater emphasis is placed on the male inventors, with full-size drawings of eight of them, but the only mention of the thousands of women workers, in what is advertised as enabling you to 'Discover Lancashire's Textile Heritage' is one large black-and-white photograph of women behind the power loom. At many such museums I have only seen men demonstrating the textile machines. At Wigan Pier, for example, the man in the mill was a former manager with a degree who had done foreign advisory work.

In many open-air museums the occupation of women that is most in evidence is that of shop assistants, mostly under the watchful eye of the male supervisor. They perform the servile and menial jobs as assistants, invariably not in charge. At Beamish there were silent women workers in the Co-op Shop, and also at the Black Country Museum. At Morwellham Quay an excellent opportunity was missed with the chandlers shop which was kept in 1914 by a Jane Martin – this was only mentioned in the 'Young Explorer's Guide'.[16] This servile view is perpetuated by the images in both glossy guidebooks and on postcards.

Many industrial museums invite us to 'Step back in time ...' and 'revisit the past'. The Beamish leaflet tells us: 'Everything you see is real.'[17] There is a danger here that the visitor will believe this and that the view of women perpetuated in such museums will become the future memories of female participants in industry.

At Killhope Lead Mining Museum, when a smallholding near to the museum became available, it was suggested that this might be an excellent way to show an area of family life and women's work previously under-represented. Miners' wages had been supplemented by the running of smallholdings, to a large extent by the women, a difficult task in such a bleak moorland environment. The idea, however, was rejected as it was decided to develop an 'underground experience' where 'you will be able to experience in a safe but exciting and authentic way the working conditions of the Victorian lead miners. Once again the women's role had lost out to the male worker and to a way to attract more visitors. I only hope that this will not always be the case, but on previous evidence I am not optimistic.

ENDNOTES

1 Jenkins, J. G., 1992, p51.

2 Ayrshire Tourist Publicity Board Leaflet – 'History and Heritage in Ayrshire', Ayrshire Tourist Board, 1993.

3 Bo'ness and Kinneil Railway. 'A Window to the Past'. Publicity Leaflet, Bowness Heritage Trust/South Scottish Railway Preservation Society, 1993.

4 The Black Country Museum Re-creating the Heart of an Industrial Community. Publicity Leaflet, 1993.

5 The Black Country Museum. Colour Guidebook (28 pages) 1992. (Published by Pitkin Pictorials).

6 'Morwellham Quay in the Tamar Valley'. Guidebook, Booker, Frank, D.A.R.T. Publication 78, Jarrold & Sons, Norwich, 1983.

7 'Beamish. The North of England Open Air Museum.' A Brief Guide. (no date)

8 'Abbeydale Industrial Hamlet'. Guidebook, Sheffield City Museums, 1981.

9 Peatman, J., 1989, pp141–154.

10 Woodhorn Colliery Museum Publicity Leaflet. Wansbeck District Council, 1993.

11 Beamish 'Washday' Information Sheet 4, 1987.

12 'Big Pit. Pwll Mawr, The Big Pit Story'. Guidebook, Big Pit Mining Museum, Blaenafon, 1992.

13 Information Sheet No.1. 'Wullie Drysdale. A Miner and his Family, 1900' by E. D. Hide, Scottish Mining Museum. (no date)

14 'Victorian Workers' Information Sheets 1–5, 1992. Yorkshire Mining Museum.

15 Wigan Pier 'Heritage Trail' Leaflet. (no date)

16 'Morwellham Quay Young Explorers Activity Guide. Part of Resource Pack for teachers. (£4.95) Published: Morwellham Quay Trust, 1990.

17 Beamish. 'Time to Return' Publicity Leaflet, 1992.

18 Killhope Lead Mining Museum. Leaflet given with entrance ticket. (no date)

WOMEN AND WEDGWOOD

Sharon Gater

We need look no further than the name of the company founded by Josiah Wedgwood in 1759 to realise that the historical reputation of Josiah Wedgwood & Sons Limited is still dominated by the great man himself, and understandably so. Wedgwood's skills as a potter, his insatiable quest to perfect the quality and expand the variety of ceramics produced were matched by his success in marketing his output through an active involvement in improving England's road and canal networks.

Born of a Unitarian family and a liberal in politics, Wedgwood's approach to all of his concerns was not hampered by any established beliefs. This almost certainly influenced his attitude towards women in all walks of life. Of crucial importance was the role of his mother, Mary, to whom apparently fell the responsibilities of his education, when at the age of nine years, formal schooling ended abruptly upon the death of his father. Such was the tradition of the Unitarian faith that Mary, though female, would have received a thorough education which she in turn passed on to her son.

When Wedgwood married in 1764, he chose as his bride a kinswoman Sarah (fig.1) who was not only to bear his eight children, seven of whom survived infancy but was also to become his 'chief helpmate'.[1] Letters written by Wedgwood to his partner Thomas Bentley paint a picture of a strong and capable woman who wrote up her husband's experiments for him and nursed him following the amputation of his leg. However, in his relationship with Sarah it transpires that he sees her as representative of a major section of the market at which his wares are aimed and he is anxious to hear her opinion on new shapes and patterns; indeed he was to write, 'I speak from experience in female taste without which I should make but a poor figure amongst my pots not one of which of any consequence is finished without the approbation of my Sally.'[2] Sarah was therefore somewhat of a guinea-pig in assessing market forces – an area in which Wedgwood was soon to recognise the virtue in pandering to female requirements. While there are many instances of his appreciation of female intelligence – his lengthy letters on the subject of slavery to Anna Seward, the 'Swan of Lichfield'[3] – the fact that he took pains to ensure a decent and modern education for his eldest daughter Susannah, and his respect for his wife for example, he was not slow to realise that women could also be manipulated to his own commercial ends.

In 1765, having secured the patronage of Queen Charlotte, he was able to term his fine cream-coloured earthenware 'Queen's Ware', a name by which this product continues to be known. Having done so, he was assured of the custom of other ladies of rank who wished to be seen to be following the best of fashions, going so far as to state on one occasion that 'few Ladies you know dare venture at anything out of the common stile 'till authorised by their betters – by the Ladies of superior spirit who set the fashion'.[4] Neither was Wedgwood averse to using flattery to secure his customers, naming shapes after them, as in the case of Devonshire vases and garden pots after the Duchess of Devonshire, 1778.

In 1774, Wedgwood had received an order for a 952-piece service from Empress Catherine of Russia, a connoisseur of Europe's finest ceramic manufacturers, which was again to confirm his standing among his aristocratic female customers, many of whose homes and estates he had sought permission to depict among the 1200 or so handpainted scenes with which the service was decorated. This was to prove of particular importance in attracting the female element to his showrooms which were in themselves an exercise in mustering the interest of his women customers. It was his intention, he claimed, to 'amaze, and divert, and please and astonish, nay even to ravish the ladies'[5] when they visited his premises in Greek Street, London.

Wedgwood was, then, prepared to go to great lengths to gain favour with the female market upon which he was of course dependent, but there was yet another faction of female society on which he relied heavily, namely that which constituted a considerable part of his workforce. Being involved in pottery production which had grown up from a cottage industry where each member of the family was responsible for a stage in the process of ceramic production, women traditionally provided much of the workforce in the industry. While it has often been assumed that they would have been allotted the physically less demanding jobs such as decorating, this was not necessarily true of the pottery industry in general. Well into the twentieth century it is possible to cite examples of manufacturers who employed women in the very heaviest of occupations such as casting sanitary ware.

FIG. I
Sarah Wedgwood. Oil on canvas by Sir Joshua Reynolds (courtesy of Trustees of the Wedgwood Museum) 1782

However in Wedgwood's case there were, and still remain to this day, jobs which were traditionally male or female – the latter centring upon methods of decorating ware and attending the heavier occupations of men. The men who threw pots on a wheel or turned them on a lathe were responsible for obtaining their own assistants and for reasons of economy were more likely to subcontract a woman or a child, hence increasing the number of women employed.

Much of Wedgwood's skilled female labour was employed in hand painting – a Miss Glisson, Miss Parrs and Mrs Wilcox (previously of the Worcester manufactory) all worked upon the celebrated 'Catherine service', Mr Wilcox admitting of his wife that 'she is an excellent copier of figures and other subjects, and is a much better hand than [myself]'.[6]

Wedgwood's 'Jasper ware', perfected in 1774, necessitated the design of bas-relief decorations with which to decorate items manufactured in this body. Many were supplied by John Flaxman junior, but others of distinction were supplied in the second half of the 1780s by Lady Diana Beauclerk, Elizabeth Lady Templetown, whose compositions of domestic scenes were cut out in white paper and converted into ceramic form by William Hackwood, and Miss Emma Crewe, daughter of Baron Crewe.

In comparison to the eighteenth century, largely regarded as the heyday of Wedgwood's success, there is little from the nineteenth century to tell us of the company's treatment of female employees and the feminine influence in general. Josiah had used his self-made wealth to bring up his sons as gentlemen who, quite naturally, spurned the filthy pottery industry in favour of the life of country squires. Their departure from the entrepreneurial class to which they were born was cemented by the marriage of the two eldest sons, John and Josiah to sisters Louisa Jane and Elizabeth Allen, daughters of the Squire of Cresselly.

The factory in the nineteenth century lacked the commitment and enthusiasm of the founder who died in 1795, and Josiah Wedgwood & Sons ceased for a time to hold its place at the top of the league table of British potters. The once innovative factory opened by Josiah I in 1769 was now becoming obsolete and logistics simply did not allow for wholesale introduction of jiggers and jolleys to be operated by steam power. Ironically this may have been one factor which made possible the avoidance of major confrontation in the nineteenth century between employer and employees as the introduction of steam power and mechanised production processes threatened the previously male dominated provinces of cup and plate making. The company therefore remained in the background on such issues and did not receive such criticism as appeared in the journal, the *Potteries*

Examiner, 1878, which carried the following attack on the increase in female labour: 'the dark vocabulary of hell itself, scarce can contain epithets strong and terrible enough to express in relation to female labour, its execrable nature'.[7]

Nevertheless, wage books housed in the Wedgwood Museum collection contain the names of many women employed in various occupations from lathe treading, assisting the thrower (that is weighing and preparing clay, removing the finished object) to freehand painting, table, decorative and sanitary ware. The work of the latter was particularly skilled and yet while they were considered socially superior to those who worked in the clay, they were not considered as artists. The studio remained largely a bastion of the Art Director and his male charges. Where the female artist is in evidence in the nineteenth century, she is more likely to have submitted designs on a freelance basis rather than to have worked on the factory site, as was the case of Helen Jane Arundel Miles, who produced tile designs for the company in 1880. At the same time, Kate Greenaway's designs were also interpreted, presumably by Art Director Thomas Allen.

Throughout the nineteenth century the company remained strongly paternalistic, maintaining much of the original village built by the founder, providing part-time education for all the young people employed, together with a library and a coffee shop. Restrictions on the employment of children under ten years of age were imposed by choice some considerable time before this was enforced by law. However, the provision of such benefits also permitted the imposition of moral judgements on the workforce. In 1873 Wedgwood sought legal advice when an employee 'but a child herself' became pregnant by an apprentice gilder. Her parents 'turned her out of doors and say she must fend for herself or go to the workhouse'. The situation, we learn, has 'created such a scandal on the works' that Wedgwood wishes to get rid of her without her consent and without becoming liable for her wages should she decide to sue.[8]

Presumably justification for such treatment was found in the fact that, according to reports of factory commissioners, the factory did everything possible to maintain a decent environment for its employees, including the provision of separate toilets for males and females, and the fact that fines and verbal warnings instead of beatings were thought to be sufficient punishments for misdemeanours.

The previous sad incident would appear to be very much an exception in the treatment of Wedgwood's female employees, who would otherwise seem to have been treated well compared with many cases cited in Dr Jackie Sarsby's excellent publication *Missuses and Mouldrunners*.[9] Sylvia Pankhurst, during a visit to the Potteries in around 1907, wrote of the haggard faces of women in general employed in the ceramic industry and the number of babies stillborn to those women. In one factory she fainted twice, complaining of a sensation of pressure and discomfort in her ears and throat and a desire to swallow and draw saliva into the mouth. Before long, she experienced that nasty, sweet taste of which the leadworkers complained. The Wedgwood factory, on the other hand, provided a complete contrast for in the production of much of their fine ware, no lead was used. Here, Sylvia was happy to try her hand at making and decorating cups. Thereafter, her son recalled, she urged her friends to buy Wedgwood.

One possible explanation for the existence of more favourable conditions at the Wedgwood factory is the influence of the women who married into the Wedgwood family and the female offspring who were frequently directly involved in the running of the company. The most obvious example here is provided by Audrey Wedgwood, daughter of Cecil, one-time Company Director and the first Lord Mayor of Stoke-on-Trent, who was killed in 1916 in the Battle of the Somme. Audrey was the first female Company Secretary and took over, single-handed, the running of the works throughout the First World War. Her work entailed the supervision of every department from the mill and sliphouse, where raw materials were prepared, right through to obtaining fuel for the firing of the ware. Each process, she learned at first hand.

The Wedgwoods had always been prominent members of the local community: Josiah II had been the first Member of Parliament for Stoke-on-Trent; as already mentioned Cecil was its first Lord Mayor; while Josiah Wedgwood IV became a local MP and was made Baron Wedgwood of Barlaston in the 1940s. The influence of their wives and daughters also extended beyond the works, sometimes in controversial areas. Cecil's wife Lucy, a former governess by profession, pioneered 'Mothers' Welcomes' in the Stoke-on-Trent area, the forerunners of infant welfare clinics; while in the 1930s, Dorothy, wife of Josiah Wedgwood V, was frequently attacked in the local press for her work in the field of family planning.

The concern of this particular branch of Wedgwood women became concrete in 1934 when four of them established a committee, who supervised the daily welfare of the company and made recommendations to its directors of the needs of the workforce.

In the twentieth century, however, it is in the field of design where women's abilities have been acknowledged as never before. One of the most startling ranges of ware was created by Daisy Makeig Jones, who began as an apprentice paintress at Wedgwood in 1909. By 1914 she had her own studio and introduced the first of a range of designs known collectively as 'Fairyland Lustre'. Vivid, imaginative and evocative of the trend in Art Deco, this mass-produced ware lasted until well into the 1930s. Daisy was also something of a character, dressing up her paintresses as replicas of the Portland Vase (the symbol of Josiah Wedgwood & Sons Limited) for the pageant staged in 1930 to commemorate the bicentenary of the founder's birth.

In contrast, in 1925, Anna Zinkeisen, who had been responsible for the murals executed on board the *Queen Mary*, used the traditional Wedgwood Jasper Ware body to very modern effects with the production of three plaques – 'Adam', 'Eve' and 'Sun and Wind' (fig. 2).

FIG. 2
Sun and Wind.
Anna Zinkeisen, 1925.
Courtesy of the Trustees
of the Wegwood Museum

Alfred and Louise Powell, disciples of the Arts and Crafts Movement, were not only talented artists in their own right but also established a school of hand-paintresses at Etruria during the early years of the twentieth century which was to set the standard in this area of production until well into the 1950s. However, it is as much the attitude towards this work as the technical excellence with which it was produced which was to prove of lasting importance and while her husband, Alfred, usually assumed the role of spokesman, in Louise's work is still visible the joy in creating a work of art. In 1919, Alfred wrote:

We must set our minds at uncovering the love of beauty-in-work. It is waiting to be called for. Instead we put our little girls – susceptible to all the usual delights of childhood, to sit in factories day after day placing little dabs of green and red on printed patterns until they turn into automatons. Their little minds stiffen up to the dull work and do it professionally, but it is a tragedy and a loss that pottery cannot afford.[10]

The teachings of Alfred and Louise resulted in the creation in 1926 of a handcraft department where hand-painted wares were produced under the supervision of their student, Millicent Taplin, herself one of the most outstanding female artists of the current century.

Women's contributions to the field of twentieth-century Wedgwood design are numerous; from Star Wedgwood and Barbara Hepworth to Thérèse Lessore, Glenys Barton and, arguably the greatest female ceramicist, Susie Cooper (fig.3), who began to design for Wedgwood in 1966 when her own company was absorbed into the Wedgwood group.

The ceramics industry does, however, involve many varied occupations and the archival accumulation housed at the Wedgwood Museum, much of which is only now being researched, suggests some of the difficulties encountered by women trying to enter into certain areas. This is apparent in an application received in 1946 from an Oxford graduate for a position in Wedgwood's laboratory. She writes:

I recognise that I have certain disadvantages for a post in any branch of industry: I am a woman, and without much practical experience. It has, I understand, been customary to employ university women in industry for personnel management, but not so frequently for production management.[11]

In fact, today, the laboratory and most other areas of the factory employ women, an increasing number of whom are employed at senior levels. Women make up approximately half of the workforce on the Barlaston site alone, numbering nearly 3,000, almost 2,000 of whom are hourly-paid factory operatives.

The entire history of Wedgwood encompasses many aspects of female involvement with the ceramics industry, reflecting the role of the woman as consumer, designer and manufacturer. This is conveyed within the permanent Wedgwood Museum display at Barlaston.

FIG. 3
Susie Cooper
modelling 'Lummox'.
Courtesy of Trustees of
Wedgwood Museum

ACKNOWLEDGEMENTS

Acknowledgement is given to the Trustees of the Wedgwood Museum, Barlaston, Staffordshire for their permission to reproduce documents.

ENDNOTES

1 Wedgwood MS E2518070. Josiah Wedgwood to?, 6 March 1765.

2 Wedgwood MS E2518183. Josiah Wedgwood to Thomas Bentley, January 1768.

3 Wedgwood MS E2618978. Josiah Wedgwood to Anna Seward, February 1788.

4 Wedgwood MS E2518766. Josiah Wedgwood to Thomas Bentley, 21 June 1777.

5 Wedgwood MS E2518232. Josiah Wedgwood to Thomas Bentley, 1769.

6 Wedgwood MS E2518245. Josiah Wedgwood to Thomas Bentley, 25 June 1769.

7 Potteries Examiner, 1878.

8 Undocumented MS Josiah Wedgwood & Sons Ltd, to ?, 13 October 1873.

9 Jacqueline Sarsby, Missuses and Mouldrunners – An Oral History of Women Pottery Workers at Work and at Home, 1988.

10 'Studio Year book', 1929; Gater, 1982.

11 Undocumented MS Dorothy Preston to Josiah Wedgwood & Sons Ltd, 20 August 1946.

THE ORGANISATION OF THE LACE INDUSTRY IN ENGLAND AND IRELAND

Pamela Sharpe

Before the Industrial Revolution, the lace industry was second only to wool manufacture in the amount of women's employment it produced. Women's employment as lacemakers was generally based in the home, although women involved in dealing in lace obviously had to travel to trade in London, and to resort centres such as Bath. As more of the processes of lace manufacture became mechanised, the more male-orientated they became. Yet in the early nineteenth century, and particularly in the 1830s and 1840s as the lace industry benefited from buoyant fashion trends, both machine- and handmade lace co-existed. In this paper, I will look at the type of lace which would have been on the market in this era and, briefly, the circumstances of lacemakers. Then I will consider how displays of lace in museums connect with what I would consider to be the themes to be explored in lace research and how museum representation can enhance our knowledge of lacemaking.

Historically, lace was made in two areas of England. In east Devon and some areas of west Dorset, 'bone' lace was made in the pillow. The development of bone lace represented a sixteenth-century move towards mass production as lace could be made far more quickly on the pillow than by the traditional needlepoint method which produced the fine laces of the Buckinghamshire and Bedfordshire industry. Both of these branches seem to have developed out of London trades, and indeed embroidery and the manufacture of lace using gold or silver threads was still London-based.

The popularity of either the west country or the east Midland product depended on fashion trends. While Honiton lace was very popular in the seventeenth century, in the eighteenth century Buckinghamshire point became the finest lace produced in England. Yet neither could ever really compete with Continental laces, and it was only because of effective government policies of protection that they managed to maintain a foot in the domestic market. Both types of lace flourished in the Napoleonic Wars, however, when the Continental blockade kept French and Flemish laces at bay. Yet throughout, the French and Flanders laces had superior designs and thread.

The end of the French Wars and the expiry of Heathcoat's patent on the manufacture of machine-made bobbin net meant a new era of lace production. The net or ground could now be machine-made, allowing for a new technique of embroidering or tambouring on to this net background. Lace finishing was now carried out by women in the Tiverton area, where Heathcoat established his mill in 1816 after Luddite attacks on his original premises in Loughborough. Finishing was also carried out in the centre of the lace industry, Nottingham, which experienced a rash of inventions to improve machine-made lace and had the largest concentration of machine-lace manufacturers. Indeed, Nottingham experienced 'lace-fever' between 1823 and 1825. The development of machine-made net also gave rise to some new laces. Tambouring net became an industry in the Coggeshall area of Essex and was connected with silk mills in the area. The early-nineteenth-century Irish laces also developed out of the invention of the net 'twist'. Limerick lace was established in 1829 as a factory-based industry combining the tambour stitches of Coggeshall with the lace running of Nottingham. Carrickmacross also developed as a form of appliqué on the bobbin-net background from 1820.

From 1841 it was possible to make patterned lace entirely by machine. This forced the hand branches either to attempt to cheapen production as far as possible – hence the continued success of Limerick, in the low wage area of Ireland – or to concentrate on particularly high-quality goods which would still sell by virtue of being handmade. Ultimately, the fortunes of lacemakers rested on whether or not they were producing to the fashion, and fashion trends could influence demand for all laces – hand- or machine-made. The continuing development of machine-made laces also created employment for women in finishing operations. While lace machines were operated by men, much of the ancillary work was carried out by women both inside and outside of the factories.

It would be correct to typify lacemaking as skilled work usually carried out for a pittance. While historically we can identify some periods of relatively high wages for female lacemakers, in the main by the early nineteenth century a very poor level of pay was common. Lacemakers were dependent on the dealer who would obtain the thread and patterns, and market the lace for her. Dealers could make large profits out of this. While dealers could be male or female, in the nineteenth century we see a move towards dealers in handmade lace being mainly female, and in machine lace being mainly male.

Work conditions were also poor. Lacemakers suffered failing eyesight through working in dark rooms in case the light spoilt the lace and in fireless damp conditions for fear of making it dirty. The awkward work posture and poor conditions led to back and neck pain, consumption and dyspepsia. As a result women tended to pass the prime age for lacemaking in their twenties. This reinforces the point that many of the lacemakers we are concerned with are not women at all, but children. As apprenticeships largely disappeared, children would be sent to lace schools to learn the skill of the trade from a tender age. Indeed it was believed that lacemakers could not acquire the necessary skills unless they started young. Lace schools included both sexes but few boys carried on lacemaking into adult life. Some men did look upon lacemaking as a source of income to be resorted to when there were seasonal shortages of work in agriculture in the east Midlands, and in fishing in Devon.

How did lacemakers see themselves? The nineteenth-century lace historian, Mrs Palliser, saw lacemaking as a 'womanly accomplishment'. Commentators also sometimes described the ability to make lace as a 'resource' to be turned to now and again when, perhaps, lacemaking was no longer feasible on a full-time basis. Interestingly, lacemakers seem to have had far more of a collective identity in France, where they met together for work evenings. In England lacemaking was more individualistic and there is no evidence of lacemakers' guilds or associations before the end of the nineteenth century. Yet lacemakers are reported to have been in processions together and to have marked 'Cattern', 25 November (St Catherine's Day) as a special day when they exchanged bobbins with either a motto or the name of the giver on them (fig. 1). There is evidence of non-conformist sects making lace together in England in the eighteenth century, but this still does not amount to the collective cultures exhibited by lacemakers working in convents on the Continent, and in Ireland. Indeed lacemaking in Ireland seems always to have been a group activity – whether in Charles Walker's factories in

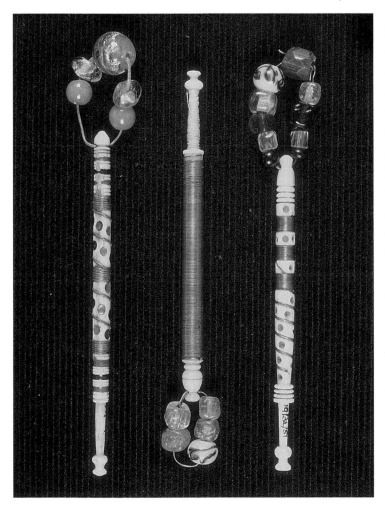

FIG. 1
Lace Bobbins.
Luton Museum Service

Limerick, the Bath and Shirley estate schools of Carrickmacross, the Presentation Convent at Youghal, County Cork, or the Convent of Poor Clares at Kenmare in County Kerry.

To build up details of women's employment in the lace industry we rely on scanty documents. There are a few mentions of lacemaking in contemporary writings, a few accounts from lace dealers, some detail in nineteenth-century parliamentary commissions and some statistics to be derived from Census returns – although what Censuses can tell us is increasingly being undermined by recent research which has demonstrated their inaccuracy. Lace history also relies on legends and handed-down stories. Histories of lace tend to regurgitate familiar facts without adding much to our knowledge. Yet if we could discover more about lacemakers and lace dealers and how they operated we could gain far more details of the hidden world of women's skilled employment. Oral history is one way of doing this – for some hand-lacemaking persisted into the twentieth century. We know from the 'lace-tells' that much of the skill required would have been passed on through the verbal communication of the past. These were worksongs used as a guide to signify which pins were to be worked to finish a piece of lace, revolving around certain numbers and forming an appropriate rhythm to make lace to, and signpost reminders about the next process to be carried out.

What we do have is the artefact: the lace itself. How can this be used to shed light on the history of the women involved in the lace trade? The ideas I have are not very original, indeed they are already being carried out in some museums. They involve moving away from concentration on the fragments of lace themselves, as means of closing the gap between the artefact and the archives. One possibility is more appreciation not only of the production of lace, but a shift of emphasis towards its consumption. Both research on lace, and displays of lace, need to make connections between the finished lengths of lace, and the ways in which they were used. These were far more diverse than just as trimmings for women's clothing – lace had a multiplicity of uses, from curtains to mosquito nets. Lace became more adaptable as the nineteenth century advanced and the techniques for cheaply making large expanses of lace were developed. Lacemaking displays are also enhanced by the accessories used in lace manufacture – such as the bobbins, pillows, patterns and order books on display at the Cecil Higgins Museum in Bedford. From the point of view of social and economic history, or of deepening our knowledge of the context within which lace was made, lace might be integrated into displays with other artefacts of textile production. For example, the concentration of machine-made lace in

Nottingham was due to the proximity of machine-made cotton and yarn supplies, emanating from the earliest factories of the Industrial Revolution, combined with plentiful doses of local ingenuity and invention which transformed hosiery machines into lace machines. As a result it is surely educational that the Nottingham Lace Centre displays framework knitting machines next to Leavers machines, and is situated in close proximity to the old Lace Market, which is currently being redeveloped. Very appropriately, lace museums want to display examples of the finest elite laces that they have. Yet these should not be allowed to detract from also displaying the low-class lace, often made by children or the elderly, such as the 'trolly' lace, made along the Devon coast from locally-produced thread in the eighteenth and nineteenth centuries.

The work of women has been the subject of what now amounts to a fairly substantial literature compiled during the last twenty years of feminist-inspired historical research. We have succeeded in producing a series of case studies, but we need more large surveys of women's employment which tackle the big questions and which place the case studies into a larger context. At the same time we need more micro-history. There are still many details to fill in of what women actually did in many craft industries. For some of us, the only resort is Shire Albums. This is where museums can be extremely helpful. The historian who is not an expert can learn very little from looking at a lace collection mounted in a glass case. The expert interpretation skills of museum staff are vital. When items, such as textiles, are put in context rather than only treated as rarified or specialised we are moving towards a position where the interactive results can only be fruitful.

ACKNOWLEDGEMENTS

I am grateful for financial assistance from the Pasold Research Fund, the Scouloudi Foundation, and the University of Bristol Faculty of Arts Research Fund for my ongoing research into aspects of lacemaking in England and Ireland, 1600–1850.

THE TROWBRIDGE MUSEUM – A MUSEUM OF THE WEST OF ENGLAND WOOLLEN INDUSTRY

Linda Wigley

A BRIEF HISTORY OF THE MUSEUM COLLECTIONS

In 1976 a permanent room was opened within Trowbridge's new Civic Hall displaying the town's local history collections. These collections consisted of topographical prints and drawings, local history material and artefacts relating to the area's woollen textile industry.

In 1982 the museum acquired a large collection of textile machinery and related equipment due to the closure of the last remaining woollen mill in the town: Samuel Salter's Home Mills. Due to space restrictions the majority of objects were housed in three separate stores in the town and were available for viewing only by appointment. More display and storage space was urgently required and over the following years the town council sought new premises in which to set up a new museum.

THE NEW TROWBRIDGE MUSEUM

Six years later, in 1988, a new site was found within the Shires shopping centre, a new town-centre development. In 1989 a professional curator was appointed by Trowbridge Town Council to set up a new museum in a grade two listed woollen mill, the last working woollen mill in the town. The entire second floor of the mill is leased to the town council and a capital loan was acquired from West Wiltshire District Council to transform the space into the new museum.

Revenue funding is from the town council's own budget and the loan is being repaid by a special levy on the Council Tax payments of Trowbridge residents. The total cost of the project, which included the provision of basic services such as electricity and water and the design and construction of purpose-built displays, was £350,000.

The museum is completely self-contained on the one floor and comprises: an open-plan public display area, a temporary exhibitions gallery, a well-equipped schools/meeting room, museum store, workshop, computer room, museum shop and toilets.

The Trowbridge Museum is probably the first purpose-designed museum in this country to be created within a modern shopping centre and opened to the public in July 1990. It is staffed by a full-time curator and education officer and a part-time assistant curator and secretary. The museum also has an enthusiastic body of 'friends' who are actively involved in its day-to-day running.

THE MUSEUM DISPLAYS – AN OVERVIEW

The Trowbridge Museum aims to tell the broad story of a West Country woollen town, its people and its history, in particular focusing on the local woollen industry. A wide range of equipment and working textile machinery is displayed with accompanying interpretive panels tracing the growth of the industry in the area from the pre-industrial period up until the 1980s when the industry collapsed.

Machines are restored to working order and demonstrated where appropriate by volunteers, most of whom worked in the local industry. A Dobcross power loom produces fine 'West of England' cloth which is sold in the museum shop and a carding machine is demonstrated to booked groups and additionally provides a carding service to the many hand spinners in the region. Reconstructions are used to interpret various machines with the majority of working exhibits located in a factory-type setting with tools, furniture and even rubbish collected from the mill itself by members of the Trowbridge Civic Trust on the day that the factory closed. Reconstructions include: Samuel Salter's mill office, a handloom weaver's cottage, a local draper's shop and a shearman's workshop.

When the textile machinery is not in use a video is available showing film clips from the mill itself taken in 1982, the year of its closure, and footage from two mills in nearby Stroud. 'Hands-on' textile activities and drama sessions take place in the school room to pre-booked groups and demonstrations of hand spinning and weaving are regularly given within the museum.

The museum displays also focus on the town of Trowbridge and its surrounding villages, from the medieval period through to the present day. These diverse displays range from Edward Fox's seventeenth-century clay pipemakers' workshop to displays on modern-day industries such as mattress making, brewing and meat processing.

THE LOCAL TEXTILE INDUSTRY

The west of England woollen industry was concentrated in west Wiltshire, south Gloucestershire and east Somerset. Until 1982 Trowbridge was manufacturing 'West of England' cloth woven using 'dyed-in-the-wool' yarn. Dyed wools were blended before spinning so that a wider range of more intense colours was produced. Only one mill now remains in the west of England woollen textile area and this company specialises in the manufacture of tennis ball and billiard cloth (Winterbotham, Strachan and Playne).

There are many different stages in the production of cloth from the raw wool to the finished piece. Generally the processes fall into four separate areas, although the number of processes undertaken varies according to the quality of finish or the type of cloth being manufactured.

The following is a simplified account of the main processes involved in the manufacture of a cloth.

PREPARATION OF THE WOOL

Wool enters the factory in large bales, which are split, sorted and then 'opened' in a machine called a willey or fearnought. After washing the wool is either dyed or left its natural colour and then carded to make an even roll of wool fibres. The carding process involves the brushing of the wool, using various sets of carding machines consisting of a number of rollers, each covered with different grades of wired cloth. The final machine is called a condenser carder and produces narrow ribbons of fibre called sliver or slubbing. The sliver is then wound on to drums, which can be easily transferred to the spinning mule.

FIG. 1
Doubling at Palmer and McKay's Mill, Trowbridge, 1903

SPINNING

The fibre is drawn and twisted into yarn and wound on to cops on the spinning mule. The spun yarn is taken off the mule, doubled on a doubling machine (fig.1), and then wound into more easily manageable yarn packages on a winding machine. The yarn is then either wound on to the warping beam or on to bobbins which are inserted into the shuttles.

FIG. 2
Weaving at
Palmer and
McKay's Mill,
Trowbridge,
1903

WEAVING

Before weaving (fig.2) can commence, the loom is set up with warp threads.
The warp is wound on to a warp beam and the threads drawn through a set
of healds or heddles (wires with eyelets through which the warp threads are
drawn, which controls which threads are lifted during weaving). The healds
are held together in a wooden frame called a harness. The threads are also
passed through a sley (similar to a metal comb and used to keep the warp
threads separate). The ends are tied on to a rod connected to the cloth beam
and wound through the loom a little way before weaving commences.

If the cloth is the same or similar to the one previously woven, the new
warp is twisted or tied on to the old warp which is still in the loom and
pulled through the existing healds and sley.

FINISHING

Once the cloth is woven, numerous finishing processes are undertaken. First
the cloth is checked – plant material is removed (spiling), knots are
removed (burling) and faults in the cloth rectified usually with a needle and
yarn (mending). The cloth is then milled or fulled; in the west of England
this is usually undertaken in a rotary milling machine, invented by John
Dyer, a Trowbridge man, in 1833. This machine shrinks and felts the cloth
in a controlled manner by friction created as the cloth passes over rollers and
through a metal tube. After milling the cloth is tentered (stretched) and the
nap raised using teasels mounted on a teasel gig. The raised surface is cut
back using a rotary shearing machine and finally the cloth is checked once
more and pressed before despatching.

The textile industry has its own terminology, which not only varies between the woollen and cotton manufacturing districts but also between regions and towns within these areas. For example; a quill in the west country is what is commonly called a bobbin in the northern textile manufacturing regions, likewise sley and reed, heald and heddle and shearing and cropping.

THE PORTRAYAL OF TEXTILE WORKERS IN THE TROWBRIDGE MUSEUM

In the woollen mills both men and women worked in a variety of jobs, sometimes both doing the same type of work, but most jobs were specific to either male or female workers. Generally women tended to do the lighter, but by no means less skilful work, for example: carding, spinning, doubling, winding, twisting-on or tying-on the warp threads, weaving, checking and mending. Men tended to do the heavier work: unpacking wool bales, feeding machinery with fibre, dyeing, maintaining machinery, weaving and the majority of the finishing processes, such as milling, tentering, raising, shearing and pressing. A few of these processes, for example weaving, were performed predominantly, but not exclusively by women.

A number of general problems arise when interpreting the textile industries in a museum context. The majority of objects finding their way into museums tend to be concerned with the preparation processes, spinning or weaving. Few museums display tools or machinery relating to the finishing process which can give an unbalanced and over-simplified view of the subject. This is a difficult problem to redress, given that the most commonly displayed processes are the most vividly exciting and understandable and therefore more easily interpreted in the museum context.

Museums have traditionally concentrated on the machinery of the textile industries and the mechanics of the subject rather than putting the subject into a human context. Only in recent years has the human element filtered into the interpretation of the industry and this provides an ideal opportunity in which to interpret the roles of both sexes in an industry which is seen as mechanical and usually associated with 'man's work'.

Textile machinery is difficult to interpret unless working, and therefore at the Trowbridge Museum widespread use is made of interpretive panels illustrated with photographs, and machinery which is regularly demonstrated (fig.3) and explained further with an audio-visual presentation. A variety of source material is used to interpret the human element of the textile industry and to fill in any gaps in the process for which no artefacts are currently available; the obvious ones being photographic and archive material. The Museum and County Record Office has an extensive collection of material depicting both male and female workers in the nineteenth and twentieth centuries. In addition the museum embarked on an oral history project in 1991, which continues to provide

FIG. 3
Hand loom weaving in the weaver's cottage display, c. 1870

enlightening recordings from both male and female textile workers in the industry. It is hoped to make use of this archive in the further development of the museum's permanent displays.

CONCLUSION

Within the Trowbridge Museum context probably the most successful method of interpretation used is the operating of the machinery by skilled workers, most of whom worked in the local woollen industry. In addition the museum aims to give a balanced representation of the processes involved in the production of cloth, whether by using machinery or other interpretive methods, a process which will reflect the roles of both male and female employees within the textile industries.

ADDITIONAL TERMINOLOGY LIST

(An explanation of a number of terms is given in the text, these have been omitted from the list below.)

Bobbin	weft carrier held in the shuttle
Cop	yarn package obtained from a spinning mule
Carding	opening the wool
Nap	fibrous surface of the cloth also called pile
Shearing Machine	a machine which cuts the surface fibres off the cloth
Shuttle	holder to carry the bobbin (weft threads) in the loom
Spinning Mule	spinning machine invented by Samual Crompton in 1779
Teasel Gig	a machine with teasel covered rollers which is used to raise the nap on woollen cloth
Weft	threads which run across the cloth, usually held in a shuttle
Warp	threads which run lengthwise through a cloth.

THE 'CIGAR LADIES' OF LJUBLJANA:
THE FORMATION OF THE TOBACCO MUSEUM IN LJUBLJANA
Taja Čepič

This paper will introduce the major features of research into female labour in the Ljubljana tobacco factory and look to the project for the protection, preservation and museum presentation of the industrial heritage of Ljubljana at the City Museum of Ljubljana. This not only includes building complexes and industrial premises, but also the movable cultural heritage, ranging from industrial products to machines, employees and their lifestyle and work in industrial plants.

Ljubljana is the capital of the Republic of Slovenia. Slovenia was a constituent part of the Austro-Hungarian Empire until 1918, after which it was a part of the Kingdom of Yugoslavia and then a part of socialist Yugoslavia until 1991, when it proclaimed its independence. The population of the Republic of Slovenia is just under two million, in other words, the population of one of London's suburbs. Its capital Ljubljana, is a city of 300,000 inhabitants. One of the chief characteristics of its historical development is that, although the capital of the country, it never was a distinctly industrial centre. However in comparison to other Slovenian towns, Ljubljana had the largest labour force in absolute terms.

The proportion of employed women is extremely high in our country, the ratio between employed men and women being 50:50. The ratio of students at secondary schools and universities is also very similar. It is also typical that after marriage and the birth of their children, women do not stop working and do not stay at home as housewives. The salary for the same job is equal for men and women, however, women working in industry mainly occupy jobs of a lower qualification rank and their numbers thin out with progression to higher positions. But, undoubtedly, women have taken over certain spheres of activity, which are now distinctly feminised, such as education, health care, culture and to some extent, law. Women are subject to considerable stress in the career race, working the same eight-hour day as men.

Unlike in other parts of the country, this high percentage of female employment has been a feature of Ljubljana since the nineteenth century, mainly because of the tobacco factory. It was established in 1871 and its chief distinction was the employment of female labour. At the end of the previous century, the factory employed almost 2,500 female and male workers, eighty-six per cent of whom were women. This represented almost seven per cent of the Ljubljana population. The female tobacco workers, or 'cigar ladies' as they were called locally, because they rolled cigars, gave a particular character to the city for decades. Most of them lived in the same district, which became accordingly distinctive.

In the mid-nineteenth century, Ljubljana was faced with a severe economic crisis. The railway connection linking Vienna, the capital of the Austrian Empire, with Trieste the largest port in the country, ran through Ljubljana (it was called the Southern Railway and its construction was finished in 1857) and brought about the downfall of some branches of the economy, namely river and road freight transport. The abolition of serfdom, a result of the 1848 revolution, increased the influx of labour to urban areas. The old forms of home production and manufacture were no longer practised and foreign capital took over the Slovenian provinces. In these conditions, the city authorities decided to propose to the Imperial Court that a new factory be established in order to help solve the grave social situation of the unemployed in the city. The founding of a tobacco factory was suggested, which would be the first in the country. A state tobacco monopoly would ensure stability for the factory's operations. Ljubljana met with the basic requirements for the establishment of this type of plant, for the railway linked it with the port of Trieste, where ships carrying the raw material – tobacco – docked, and the city had enough cheap labour and a promising market.

The factory was established in March 1871 and twenty-two female workers started producing cigars, which were at the time the most popular tobacco product in the country. A year later, the factory employed almost 1,000 women and the construction of a new factory building was undertaken. Austrian tobacco factories established and built in the nineteenth century do not differ greatly in architecture, production process or the organisation of operations. The building complex of the Ljubljana tobacco factory is characteristic of Austrian industrial architecture in the second half of the nineteenth century. The Ljubljana tobacco factory was one of the 'major' category tobacco factories and was thus one of the most important. In size, it was the third largest in the Austrian part of the Empire. The management and administration of the factory was divided by job classification into special categories, but the position of the administrators grew worse towards 1914 and became very similar to that of the workers. Mention should be made of the national problem with regard to the factory's administration and labour force, for the former was German and the latter Slovenian, which caused certain tensions and conflicts before the First World War.

The Ljubljana tobacco factory needed a high number of workers, and these were provided by women and girls from Ljubljana and outlying villages. In comparison to other industrial plants in the city, the position of those employed in the factories of the state monopoly was more favourable. They were provided with a permanent income, sickness and old-age insurance and, what was most important, permanent work. Thus they enjoyed social security even in old age. At the beginning of the twentieth century, a health service with three doctors, a factory kitchen, bathrooms, a workers' library and after 1912 a creche, was available in the factory. But the reality often differed from the declared rights.

The position of the tobacco factory workers was in all respects defined by the 'Working Order of the Imperial Royal Tobacco Factories'. The workers were accordingly divided into permanent, temporary and occasional categories. The employment age limit was determined for newly-employed workers. The lower age limit was sixteen and only exceptionally fourteen, while the upper age limit for newly-employed workers was thirty-five. For juvenile workers under eighteen, the Order demanded that they be additionally educated mainly in crafts and at Sunday schools, which represented an additional burden for adolescents. As in any other country, child labour was nothing unusual in nineteenth-century Austria. A court decree of 1842 allowed the employment of children above twelve and only exceptionally of those above nine, who were permitted to work 'only' ten hours a day, while children between twelve and sixteen years of age were permitted to work twelve hours a day. A law from 1859 prohibited the employment of children below ten years of age in industry and in 1885 an important law was passed prohibiting the employment of children under fourteen in industrial plants. But despite the strict legislation, the employment of children was still practised, as shown in a comprehensive survey of child employment carried out in 1908.

The 'Working Order of the Imperial Royal Tobacco Factories' determined the maximum working hours, their organisation, the accounting and paying out of wages and also the rights and obligations of the supervising personnel. The order clearly defined that respect should be paid to management, foremen and guards by workers and that demonstrations were prohibited. Furthermore, workers had to come to work 'clean and sober'. Having arrived at work in the morning, their names were called before the start of work at their work stations. Visiting of different departments was prohibited, but praying and singing 'decent songs' was allowed during work! The workers had to be informed about work security measures. The order defined precisely when they were allowed to eat. Liquor was prohibited, as was (ironically) smoking or any other form of tobacco consumption in the premises and warehouses. The so-called 'visitation' was a regular form of control of workers after working hours. The women employed as these 'visitors' were in actual fact paid controllers and authorised to examine the workers' clothes and bags etc. Whoever was caught stealing tobacco was fired immediately.

The workers were organised into two professional organisations or unions: one Christian and one Social Democratic. The lack of unity of these organisations often presented obstacles to the demands for the improvement of the workers' position.

As mentioned above, eighty-six per cent of the Ljubljana tobacco factory workforce were women who came from the city and nearby communities. The working day of nine hours, from the beginning of the twentieth century onwards, with the one-hour break at noon, meant that they were away from home practically all day long. If we consider the poor transportation and the fact that many of them walked to work, working at the factory was extremely strenuous. Nevertheless, there was an extremely low turnover of labour. Despite numerous childbirths (maternity leave consisted of six weeks before and after childbirth), the workers remained faithful to the factory. Since the problem of child-minding was extremely acute, a creche for young children was organised in the tobacco factory in 1912. One of the characteristics of the factory was that it was a 'family factory', as it still is today. Entire generations of the same family were employed there – the mother, daughter and granddaughter. Tobacco workers were highly prized brides and they often remarried, some even several times, after the death of a first husband. The so-called 'team books' (lists of generations employed in the factory) even include a few divorcees, which was something unheard of at the turn of the century in a Catholic country such as Slovenia.

It is interesting that one-third of the women workers never married. They represented a considerable financial resource to their families and they paid for the education of many of their nephews. At the same time, a steady income provided for the payment of taxes on farms near the city. Relatively good, regular income, the pension enjoyed by the women workers after thirty-five years of employment and good labour organisation, meant that small neighbourhoods of modest family houses began to emerge at the end of the previous and beginning of this century in the vicinity of the factory. Built by tobacco workers with the help of loans, these still serve their purpose today.

However, there could also be problems for the workers. According to recorded oral statements, many 'cigar ladies' were of ill-repute, although this was rarely justified. Illegitimate children were frequent, although they were regarded as a serious disgrace. Many young girls who came to the city with high-hopes were disappointed. Some of them took their own lives, which shook the city, and the tragic fates of 'cigar ladies' entered Slovene literature. Despite the provision of surprisingly good working environments, as listed earlier, the processes caused a great deal of illness. Fine tobacco dust, which was impossible to avoid, was the chief cause of lung disease. Most lives, as many as fifty-two per cent of all deaths, were claimed by consumption, followed by stomach and lung catarrh, various viral diseases, gout and anaemia. The fact was mentioned in the press that seventy-five out of one hundred women workers were unable to work or died before they reached the age of forty.

Enjoying a higher social status than other industrial workers, if also the associated bad health, the tobacco workers liked to stress this difference in their appearance. In clothing, they imitated the lower bourgeois classes, and they attended various social events organised mainly by their professional organisations, such as dances and excursions. Most of all, they were famous for their self-conscious bearing, which was undoubtedly the result of their economic independence. The tobacco worker was often the only provider in the family.

As the capital of Slovenia, Ljubljana has been a cultural, transport and educational centre for decades, although not a typical industrial area, and thus there has been little interest in preserving or exhibiting this part of our history in the city museum. Lack of sentiment towards the material remains of the past in its factories has been the reason for the rapid disappearance of traces of the past in the last two decades.

In Slovenia, no regulation or law requires consultation with a professional organisation prior to the destruction of potential movable cultural heritage, with the exception of archive material. The situation is completely different with the immovable cultural heritage (for example, architecture) which is controlled by a special professional organisation charged with the task of preventing demolition of, or unprofessional changes to, potential architectural monuments. Nevertheless, attitudes started to change in Slovenia in the late 1980s, and the first museum exhibitions began to appear in factories, representing part of the new marketing methods. These accorded greater significance to heritage. The project for the preservation and museum presentation of the Ljubljana industrial plants was started in co-operation with the tobacco factory of Ljubljana, based on equal partnership between the museum and the factory.

When the preparation for the exhibition was undertaken in 1988, there was not a single object, document or photograph in our possession that might represent a material remnant of the past work, life or production of the factory with its 120 years of history. Due to outside forces (the moving of the equipment of cigar production departments to another factory outside Slovenia, in Serbia) the factory itself was left with an extreme scarcity of material, although a great deal of material was preserved in the city archives. Through extensive fieldwork in co-operation with well-organised retired workers and private collectors from across the country, more than a thousand different objects have been collected. The field recording of oral sources has also been carried out (the oldest interviewee was born in 1888 and started working in the factory in 1906).

The first step was an exhibition opened in the museums cultural information centre in spring 1991, which was warmly received. This was also helped by the family ties linking a high number of inhabitants of Ljubljana to the factory. The exhibition facilitated a greater influx of exhibits, these being contributed by the visitors themselves. This was followed by the opening of the tobacco museum in the premises of the factory a year later. Located in the former warehouse of the main building, where cigars used to be produced, the museum is dedicated primarily to the presentation of the role and significance of the factory in the city, its workers and their lifestyle. It also narrates the history of tobacco, the main point being the differences between smokers and opponents of tobacco in previous centuries. The greatest problems were encountered in collecting personal objects and material remains of the living conditions of tobacco workers. Although we received a detailed description of what the dowry of a woman worker married in the 1930s comprised, the worker had not preserved a single item, despite the fact that the china and glassware had been bought at the most prestigious merchant in Ljubljana. Gold rings typical of women tobacco workers were also of great interest. One of those acquired for the exhibition was lent to us by a colleague from the National Museum and it represents the dear memory of her old aunt, who worked at the factory.

At its opening, the museum was proclaimed a part of the cultural heritage and the City Museum and the tobacco factory signed a special contract for the development of the museum, which was necessary as the tobacco factory was taken over by foreign investors in 1991.

The successful setting up of the tobacco industry museum encouraged some other factories in Ljubljana, taking pride in their tradition, to consider establishing a similar type of museum collection. However, progress is hindered by the transition of factories from state to private ownership. It is difficult in this transitional period to ensure the interest of new owners, that is the management, and the guarantee of a constant financial flow contributed to this kind of partnership by the factory.

Lastly, an important aspect in this experience of co-operation with the tobacco factory is the fact that they did not set conditions in our partnership with regard to the content of the displays, so that research and scientific findings on the harmful effects of smoking are also presented in the exhibition.

'VILE CREATURES':
HOMEWORKING IN SPITALFIELDS, LONDON, 1880–1909
Diane Atkinson

'A London homeworker carrying skirts'. *The Mansell collection*

'This photo-essay is an introduction to the long-running and impassioned debate on sweated labour which exercised the minds of the 'great and the good' from the 1840s, when Thomas Hood's poem 'The Song of the Shirt'[1] exposed the scandalous working conditions of seamstresses. Homeworking was described as 'sweating', a shorthand term for the three lethal ingredients of long hours, starvation wages, and insanitary conditions. A broad coalition of politicians, social reform campaigners, the clergy, the medical profession, trade unionists and feminists was formed to promote legislation aimed at eradicating the sweated working conditions of hundreds of thousands of Victorian workers.

Working-class women who worked in their own homes throughout the United Kingdom, and especially those in Spitalfields, east London, were subjected to the closest and most hostile scrutiny of all women workers. In the summer of 1906 the National Anti-Sweating League sponsored the groundbreaking Sweated Industries Exhibition which proved to be the catalyst for Britain's first piece of minimum-wage legislation, the Trade Boards Act of 1909.

On 2 May 1906, Princess Henry of Battenburg opened the *Daily News*'s Sweated Industries Exhibition at the Queen's Hall, Langham Place, London. The aim was: 'to bring into fresh prominence a social evil which, though long recognised and deplored by all parties, remains to this day without a remedy'.[2] The exhibition committee wished it to be 'very clearly and definitely understood that they are not either in this book [the catalogue] or by means of the exhibition, condemning employers of home industry workers as such'.[3] The fifty-six members of the exhibition's council included the most eminent people of the day who were concerned about homeworking. They included eight MPs, George Cadbury, Robert Blatchford, George Bernard Shaw, H.G. Wells and Clementina Black, Margaret Irwin and Mrs Ramsay MacDonald, leading lights of the women's trade-union movement.[4]

The exhibition was to:

> '… acquaint the public with the evils of Sweating, and to cultivate an opinion which shall compel legislation that will mitigate, if not entirely remove those evils. Such legislation does not either necessarily or primarily mean that home industry is to be forbidden by law; it does mean that it must be regulated by law, that it shall be done under conditions which shall guarantee the public no less than the worker from disease. '[5]

Six hundred 'society' visitors paid a shilling each to see the exhibition on the first day:

At three o'clock the gathering wore very much the aspect of a society crush, almost as though the attractions were a flower show or a West End bazaar. The dame of high degree and the well-grounded gentleman of leisure had come to make personal acquaintance with the lamentable human facts to which Princess Henry of Battenburg by her gracious presence ... had desired to draw public attention. The visitors paid 'rapt attention' to the display of homeworkers and their goods and expressed 'amazement and dismay' ... Society came and shuddered and expressions of sympathy and indignation fell from these gentle-natured folk.[6]

Gertrude Tuckwell's emotional lecture, 'Wages and Hours', cited a number of case studies:

The workers in the hall represented thousands of homes of our great towns and represented them inadequately as many of the hearers would know ... The very things they (the audience) were wearing might be sweated and surely if it were so, they knew the clothes would burn into them like the fabled shirt of Nessus. For the sweater is the purchaser, the whole nation, you and I.[7]

Forty-four homeworkers and twenty-two stalls were the exhibits. Worker Number Three made matchboxes at a rate of two pence a gross. She earned on average less than five shillings a week and had to buy paste and string to tie the bundles together and firing to dry the wet boxes. Two hours out of the twelve were lost collecting and delivering the work. The rent for the small room where she and her five children lived was two shillings and six pence. Her details were typical of the other homeworkers who were exhibited.[8] The thirty thousand visitors, approximately two thousand a day, were not permitted to give the homeworkers gratuities.[9]

The editorials of the *Daily News*, the lectures which were given at the Queen's Hall, and the articles in the official catalogue, convey the politics of the anti-sweating debate. The sponsors, the *Daily News*, set the tone of the debate and warned that the reality of homeworkers' lives was far worse than the exhibition had been able to portray and that their working and living conditions were an affront to the sanctity of the home:

No exhibition, however faithful, can reproduce the milieu which makes these home industries not only a struggle against starvation but a continual outrage upon the decency of family life. The furniture huddled into a corner to make room for material and machines, half-finished garments littered across the untidy bed ... the unkempt children staggering under enormous bundles ... But it is something we have the opportunity of seeing, many of us for the first time in our lives.

Even worse, homeworkers in the East End of London were imperilling the race:

> **In nine cases out of ten the woman was absolutely compelled to take in some form of home industry. It was impossible for her to look after the children properly. Could they wonder at the high mortality among the children when the mother had to slave from morning to night?**[10]

Margaret Irwin, a leading member of the Scottish Council of Women's Trades, was appalled at the cost to the homeworkers themselves. She referred to shirtmakers: 'the hopelessness of their outlook and the relentless, unremitting daily toil that goes in with them year in year out and which even sickness is scarcely allowed to interrupt'.[11] Along with other contributors to the catalogue, she voiced the public-health fears long associated with homework:

> **The sympathy of the community is easily roused. What is more difficult to awaken is the sense of the terrible risks to which not only the workers but the purchasing public are exposed through the making of clothing, and other articles of general use in insanitary houses. One often finds in the worst of these homes that the woollen shirts, shawls and other articles of clothing on which the workers have been engaged during the day are used as coverings for the sick or do duty as bedclothes for the members of the family generally.**[12]

Irwin reminded readers of the reputation for poor hygiene and housewifery enjoyed by sack-sewers: 'without exception their houses were indescribably filthy. Some of them were entirely destitute of furniture and in others the sacks, dirty and vermin-infested would be used at night for bed and bedclothes.'

Thrift and pride were said to be the first casualties when homeworkers' wages fell to starvation levels, when they were 'benumbed by a sense of utter hopelessness'.[13] The spread of infectious diseases through home industries, the decline in mothercraft and housewifery and the defilement of the home were the crux of the campaigners' concerns.

Legislation was perceived to be the answer to the worst excesses. Minimum wages for the most sweated trades via Wages Boards (later called Trade Boards), and the licensing of homeworkers' premises were the most discussed remedies, and two Bills were canvassed aggressively and promoted at the exhibition. Sir Charles Dilke's Wages Boards Bill, and the Women's Industrial Council's Bill for the Better Regulation of Home Industries (first drafted in 1899) were recommended by the exhibition organisers.[14]

The thirty-two illustrations in the exhibition catalogue are some of the earliest representations of homeworkers in their own homes. Interrogation of the images reveals them not to be squalid or especially poverty-stricken and barely living up to the reputation that homeworkers enjoyed. The five selected here, including the front cover, are typical of the rest of the material. The catalogue advised readers that the photographs had been 'taken in most places by false light and have not in any way been altered or, with two exceptions, touched up'.[15] The photographs show homeworkers from Spitalfields, although the location is not given.

FIG. 1
Cover of the *Daily News*
Sweated Industries
Exhibition catalogue
1906

Fig. 1 is the drawing which appeared on the front cover. The central figure is the mother making matchboxes, assisted by a bedraggled daughter, accompanied by a toddler and a baby. The room is small and crowded and bare. We see bare boards, a bed, a table, a chair; the patched washing is drying overhead. The matchbox-making industry is not only trespassing into their private space, but not paying them an adequate wage. The toddler seems to be eating its mother's work. It is a scene of misery and neglect in an unloved room.

Fig. 2 is a photograph captioned 'Sack-Mender'. The scene, of a young woman alone in her room, seems to have been posed to look downcast and oppressed by the pile of sacks next to her, which are taller than she is. She avoids looking at the camera. Her hair is neatly tied; she wears an apron and she owns a straw boater. Margaret Irwin's description (see above) is not entirely borne out by this particular image.

FIG. 2
'A sack-Mender'.
c. 1906

Fig. 3 is of four women making match- and tin-tack boxes. The room is full of furniture, the walls are covered in framed prints and photographs and the mantelpiece is decked with ornaments. A Vesuvius of industry, we

FIG. 3
'Match and
Tin-tack
Box-Makers'.
c. 1906

are manipulated to think, has erupted among this mother and her three daughters. The Liberal MP, Mr L. G. Chiozza Money, wrote the accompanying article. Again, his description does not marry up with the image. Matchbox-making was:

frequently carried on under the most distressing conditions ... made under the most filthy and revolting conditions. The nice clean-looking box of matches may have been fashioned by a consumptive in a room reeking with pestilential matter.[16]

Fig.4 is of a mother and her three children, making trousers. Their home has been taken over by other men's trousers. The daughter helps her mother and the two boys, both quite well dressed, who probably delivered the completed work and collected fresh supplies from a local warehouse. The paper-doily shelf trimmings bear witness to some level of affluence.[17]

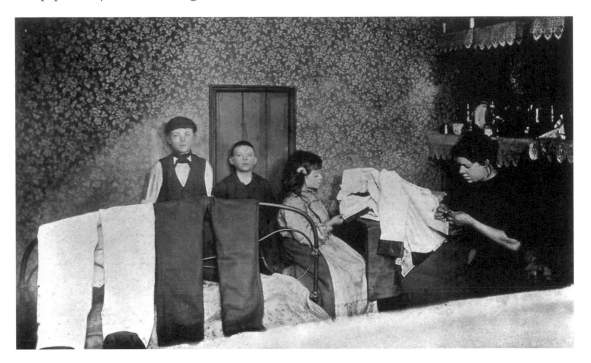

FIG. **4**
'Making Trousers'.
c. 1906

Fig. 5 shows a family of bristle-pickers employed by the brush-making industry. The mother and two of her four children are engaged in this work. They are all properly dressed, and we can imagine they are properly shod. Their home is full of things. Rather than a picture of domestic neglect it is cheerfully cluttered and cosy. It is a God-fearing home, witness the 'God Bless Our Home' framed motto. The mother has not tidied the dishes away, but there are plenty of dishes to tidy away when she has finished her work. This mother and the others who did this work came in for criticism by Mrs Hogg, a founder member of the Women's Industrial Council, who wrote the article which this photograph illustrated:

> It is one of the melancholy features of the neighbourhood to see sickly children, hardly more than infants, staggering along in the wind … with every muscle of their rickety little bodies strained beneath the load upon which the chance of next day's dinner depends … It is only by seeing the homes of brush-drawers [makers] that it is impossible to realise all that is implied in the carrying on of a trade in one single room or the misery of these lives of endless toil.[18]

FIG. 5
'Bristle-Pickers'.
c. 1906

These five images invited readers to share the exhibition organisers' outrage at the practice of homework. To Edwardian middle-class eyes these photographs displayed poverty and married up with their perception of what homework involved. However, these images tell us as much about the people who commissioned them as the women workers they were illustrating. John Tagg's *The Burden of Representation: Essays on Photographies and Histories* (1988), reminds us that we use photographs as 'evidence' at our peril:

The camera is not neutral and the images it produces are highly coded, and the power it wields is never its own. As a means of record it arrives on the scene imbued with a particular, powerful authority to inform daily life. This is not so much to do with the power of the camera but the power of the machinery which deployed it and guaranteed the authority of the images is constructed to stand as evidence.[19]

We may choose to interpret the images in the catalogue differently, but at the time it is likely that anyone would feel disturbed by the gloomy rooms, the cluttered living arrangements and the sight of mothers and children working. The paraphernalia of homework, and its intrusion into private spaces where the absent father was present, was the point of these photographs. These images remind us of the invention of the factory which posited the innovation of 'The Home' as a refuge from waged labour. The secret horror of these photographs to well-meaning middle-class contemporaries was the eruption of work into a space that two generations had sanctified. The Englishman's home had only recently become his castle, and the division of economic activities into what was considered to be their appropriate physical location was a novel and much-prized Victorian invention, which ignored the use of the home as a workplace by all workers until industrialisation.

POSTSCRIPT

The Trade Boards Act of 1909 was the direct outcome of the thirty-year campaign waged by 'the great and the good' late Victorian and Edwardian society. The Act legislated for minimum rates of pay in ready-made wholesale tailoring, cardboard box-making, chain-making, machine-made lace and net finishing. It took five years for all the minimum hourly rates to be set and put into practice: three pence farthing per hour in ready-made wholesale tailoring; two pence half penny per hour in chain-making; three pence an hour in cardboard box-making and two pence three farthings in lace and net-finishing. While the Act was not framed exclusively for the benefit of homeworkers in these trades, it was envisaged that they would be the first and most numerous beneficiaries as these were the trades that had a large homeworking force integral to their mode of production.[20]

Spitalfields homeworkers did not necessarily enjoy immediate financial benefits from the Act. In 1915 a survey of East London revealed that only 24 per cent of the homeworkers surveyed reported higher rates of pay as a result of the Trade Boards Act. Most homeworkers did not feel confident enough to challenge the rates offered by their employers. Others were ignorant of the Act or were afraid to report under-paying employers to the inspectors whose job it was to enforce the agreed rates of pay.

In the 1920s, homework disappeared from the public domain. By 1921, a further twenty trades had been added and over two million women, mostly homeworkers, were now included within the scope of the 1909 Act. All the key players in the homework debate died during this decade and homeworkers inevitably slipped from the public interest which was overtaken by the socio-economic and political consequences of the First World War. It was thought that homework died out, but oral testimony tells us that it survived, became more hidden and even more badly paid.

After the Second World War the wages of low-paid workers were monitored by Wages Councils which replaced the Trade Boards. The work of the Councils and that of the low pay unit, which 'rediscovered' homework and homeworkers in the labour market in the 1970s, and organisations such as the National Homeworking Unit is beyond the scope of this paper. In 1993, the little wage protection that (some) homeworkers enjoyed was lost by the abolition of the Wages Councils, an Act which had been high on Mrs Thatcher's agenda.

There are over a million women working in their own homes today. Some earn as little as twenty pence an hour. Even 'teleworkers' – those who work at computer screens in their own homes – often earn low rates of pay. Despite the thin veneer of glamour which comes with technology, teleworkers are just as isolated, just as badly paid, just as hidden and just as disadvantaged with just as few employment rights as their 'sisters' who work in the more traditional manufacturing areas of homework. With the rise in male employment and the growth of female part-time work, all the indicators are that homework can only increase and that conditions will probably not improve.

ENDNOTES

1 Thomas Hood 'The Song of the Shirt', is quoted in Walkley, C., 1981.

2 Morning Post, 4 May 1906, Gertrude Tuckwell Collection, Reel 5, File 217.

3 'Sweated Industries Catalogue', op cit, p9.

4 Ibid, p4.

5 Ibid, p10.

6 Daily News, 4 May 1906, Gertrude Tuckwell Collection, Reel 5, File 217.

7 The Greek Myths, Graves, R., 1955, Vol.2, pp113–4, 193, 200–2.

8 'Sweated Industries Catalogue', op cit, p21.

9 Black, C., Sweated Industries and the Minimum Wage, 1907, p.ix Lectures were given at 3.30 p.m., and included: 'The evils of Home Industrial Work'; 'Labour as a Commodity'; 'Cheap Clothing and Nasty'; 'Trade Unionism and Women'; 'The position of Women in Industry'; and 'Foreign Methods of Dealing with Sweating'. 'Sweated Industries Catalogue', op cit, p7.

10 Daily News, 5 and 7 May 1906, Gertrude Tuckwell Collection, Reel 5, File 217.

11 'Sweated Industries Catalogue', op cit, p44. The East London Observer reported a sad case of a local homeworker: East London Observer, 29 December 1906, p3.

12 'Sweated Industries Catalogue', op cit, p45.

13 Ibid, pp49–50.

14 Ibid, pp27–30.

15 Ibid, p6.

16 Ibid, pp95–8.

17 Ibid, pp86–9.

18 Ibid, pp91–5.

19 Tagg, J., 1988, pp633–4.

20 Schmiechen, J., 1984, p174.

WOMEN TELEGRAPHISTS AND TYPISTS, 1870–1890   Anna Davin

In the last decades of the nineteenth century, the expansion of the commercial and distributive sectors of the British economy, along with the growth of bureaucracy in local, national and imperial government, created a rapidly increasing demand for literate and numerate office labour. Men's employment in these sectors was growing fast, but employers found it advantageous to supplement them with a new and low-paid workforce, whose inexperience and diffidence made possible their greater exploitation: women. Women's employment in the civil service was explicitly recommended on such grounds: they were better value for money than the men who would accept the same rates of pay, and they were more docile, less likely 'to combine for the purpose of extorting higher wages'.[1]

The new labour need was matched by two groups of potential employees: single middle-class women, whose employment was ceasing to be socially unacceptable, and girls of the upper-working-class who, from the 1880s, were emerging from the board schools (set up following the 1870 Education Act) well-trained and ambitious for respectable work of the kind sometimes already done by girls of the lower-middle-class. The numbers of female clerks recorded by the Census rose rapidly, in London there were 557 in 1871, 2,327 in 1881, and 6,793 in 1891.

From the middle of the nineteenth century the middle-class dogma that ladies never did paid work began to be undermined. This shift in opinion came to affect employers, parents and women themselves. It introduced the possibility of employment that was respectable even for a lady; and it allowed the unmarried or widowed woman (though not the wife) to earn her own living without losing status. New areas of work were opening up, notably in offices, the new department stores and teashops, where speech and comportment, and sometimes family, qualified (or disqualified) the applicant. Employment practices were often paternalist, aimed at securing the welfare of the young ladies, the reassurance of their parents, and the satisfaction of the employers. Clerical work was a classic example.

The 1851 Census showed a preponderance of women in the population, especially in the middle class. 'Natural' surplus was reinforced by other factors. Numerous eligible men were claimed by service abroad (in the imperial army or the administration of outposts, for instance) or foreign trade, or emigrated, or were reluctant to give up the joys of bachelorhood for the responsibilities of a family. All this meant, as feminists were quick to point out, that the many young women whose training and education had pointed exclusively towards marriage and homemaking would in fact not all be able to marry. Late proposals and long engagements resulted from the great importance attached to marrying only on a sufficient and stable income, and young ladies might remain dependent on their fathers for many years. The resulting strain on family finances, especially where there were numerous daughters, could mean endless difficulties. Another predicament could arise if a breadwinner died without leaving proper provision for his widow and orphaned daughters: they were left without resources, yet had been educated only for dependence and leisure.

Consequently, even ladies might need paid employment, and this was increasingly recognised. The most accepted option was to become a governess; but in the second half of the century, with the development of high schools and as standards of teaching rose even for girls, openings for governesses were fewer and expectations higher. Many young ladies were themselves too inadequately educated to attempt governessing. Others, though better qualified, rejected it as blinkered drudgery and looked for other ways to support themselves while not abandoning their status as ladies.

Many young women of the lower-middle-class, of course, already went out to work, and certainly did not consider that they lost status by doing so. The diarist, A. J. Munby, recorded meeting one such in Caldwell's Dancing Rooms (Dean St), in 1863. She was 'a bona fide female city clerk', employed as a copyist at a mercantile house in Old Broad Street. He was fascinated, and even danced with her (though he 'really could not spin round with the rapidity which she required'), so that afterwards, over refreshments (she drank sherry and soda water), he could obtain 'an account of her business and habits'. 'She was twenty-two, and had been three years a clerk under her present employers. It was the only business she had ever been engaged in: and it took a good deal of influence to get her place.' She worked in one room with several other girls and a number of male clerks, all doing the same kind of work: copying invoices and letters. The male clerks were pleasant companions enough, but there was no flirting: 'when you're all in business together it's different; and besides we've no time'. She sat on a high stool – 'our sleeves get worn with leaning on the desk, and our cuffs get terribly inked' – all day, from nine to five, or from twelve to eight: 'I've been on late duty this week.'

She was careful to call her fellows 'ladies' and 'gentlemen'; she travelled first class(!) on the 'underground railway' she behaved to me with an air of calm equality. On the other hand, she was ready to talk and dance with Severn and

**myself without any introduction; to make me her companion homewards, and
to chat freely with a stranger about her work, her dress, her daily ways. But
again, she did all this … out of a kind of manly frankness and affability … She
was a city clerk, and moved among men as other city clerks would.**[2]

Gentility, of birth or of aspiration, was clearly of potential advantage to
employers. Unlike the factory girl who would answer back, argue, even walk out
on the job and quite possibly be followed by others, a 'lady' would avoid
unseemly wrangling or confrontation of any kind and put up with difficulties
as best she could. And in some cases, notably in the Civil Service, women were
also conscious that their employment represented a breakthrough for women
and hesitated to compromise such employment in the future by making
unacceptable demands or by appearing as less than ladies.

Employers' labour needs and the ready supply of women to meet them
influenced the expansion of clerical employment for women. It was also
affected by technological innovation, most notably in this period the telegraph,
the typewriter and the telephone. Of these I focus here on the first.

Female clerks were employed by the telegraph companies from the early
1850s. They worked as counter clerks and as manipulators; that is, they took
down and transmitted the messages which customers brought in to their
company's branch offices. They also had to keep detailed records of
transactions and at the end of the day to balance their books. So they needed
to be literate and to be able to keep books, and to have learnt to use the
transmitting equipment. A. J. Munby, in his diaries during the early 1860s,
not only noted each time he mentioned sending a telegram the female clerks
who served him, but (in 1861) also gave in some detail a conversation with
one whose acquaintance he made.[3] Lizzie Gregg, aged twenty, with five years'
telegraph experience behind her, was working in a branch office of the
Electric Telegraph Company in Fleet Street. It was run by four clerks, all 'girls';
the chief of these received a pound a week, and Lizzie herself, Munby
estimated, probably fifteen shillings.

**The hours are from ten to seven; but sometimes nine to five or twelve to eight
… No time allowed for meals, but we have our dinners sent in from the
London, and get it when we can. Find odd times to work [this may perhaps
mean sewing or knitting – A.D.] and read (novels) during the day. Have 'to sign
a great paper' about secrecy before you become a clerk.**

The transfer of telegraph business from the companies to the Post Office
in 1870 involved a considerable effort of reorganisation and expansion, in
the course of which the number of women clerks (in London alone) grew

from 363 to 752, an increase proportionally greater than that of male clerks. Eighty-one of these were 'counterwomen', who did not need technical training. The rest were 'manipulators', who did. One of the civil servants involved in the transfer, R. W. Johnston, recalled the search for operators with previous experience: 'It became evident, as the day of transfer approached, that we should be terribly shorthanded, and I was given *carte blanche* to engage all the 'skilled hands' outside the service I could lay my hands on.' One enterprising young lady, who applied declaring that she 'knew all about the telegraph', turned out to have an exclusively theoretical knowledge, 'gathered from books and from a study of official forms'. Johnston engaged her anyway, being taken with 'her naiveté and intelligence', and by 1894, when he was writing, she was in 'one of the most responsible positions in the female branch of the service'. Wherever possible, they brought back 'clerks who had left the service of the telegraph companies for other occupations', and among these were many women, especially 'female clerks who had married, and who in accordance with the practice of the … companies had been dismissed'. To train new recruits, schools were set up, first one for girls (in November 1869), then one for boys (February 1870). Although the training period of two or three months was unpaid, and the probationer's wage after that was only eight shillings (ten for males), there was 'a superabundance of applications': 154 male and 269 female telegraphists were produced by these schools in the first year. Another scheme, which offered a one pound bonus to 'persons already in the service of the Post Office, and their friends and relatives' if they learned telegraphic techniques, furnished in London 196 female clerks and only 139 male.

The extension of female employment in the telegraph service was promoted by Frank Scudamore, who was in charge of the reorganisation and who wrote the accompanying report on it. His arguments, cogently presented in the report, were as follows: that women's dexterity made them particularly skilful manipulators; that they took more kindly then men or boys to sedentary work, and bore long confinement with more patience; that they were cheaper ('the wages which will draw male operators from but an inferior class of the community, will draw female operators from a superior class'); that being thus superior they were likely to write and spell better, and to raise the tone of the whole staff; that they were less disposed than men to combine for the purpose of extorting higher wages; and finally that there would always be fewer of them on the pension list because those who married would be likely to retire. It is clear, both from Scudamore's summary of his propositions and from later Civil Service discussions of female employment, that economy was thought to be the strongest of the arguments in their favour. Additionally, unrest among male telegraphists after the transfer may have made the females' supposed docility an extra attraction. Male telegraphists, according to H. G. Swift in his *History of Post Office Agitation*, were, under the companies, 'an independent Bohemian lot, and nomadic in their habits', rambling from one company to another as it suited them, and making up for a uniformly poor wage by such expedients as 'keeping the office open after hours and making their own charges, levying taxes for porterage on messages, taking allowances for string, paper and other material, and so on'.[6] The transfer put an end to these unofficial emoluments without improving men's official wage; and Civil Service bureaucracy checked their casual ways. They chafed under the new discipline, formed a Telegraphists' Association, and in December 1871 struck and were locked out. Their action was unsuccessful, but it probably reinforced Scudamore's views.

For female telegraphists, on the other hand, Post Office control had its advantages. In the early years at least the Post Office did not 'punish marriage with dismissal'.[7] Far from turning off its employees at the age of thirty, like the telegraph companies, it rewarded long service with improved pay, and advancing years were crowned eventually with a pension. Medical attention was free. Conditions compared favourably with those of all other employment open to women. The female clerks were provided morning and evening with tea and coffee and bread and butter; they brought their own dinner, but could have it cooked in their own kitchen and ate it in their own dining room, without charge for attendance, fuel or anything else.[8] (Elsewhere, in the exceptional cases where eating facilities were provided, they were likely to be an excuse for a wage deduction.) They also had cloakrooms and lavatories. They worked only eight hours a day, and unlike their male colleagues they were not expected to work on Sunday or at night. This was a recurring source of tension, but in fact it secured the men's continued employment, which otherwise might well have been at risk. The balance between numbers of male and female clerks was a subject frequently raised in subsequent years: the Post Office tried to keep up the numbers of men so that night work could be shared between many instead of falling exclusively on a few; while the Treasury deplored the 'serious increase of expense, clerk for clerk' and wanted to reduce male employment.

There was resistance to female employment both among the male telegraphists and their superiors. The latter expressed themselves more guardedly, at least in their evidence before Civil Service Commissioners, our main source for their views. They gave praise only grudgingly and stressed the high rate of absence among women (5.5 per cent to men's 2.5 per cent) and their incapacity for night work. Such reservations, together with concern at the unexpectedly high rate of resignations among the men, presumably explain the steady swing back in favour of men's employment which took place from the mid-1870s. But the men's sense of threat remained, erupting from time to time in prejudiced and resentful complaints about the incompetence and unreliability of women. A debate in their journal, the *Telegraphist*, in 1885, provides fine examples of such assertions. Here is one of the more moderate contributors, who acknowledged that some female labour was all right, though felt that it injured the telegraph service by placing extra burdens on the men. In his view:

> **Billiards, coursing, racing, cricket, yachting, shipping, money, and other descriptions of special work, female clerks as a rule are not well qualified to deal with, and therefore it is advisable that the policy of employing ladies should be followed with caution, so that there may always be a fair proportion of male clerks.**[9]

The ladies' defence was spirited, both on particular grounds and on their general right and need to work. The arguments are still familiar.

> **It is argued in our disfavour that girls only resort to telegraphy as a means of procuring pin-money, and that therefore the salaries are frittered away on us which should be paid to male clerks ... Very many of us have no other resources, and depend *solely* upon our remuneration as a means of subsistence.**[10]

Despite recurrent alarms about the expense of the Telegraph Service and attempts to increase the proportion of women employed for economy's sake, the men's lobby seems to have had more success. In 1872 there were 688 men in the London Telegraph Service and 1,038 women. Twenty years later the men's numbers had trebled (2,468) and the women's had stayed almost the same (1,316).[11]

Who were the young women attracted to this work? In Munby's first diary references he described the 'nice looking well drest girl' whom he met every morning 'trudging citywards to her work as he set off to Whitehall for his'. It was Lizzie Gregg, whom he had met already at a working people's dance at Salter's Hall, and he observed that she was 'one of the self-supporting women of the future'.[12] In his references to other clerks such words as 'respectable' and 'well drest' recurred, and, less often, 'ladylike'. When he got to know her better he decided that Lizzie's family belonged to 'the highly respectable or lower-middle-class', and she herself therefore 'came short of ladyhood by differences much more subtle than those one observes, for instance, in a milliner'.

Lucy Brightman, another telegraphist whom he knew, probably had the same kind of background. Her father kept a small grocer's shop in the Adelphi; she herself, after working as a telegraph clerk at Lothbury, was now 'improving her position and learning French, as a nursery governess at the West End'.[13] Most of the clerks at Lothbury, according to Lizzie, were the daughters of tradespeople, but some few of clerks or professional men: one was a doctor's daughter, and two, sisters, daughters of a clergyman.[14] To the outsider the young women were 'evidently drawn from the middle rank of life'.[15] Civil Service authorities seem to have expected them to be the 'children of the lower-middle-class'.[16]

Under the Post Office, entry was through examination in dictation, writing and arithmetic ('easy sums in the first four rules'). Applicants had to be between the ages of fourteen and eighteen; and they had to get through a medical examination with special reference to their eyesight and hearing.[17] They could try to improve their chances by attending one of the telegraph schools, like Lundy's in City Road or the Central Telegraph School near London Bridge.

In the Civil Service hierarchy, however, among the various employments being opened to women from the 1870s onwards, telegraphy stood lowest. Such non-technical appointments as clerkships in the Saving Bank Department carried higher salaries, involved shorter hours, and were reserved for 'gentlewomen of limited means, daughters of officers in the Army and Navy, of civil officers of the Crown, of those engaged in the clerical, legal and medical professions, of literary men and artists'. And unlike the humble telegraphists, these ladies worked 'entirely apart from clerks of the male sex', following a warning by the Civil Service Inquiry Commissioners that they would not recommend the further employment of women unless they could be placed 'in separate rooms, under proper female supervision'.[18]

Similarly, in the business world some firms insisted on class qualifications for their lady clerks, however humble the tasks for which they were required. The Prudential Assurance Company accepted only the daughters of professional men, some sixty or seventy of whom in 1875 were 'copying letters and other documents and writing out dockets connected with the life policies issued to the poorer classes'.[19] The Bank of England began to employ women only in 1894, to count and register banknotes, and they had to be nominated by one of the directors and to sit a special entrance exam unless they had already passed the Oxford or Cambridge Local Examinations. (This high academic level would effectively exclude candidates from the working- or lower-middle-class.)

As the typewriter came into use, in the 1880s, the operators were often female. Rival firms each with their own model would organise lectures and exhibitions to publicise their wares, at which interest in the novelty would be enhanced by having a lady operator demonstrate its paces. There may also have been more potential operators available among women: suitable men would be more likely to have jobs already and not be free to learn at the new school.

A single typewriting enterprise would have many functions. It would sell typewriters to firms or individuals, providing an operator to the one and basic instruction to the other. To convince the cautious of the machine's usefulness it would also supply machine and operator on a temporary basis by the day, or week, or longer. In this way, with the typewriter as Trojan horse, many a city sanctum was invaded by females, and the normal system of controlling entrance to clerical posts by advertisements, interviews and references was completely bypassed. The typewriter firm would also provide a copying service, sometimes putting the work out to freelance typists working at home, sometimes having it done on the premises by girls installed near the window so that passers-by would stop and watch. In this way the idea of women typists became familiar.

The importance of learning shorthand as well as typewriting was continually stressed in advice to would-be clerical workers.

> **Typewriting and shorthand are twin arts, and young ladies who aspire to succeed in one of them must make themselves proficient in the other. A typist who cannot write shorthand is very much like a pianist who cannot read music.**[20]

Without shorthand, according to a writer in 1892, a girl typist in a business house would earn 15s to 20s a week (already a high salary compared with much women's work); with shorthand she could earn 30s and upwards.[21] Classes and schools sprang up to meet the demand for training. The list of London schools published in *Pitman's Year Book* grew longer each year: twelve in 1892, eighteen in 1894, twenty-six in 1898 and thirty-nine in 1899; and it was no doubt incomplete, listing actual institutions rather than the informal evening class at a clerk's suburban home. The larger establishments had elaborate syllabuses, large staffs of specialised teachers, day and evening classes, and 'separate tuition for ladies, gentlemen and youths'. The Kensington School of Shorthand offered 'high class instruction by means of private lessons or small select classes … to the sons and daughters of gentlemen and gentlewomen careful as to surroundings and associations'. Their fees were also select: the minimum for a course in typewriting was two guineas, payable in advance. At the South-Eastern School of Shorthand in Newington Causeway, on the other hand, thirteen weekly lessons cost 7s/6d, or a three-month proficiency course with unlimited practice, twenty-five shillings.[22] Some schools were highly profitable: the London College of Shorthand was reported in 1887 to have realised a net profit of over thirty per cent on the capital employed.[23]

By 1895 it was being asserted that 'the great influx of women into the commercial world' had considerably reduced the price of skilled stenographic labour, so that there was no inducement for the competent male stenographer to enter the field.[24] A general shortage of male operators was claimed in articles and advertisements in the clerical journals, with such comments as, 'it would almost seem as if young fellows were leaving the stenographic field to the ladies'.[25]

Although women asked 'that for the same work, performed under the same conditions, they should receive the same pay as their masculine colleagues',[26] there does not seem to have been any strong movement for equal pay, either by women or by men anxious to prevent undercutting. Lower pay was sometimes explained by assertions that women were in fact less useful in the office. The Principal of the Yost School of Shorthand, for instance, 'had not the slightest hesitation in saying that the sexes were equal in the acquisition of phonography', but 'as to the application of the art when acquired he thought somewhat differently'.

In some cases their attire was against them; in other cases they would not keep their status ... Many ladies did not treat business as seriously as they ought to do ... If the ladies would endeavour to make themselves more worthy of the honourable positions they were striving after, they would improve their positions.

The numbers of female clerks continued to grow. The 1891 Census recorded 17,859 female clerks in England and Wales; in 1901 the figure was 54,346, and this did not include Civil Service clerks (8,546 in 1891, 11,145 in 1901) or telegraphists and telephonists (4,356 in 1891; 9,057 in 1901), or bank, law and insurance clerks. Pitman's School was said to take 2,000 young ladies a year.[27]

As their numbers multiplied, stratification developed more clearly. There were women entrepreneurs, running secretarial schools, copying offices and employment agencies; there were self-employed freelance typists working at home with their own machines; there were the employees in copying offices; and there were the clerks employed by particular firms or in government or LCC offices. Among these last there were further divisions, which concerned qualifications and function and resulted in very different rates of pay. The list of vacancies on the National Phonographic Society's employment register categorised jobs as being paid £1 a week or less (in this group there were only women's posts), over £1 and under 30s, over 30s and under 40s, over 40s, and over 50s. The last two groups contained men's posts only.[28] Some few women did in fact reach this higher range of salary, but presumably not through advertisements or employment registries.

A demarcation commonly made by those who wrote on the subject distinguished secretaries – professional women of some education and standing, whose salaries were said to range between £100 and £300 a year; clerks – less qualified, but 'reliable and efficient', receiving £50 to £140 a year with typing, shorthand and perhaps a language; and typists – 'uneducated girls who fly to typing and shorthand in preference to domestic service or a place behind the counter',[29] who would get about 15s a week or sometimes even less. The typist's day was longer, her work more routine, her conditions and pay worse than that of her superior sisters. Nevertheless, 'the gentility of the typist's calling proves a strong attraction'.[30] As Gertrude Tuckwell pointed out in 1908, the girl clerk working for ten shillings a week in a crowded basement late into the night was a sweated worker, but never seen as such because 'the gentility of the occupation appears to lift it out of the category and to form its own reward'.[31]

Technological change, then, did play some part in opening up clerical employment for women. But technical skills were at the same time discounted in relation to social status. The average female telegraphist or telephonist had only limited opportunities to move up into better-paid work; while the typist who hoped to become a well-paid secretary had no hope without other skills (especially shorthand) and experience. And even then non-technical factors (background, accent, dress, general education) influenced the jobs open to her and the level of pay and status she could achieve. In the new sector of female clerical work, technological skill ranked lower than administrative, and class background was most likely to determine the individual's position in the hierarchy.

ENDNOTES

1 Report on the Reorganisation of the Telegraph System, LC. 1871 xxxvii (c.304).

2 Munby, A. J., MS Diaries, 10 April 1863: vol. 18, p155 and following. (My thanks to the Master and Fellows of Trinity College, Cambridge, for permission to consult and to quote from these diaries.) See also Hudson, D., 1972.

3 Munby Diaries, 10 June 1861: vol. 8, p274.

4 Report on the Reorganisation of the Telegraph System.

5 Johnston, R. W., July 1894, p367.

6 Swift H. G., pp135–7.

7 Scudamore's phrase, in the report already quoted. He did anticipate, however, that 'as a rule those who marry will retire, and those only will return whose life is less fortunate and prosperous than they had hoped'. And in 1875 a Select Committee were informed that a woman employed as a clerk would on marriage be discharged: LC. 1876, xiii (307), evidence of C. H. B. Patey (q.644). By 1912, resignation on marriage was required (GPO Staff Rule Book, Section 20).

8 Report on the Reorganisation of the Telegraph System.

9 'Saul', in the *Telegraphist*, 2 February 1885.

10 'Efel', in the *Telegraphist*, 2 February 1885.

11 Statement showing the number and wages of telegraphists, 1872 and 1892: LC. 1895, ixx (202).

12 Munby Diaries, 19 January 1860: vol. 4, pp34–5.

13 Munby Diaries, 24 May 1862: vol. 13, p177.

14 Munby Diaries, 10 June 1861: vol. 8, p216.

15 *City Press*, 10 September 1870, (quoting from *Edinburgh Review*).

16 Letter from the Treasury on recruitment to the Post Office Telegraph Schools, 26 September 1873: Public Record Office T.19, vol. 8, p2.

17 The examination was made harder in 1885 by the addition of a fourth subject, 'Elementary Geography of the United Kingdom', and the substitution of 'first four rules, simple and compound', for 'easy sums in the first four rules', in arithmetic. And in 1888 the age for starting was raised, from 18 years to 20.

18 *Fraser's Magazine*, 12, p335, September 1875; LC. 1875, xxiii (c.113), p18.

19 *Fraser's Magazine*, 12, September 1875, p340

20 *Phonetic Journal*, 4 April 1891, p209.

21 *Counting House*, September 1892, p228.

22 *Pitman's Shorthand and Year Book*, 1892.

23 *Phonetic Journal*, 1887.

24 *Phonographer and Typist*, August 1895, p131.

25 *Phonographer and Typist*, April 1895; see also Yost advertisements and *Quarterly Journal of the National Phonographic Society*, August 1895, p60.

26 *Phonetic Journal*, 1 July 1893, p401, editorial quoting recent article in *Manchester Guardian*.

27 *Typist's Review*, March 1902. See also LC. 1911, (Cd.5693) xxii, Special Report on … Typewriting Offices.

28 *Quarterly Journal of National Phonographic Society*, August 1896.

29 *Women's Employment*, 12 April 1900.

30 *Women's Industrial News*, June 1898.

31 Gertrude Tuckwell, in *Women in Industry from Seven Points of View*, Duckworth, London, 1908.

CHAPTER 5

THE INDUSTRY OF WAR

ORAL HISTORY: ATTITUDES TOWARDS WOMEN
Margaret Brooks

War fits easily into a conference on industry. In large-scale conflicts such as those we call the First and Second World Wars, the war itself is the industry of the whole country at that time. It is larger and more pervasive and has more impact on individual lives and on society than any conventional 'industry'. No one is unaffected, including civilians and pacifists. A smaller, more contained war – of which of course there are by far the greater number – may be the industry of only a part of society, though even this can be far-reaching.

What is it about war that makes this industry particularly significant to individuals? And how and where does the industry of war touch women?

I merely offer an introduction, using one of the many types of records available. Even using only oral evidence the potential for studying the realm of gender, peace and war in this country is very great. Unlike other media we collect for museums, teaching, or research, oral history necessarily includes the contributor. Oral history is no more nor less 'true' than drawings, letters, costumes or photographs – just a particularly powerful and direct method and product of collecting. It is especially helpful and relevant in studying under-represented or under-appreciated groups, including women.

Oral history provides interesting and evocative details of women's role in the industry of war, complementary to other documentary sources. Certainly there are detailed descriptions of working conditions and procedures but the glory of oral history is in its underlying question: how was it for you? The First World War munitions worker whose skin and hair turned yellow (and whose friend had her eyes blown out); the Timber Corps or Land Army worker wearing trousers for the first time; the mother catching a seagull to feed her hungry family; how was it for them? Oral history of war might investigate a great range of aspects of women's lives. Generally it records daily life and routine, work both in and out of the home and important adjuncts such as food, shelter, clothing, hygiene. Concepts – such as freedom, camaraderie, bereavement – arise from practical questions about experiences and events. You will note that most of this relates to men in the industry of war as well.

The extracts below are from the Sound Archive of the Imperial War Museum in London, recorded between 1973 and 1993. The museum holds over 22,000 hours of tapes recorded by many nationalities, but all of these here are British. They are a few examples of women's comments on their position during wartime or people's response to women in war as perceived by the women.

Women are associated with the cosy domestic scene in which there may be very hard work indeed but which is, somehow by definition in the public mind, not war work. Women have always worked on the land or in manufacturing, but image has little to do with reality, rather with a mental shape or space. How can such an image be altered? Not by being but by behaviour. In the First World War, Mary Lees was sent alone to work on a small farm which did not use (and did not want) female labour. She joined the Women's National Land Service Corps, subsequently the Women's Land Army, in Devon in 1917 and later worked in the Air Ministry in London. This was her first day on the Exmoor farm of a Mr Tapp:

> **And I rode right up on to the moor, came into the yard. And there was old Tapp standing there. Very upright. Coal-black hair. Bright pink cheeks. Riding crop under this arm and sort of breeches, you know, and gaiters. And in this hand he was holding a sack and a pair of shears. Well, I rode up, you see. He didn't take the slightest notice till I got off the horse, came round the horse. 'Put her over there in the shed,' he said. So I took her over, put her in the shed. I came back. Still he didn't speak. I thought, well, what's the matter with him? He handed me the sack and the shears. 'Now,' he said, 'go up the road, first gate on the left down over, under the hedge,' he said, 'you'll find an old ewe. Her's been dead three weeks. I want the wool.' So I thought, all right, try anything once, that's my motto. So I took them and went down. And of course, the old sheep, I didn't need the shears. The body was bright blue. So I plucked off all the wool and I sat her up in the hedge. I can see her now with her feet sticking out like that. And I went back and he was still standing there. I said, 'Oh, Mr Tapp, I didn't need the shears because the wool really came out quite easily. I think perhaps I'd better have a spade, hadn't I, and bury her.' And do you know, he looked at me. 'Gor,' he said, 'you done it?' He said, 'I were testing you. Will you shake hands?'**
>
> **IMPERIAL WAR MUSEUM SR 506/7/2**

One compelling factor behind middle- or upper-class women's enthusiasm for work on the land, in the armed services, in nursing, was the prospect of freedom. Scores of women have spoken explicitly of their wish for liberation from the domineering Victorian paterfamilias and the strict social codes.

Mary Lees was breaking new ground for herself, her gender and for old Farmer Tapp, but she still fits into an image, popular then as now, of the cheerful plucky girl battling through adversity. The next extract comes from a woman who felt that she really upset people. Their reaction to a woman soldier was so harsh that her life, though liberated by war, was also circumscribed in that she was denied access to conventional social niceties. Emily Maud Victoria Rumbold (fig.1) was a non-commissioned officer in the Women's Army Auxiliary Corps, working as a clerk and storekeeper in England and France from 1917 to 1919. She recalls here her first days in uniform:

FIG. 1
Emily Maud
Victoria Rumbold.
Imperial War Museum

We were passing this house to get to our billet, which we'd been advised to go to and as the lady came down the steps and we passed quite close to her we literally – skirts were long in those days – she literally gave us one look and drew her skirts aside like that. We should've contaminated her, I expect she thought. And well, they simply, as I say, almost drew aside their skirts, the women did. But didn't take the slightest notice of me otherwise until a gentleman gave me a magazine: he was the only one who said a word. I could tell the feeling was quite hostile. One particular canteen was really – because we had no YWCA of our own at the time and had to go to other canteens – the women there gave one look at us and said, 'We don't serve women here.' And they sent a complaint to our officers at the camp and said that they were not going to serve any English women at their canteens, so our officers were very furious about that. And of course we were rather furious because we had nowhere to get cups of tea or buy soap or anything. We were told that we were not to queue with the men at this little mobile hut where the drinks were served, tea or coffee, but we were to stand and wait at the side, which we did. And this man who was in charge said to the French girls 'Take no notice of the women; just serve the men.' And that was that.

IMPERIAL WAR MUSEUM SR 576/7/3

That was the First World War, behind the lines in France. The following extract comes from a recent woman soldier, also near the fighting front. No one would now shrink from her in the street or deny her a cup of tea in the canteen, but she felt circumscribed or denied by being ignored. In both these extracts the main adverse response to the speakers comes from other women. I doubt that this is really the case, but I suspect that the pain and significance of these responses are worse because they came from women.

Susannah Emma Grey (fig.2) was an officer in the Joint Forward Interrogation Team, First Armoured Division, handling prisoners of war in Saudi Arabia and later Iraq and Kuwait during the Gulf conflict in 1991. She is discussing the visit of a woman journalist:

FIG. 2
Susannah Grey in the Gulf. 1991
Imperial War Museum

She's a man's woman and she's obviously very ambitious, career-orientated. When we knew that they were going to be eating with us that first evening when they arrived – it was in this old hangar , in this quarry – being one of three women I thought well, she's going to be fascinated to talk to the women here, to get our point of view. I didn't want to be interviewed, but I just thought she'd have been interested on a personal and professional level. I remember seeing her and I smiled and said hello to her and she never ever the whole time, never chatted to me. I think once she did but it was only because she wanted something. Time and time again – I didn't come across women very much but they really let women down. I was quite angry about it.

IMPERIAL WAR MUSEUM SR 12280/11/4

The First World War women and their fellow-workers, whether they had positive or negative wartime experiences, gained a sense of competence, value or independence from their participation in the industry of war. But this is remarkable. This isn't what war is about: it's about territory and power and coercion and destruction. In attempting to overturn certain aspects of existing world order, war has had the effect of over-turning others, including many people's lives and attitudes. Then, after the First World War, many women felt thrown back like fish. The following three women recalled their own and the experiences of other women at the end of the war.

Ruby Adelina Ord was a chemist with Boots in civilian life and worked as a field indents clerk with the Women's Army Auxiliary Corps in England and France between 1917 and 1919:

Well immediately after, you see, one was occupied with trying to get a job, so I suppose that was the principal thing. It was very difficult if you'd been a WAAC because we weren't looked on with favour by the people at home. We'd done something that was outrageous for women to do, you see, we'd gone to France et cetera and left our homes. It was dreadful. I think there's always terrible discontent because people think they're fighting or working for something that's going to be an uplift and it's going to make everything better and it doesn't; it makes everything worse.   IMPERIAL WAR MUSEUM SR 44/5/5

Jane Cox was a civilian needlewoman who worked in London 'khaki' factories, making soldiers' caps and badges:

It learned women to stand on their own feet. It was the turning point for women. Men became a little bit humbler; they weren't the bosses any more. Because, years ago, once you were married you stopped at home. The men could go up the pub but a woman couldn't. But during the war the women learnt and they've been learning ever since.   IMPERIAL WAR MUSEUM SR 705/6/6

Caroline Rennles worked on munitions, including the arduous and dangerous shell filling at Woolwich Arsenal:

Of course there was no work when the war ended. Oh starving nearly, we were. Thank God I'd a good mother. I know they put us down to this factory, breaking up the bullets. And then as far as I can remember they threw us all out on the slag heap. Nothing. We walked to the Houses of Parliament, protesting against all being thrown out like we was. It's stupid, war: don't you think so? Where are we now? There's all these lovely boys been killed, haven't they, and women worse off than ever and all. So what's the good of war, love?

IMPERIAL WAR MUSEUM SR 566/7/4

The demonstration she spoke of, by thousands of women, was dispersed by mounted police. Our interviews on the industry of war include accounts of numerous other protests and demonstrations and of people's attitudes and reactions.

Ann Pettit was an organiser of the first anti-nuclear march from Cardiff to Greenham Common in 1981 and she lived in the peace camp on and off during the 1980s. Here she describes the difference it makes taking part in a specifically women's anti-war demonstration:

> Once it became a women's protest, clearly defined as a women's protest, then all these kind of more imaginative ways of making your protest were enabled. It was a kind of explosion of the imagination that took place. I remember the idea of women webbing themselves up. You know that wonderful photograph of a row of policemen standing there literally scratching their heads in puzzlement. You know, a sort of caricature puzzlement as he looks down at two or three women who are lying across ditches. The work of expanding the camp to take in all the extra personnel to service Cruise was still going on and this involved digging ditches across the peace camp to take the sewage pipes. So this involved all sorts of opportunities for disrupting their work and the women did it by lying in the ditches – or lying across them – and webbing themselves up. The web had become one of the symbols by then, with wool. All they'd done was just to tie wool around themselves and between themselves. So when a policeman picked up one person she was all tangled up with wool into the next one. All it needed was a pair of scissors, for God's sake, but they just didn't know how or where to begin approaching this new thing. And it took them ages to move them away and they lost a whole day's work. It was as simple as that.
>
> **IMPERIAL WAR MUSEUM SR 12745/7/4**

There can be no clear and simple measurement of the value of this industry of war: self-esteem and independence in exchange for suffering and bereavement, the loss not only of people but of towns or countries and a period of one's own life. But that is not the issue: wars have happened, what about the women? We need to collect the evidence. To conclude with one more woman's words.

Mamie Freda Colley had been an army schoolmistress at Changi School in Singapore since 1937 and was interned under painful and degrading circumstances (about one-third of the women and one-half of the men died) on Sumatra between 1942 and 1945. In this extract she describes the changes the war made and her lasting reactions:

> Well it seems strange but I think for the first time in my life I had become an independent person in my own right. I'd been the youngest in my family with all sisters. When I was young I was always told what to do, more or less. I wasn't very independent. And in the army one isn't exactly independent; you do what

the army tells you. And I married fairly soon after I started teaching. My husband was several years older than I was and I automatically took it for granted that he made the decisions and so on. I was quite content to go along like that. But then of course it became quite different. Interned, I had to be myself. And I did find that perhaps I was a bit of a different person from what I'd always thought I was. I found my independence. I found that in a tight spot I had enough there to depend on myself, something I think I'd have doubted if anyone had told me that I'd got to do this and face this. I should've said I could never do that, that I'd never survive. But you see, I found I did have the strength; I did have the will. I did have it somewhere there that I could be myself and survive. That was one very great thing. And I also came away with an extremely high regard for members of my own sex which I didn't have before. I used to rather shy away from women's company; I was much more at home in men's company. I really found women boring and vapid. But when I came out of the camp I had a very healthy respect and regard for women which I have retained for the rest of my life. I know that women are dependable. And women are strong, extremely strong in a crisis. I do admire women very much and I know how very reliable they can be and how very strong.

IMPERIAL WAR MUSEUM SR 6229/11/11

WOMEN'S WORK IN THE FIRST WORLD WAR

Anita Ballin

This paper examines the types of industry in which women began working during the First World War. Using photographic evidence, it briefly considers what difference this experience made to their own attitudes and behaviour and how men viewed these changes.

First, we need to consider the context into which women's work in the First World War fits. There was certainly nothing new about women working and nothing unusual about women working in industry. While one and a half million women were employed in domestic service at the outbreak of war, two million were employed in industry, mainly in the textile industry and the infamous sweated trades, many of which could be carried out in the home (mending sacks, making intricate flowers for the millinery trade etc). What then was new about the employment of women in the First World War? The answer must be both vastly increased numbers and a far wider range of jobs. Employment spread beyond just poor, working-class women to many well-to-do middle- and upper-middle-class women.

However, it was slow to happen. The familiar photographs of women as tram conductresses, munitions workers, Land Army girls or Wrens do not date from the early part of the war. It took a major shortage of weapons in 1915 and a severe labour shortage following the introduction of conscription in 1916 to convince the male heads of government and industry that women could play more than a minor working role. Thus the first year or so of the war is characterised by women's traditional war role: as voluntary helpers, 'ladies bountiful' or Florence Nightingales.

Upper- and upper-middle-class women packed up food parcels to send to soldiers: part of the great industry of 'comforts' for soldiers. Collecting money for the many charities that sprouted and flourished in the war was another favourite female occupation: for example money for 'poor little Belgium' or 'poor little Serbia'.

Nurses, either as properly, trained professionals, or as volunteers (VADs), often young women from well-to-do backgrounds, tended the wounded in areas of conflict.

It was largely through the discontent and frustration of the wealthier, better-educated women who wanted to do more than roll bandages or rattle collecting tins that many of the changes began to take place. It was, after all, Mrs Pankhurst who hatched the clever publicity stunt with Lloyd George to hold a huge demonstration on 17 July 1915, known as 'The Right to Serve' March, in which large numbers of women demanded a greater role in the war effort. Among the marchers were many Suffragettes, ready and willing to throw their considerable energies into the war effort. The march was prompted by the famous 'Shell Scandal' in May 1915: the news that British soldiers were prevented from fighting effectively by a dire shortage of high explosives. A highly explosive debate in parliament ensued and resulted in

FIG. I
TNT shop,
Woodwich Arsenal.
Imperial War
Museum.
(IWM Q27889)

the establishment of a new Ministry of Munitions with Lloyd George at its head. New munitions factories under direct state control were established and existing factories now came under much closer government supervision. A new degree of state interference in working conditions crept in, which brought with it better welfare provision but lacked the vital element of labour. The obvious solution to this was the employment of women and Lloyd George, himself a former target of the Suffragettes' campaign when his house in Surrey was attacked in 1913, now championed the movement to bring women into new spheres of war work. He was also astute enough to recognise that his old adversary Mrs Pankhurst was an excellent publicist and organiser of demonstrations. She was, therefore, given a substantial grant by the Ministry to organise this deputation of women, who would march through central London and present their demands to Lloyd George. 'If the country is to be saved,' said Mrs Pankhurst, 'women must be allowed to help.'

The march was an impressive affair with banners and even male brass bands to add excitement and drama. The result was the establishment of a National Register, listing all women between fifteen and sixty-five who could work. It was a turning point: women came forward in large numbers to offer themselves for munitions and other war work.

Opposition was considerable. The trade unions were extremely worried about 'dilution'. Allowing unskilled women into skilled male preserves such as munitions could endanger the status and perhaps even the wages of their male workers. Eventually the needs of the vast technological war machine prevailed and women were admitted, but only on condition that they relinquished their jobs when the war ended.

Improved welfare benefits and better working conditions such as washing facilities, rest rooms and canteens became the norm rather than the exception during the war. Skills were quickly acquired and many women enjoyed their new role. However, there were negative aspects. The women in figure 1 are working in the TNT Shop in Woolwich Arsenal (London) supervised by Lilian Barker. Working with TNT powder could have some very nasty effects. Not only did their skin get dyed yellow, but they frequently suffered various symptoms that became known as TNT poisoning.

The medical journal, the *Lancet*, reported in August 1916 a series of case studies of women who had been so affected. To quote from one:

Case 2. Patient aged 37 single. Time at work on TNT: four weeks. When examined before starting work on TNT she was quite fit physically. April 27th: First visit to the surgery. Complaint: sickness; diarrhoea; severe headache … keeps having turns of diarrhoea and sickness and vomited only stuff 'just like castor oil, only all green and very bitter'. Vomited four or five times a day. Face pale, flabby … tongue dirty yellow; lips slightly blue … hands slightly yellow …

She was taken off work. When she returned to work a month later she was not allowed back on TNT. By 24 June the report concludes she was 'quite well. Good colour; good appetite; good spirits.'

She was relatively fortunate and made a full recovery. One hundred and four women died from TNT poisoning.

Another major danger was from explosives. Figure 2 shows the large quantity of explosives about and faulty machinery or human carelessness could result in calamity. There was also the external danger from German air raids, munitions factories being a major target. Two hundred and thirty-seven women died in explosions.

Why, then, did so many thousands of women flock to work in munitions? There are many possible answers: patriotism; a sense of doing something worthwhile for the war effort, particularly, perhaps, if your boyfriend or husband was away fighting; and, of course, money. It was by far the best-paid job a woman could get and for the many who had been used to the appalling wages in service, five shillings (25p) per week, the prospect of earning £4 a week was indeed attractive (to translate those figures into today's equivalents, it is like comparing a weekly wage of £10 with one of £160).

FIG. 2
Working with explosives.
Imperial War Museum.
(IWM Q30011)

By 1918 ninety per cent of the workforce in munitions was female, and women were moving into other areas of industry.

The Imperial War Museum has a wonderful collection of photographs of women's work. Two photographers, Horace Nicholls and G. P. Lewis, made a special feature of photographing the home front and between them produced 4,600 photographs. Nicholls particularly enjoyed seeking out the unusual, although one criticism of his work might be that he tends to glamorise his subjects somewhat, so many of the images being happy, smiling women enjoying every minute of their job! Nevertheless, many of these photographs have become symbols of women's contribution to the war effort. For example the famous image of the coke heavers shown in figure 3, or tar-sprayers photographed on the roads of London (IWM Q 30875). Perhaps less romanticised are the photographs of G. P. Lewis. One, for example, of women packing flour at the Rank and Sons Mills in Birkenhead shows women far too busy even to notice let alone smile at the camera (IWM Q 28268). The image of a woman shovelling refined sugar (fig.4), about to be put into bags ready for sale, beautifully demonstrates the stringent hygiene regulations at the Greenock sugar refinery!

Outside the strict sphere of industry, women were also moving into many new areas which all contributed enormously to the whole war effort: transport, farming, the police and the armed services. In farming as in coke heaving or munitions, women were beginning to wear practical clothes suited to the job: breeches, trousers, boiler suits. In the case of the Women's Land Army, women in corduroy breeches are a far cry from Tess, in her

FIG. 3
Women coke heavers.
Horace Nicholls.
Imperial War Museum.
(IWM Q30859)

milking parlour in *Tess of the D'Urbervilles*. The impact of these changes is difficult to assess, but changes in dress as well as changes in jobs could not go unremarked and inevitably many men were horrified by women doing what they considered unfeminine jobs wearing unfeminine clothes. Men at home simply became accustomed to it, but what about the men away fighting? What was their reaction to the news that their sisters, wives or girlfriends were going to work in what had traditionally been a male preserve and might even don trousers?

In the Imperial War Museum's Department of Documents, among a huge collection of letters, diaries, memoirs and so forth, there is an interesting correspondence from an ambulance driver, George Wilby, to his fiancée, Ethel Baxter. It spans the period from his enlistment in 1915 to his return to England in 1919. He served both in France and in East Africa. Throughout he addresses Ethel as 'My dear little girl' and it is obvious from what he says that he expects to be consulted

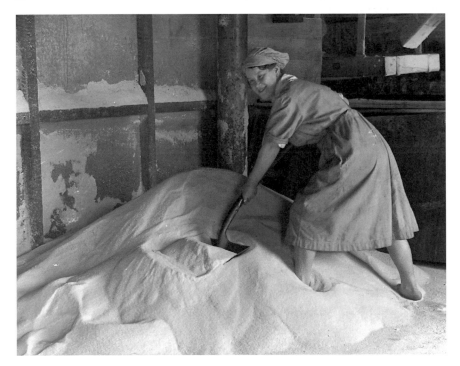

FIG. 4
Women shovelling
refined sugar.
G. P. Lewis.
Imperial War
Museum.
(IWM Q30859)

about every decision in her life down to the purchase of a chest for her clothes. His tone is obviously loving and affectionate, but also very condescending. As in many relationships of the time, one suspects there is quite a gap in age between them, but this may not be so. We can only imagine what she is writing to him, but his replies seem to me quite revealing about the sort of changes that may be happening to her. In August 1918 he had written:

> **... and whatever you do, don't go on Munitions or anything in that line, just fill a woman's position and remain a Woman (capital W) – don't develop into one of those 'things' that are doing men's work, as I told you in one of my letters, long ago, I wanted to return and find the same loveable little woman that I left behind – not a coarse thing more of a man than a woman – I love you because of your womanly little ways and nature, so don't spoil yourself by carrying on with a man's work – it's not necessary, my sweetheart.**

His next letter, dated 3 October, reads:

> **My dear Little Girl,**
>
> **I have just received your letter, dated June 18th in which you tell me that you are now working in a munitions factory – Well, I'm not at all pleased about it – in fact I am very cross with you, Darling, you shouldn't have done such a thing, especially after I almost begged of you not to – the work is much too rough and hard for a girl like you ... Fancy my little girl helping to make shells to blot out human lives – you know, Darling, you weren't made for such a thing – you were really made to bring lives into the world ... Bye-the-bye I hope you don't wear trousers on your job, sweetheart – I think it's so disgusting – and I hope you will never put such things on, anyway if you do, don't ever let me see you in them, take them off before you come into my sight – otherwise I shall pull them off for you, and I shan't be at all gentle about it neither, and whatever you do, don't lose your womanly little ways or nature. I love you because you are such a perfect little woman ... and I want to come back and find the same ideal little woman that I left behind.**

The tone of his letters suggests a male–female relationship fairly typical of the time: he is accustomed to giving his permission before she carries out any new action. We can only assume that she has gone along with this up to now. But by 1918 she is making her own decisions and doing work that she knows he considers unfeminine and probably even wearing trousers! George returned from the war alive and the correspondence continues till late 1919 when he is in a military hospital in Devonport. The signs are that they are to be married soon. But did they live 'happily ever after', as George had so often promised in his letters? Well, it seems they did as George's widow donated the correspondence to the museum after a long married life. Perhaps they both did a bit of adjusting after the war.

What about women's attitudes to the changes brought by the war? Undoubtedly women's achievement was two-edged: on the one hand they had learned new skills, gained new confidence and, through greater financial rewards at work, had a new economic independence. Their clothes and social habits (smoking and drinking in public!) demonstrated a greater sense of freedom, but at the end of it all there was unemployment and a sense of being thrown on the scrap-heap. The deals done with the unions gave them no choice. But having tasted freedom and relatively high wages, it was hard to contemplate a return to the old restrictions of domestic service and many vowed never to go back, however hard things became. I think the words of Jane Cox[1] who participated in the Imperial War Museum's oral history programme, sum up the situation quite well: 'The war,' she said, 'learned women to stand on their own feet. It was the turning point for women. Men became a little bit humbler. They weren't the bosses any more.'

ENDNOTES

1   Brooks, M., this volume.

SCOTLAND'S FORGOTTEN LUMBERJILLS

Dorothy Kidd

At the beginning of 1991 planning began for the new Museum of Scotland. Scheduled to open in 1998, this aims to tell Scotland's story from the earliest times to the present day.

I was asked to work on Scotland 'At War' in the twentieth century, with particular emphasis on the role of women in wartime. When the *Courier* featured an article on the Women's Timber Corps (WTC)'s forthcoming second reunion I contacted one of the organisers, Bonny Macadam, and was very kindly invited along. Thanks to this initial approach we have been able to collect a great deal of material relating to the WTC. The museum has been given a complete WTC uniform, along with a number of items of equipment and original documents, and dozens of photographs and archival papers have been copied. I have also so far interviewed four former members of the corps and several more have sent in their own written reminiscences.

For the 1992 season at the Scottish Agricultural Museum at Ingliston near Edinburgh, we mounted a small exhibition on the WTC, both to mark the fiftieth anniversary of the corps' formation in 1942 and as a way of thanking all those members who had made it possible to record a piece of history which was well on the way to being forgotten.

Since then, new information has continued to come in. A second, smaller, exhibition was put on in the Museum of Antiquities in Edinburgh and further media interest was aroused with BBC Radio Scotland interviewing a former member, and Vanessa Collingridge, a freelance journalist, conducting further interviews and giving a talk in Glasgow's Royal Concert Hall in the autumn of 1994. More photographs have been sent in for us to copy, other contacts have also been established, and further recordings will be made in the future.

The following accounts of life in the Scottish WTC are taken from the interviews I conducted and from the written reminiscences which were sent in. They reflect the experiences of women with very different characters and backgrounds, but who all remember their wartime work as a remarkable and precious time in their lives.

THE WOMEN'S TIMBER CORPS

During the Second World War, as in the First World War, women were needed to take over the jobs of the men who had gone into the armed forces. Agriculture and forestry in particular had to be kept going to feed the nation and provide essential timber for industry.

In April 1942 the WTC was formed as a distinct branch of the Women's Land Army, specialising in timber production. This is how the corps was remembered in the foreword to a book published shortly after the war:[1]

> It is difficult today to recapture the atmosphere of the first months of 1942 when the idea of the Women's Timber Corps was born. Singapore had fallen; Egypt was threatened; the Armies of Russia had been forced far back from her frontiers; the Battle of the Atlantic was at its height; more and more men were being drafted from industry into the Armed forces.
>
> Timber is one of the most vital munitions of war, but the manpower available was not sufficient to supply our minimum needs. In this emergency an appeal was made to women to help with home timber production.
>
> Many people would not believe that women could, or would, take the place of men. Experience during the past three years has triumphantly proved how wrong they were.
>
> All honour to the girls who, as volunteers, faced exile from home, the cold and mud of winter, long hours and heavy work, to do a job of first importance for their country.
>
> Here is a memento of their success which all should read.
>
> GERALD LENANTON,
> (Director, Home Timber Production Department,
> Ministry of Supply).

As the United Kingdom's principle timber-producing area, Scotland provided almost half the 3,000 or so women employed nationally. Women from all walks of life, from the age of seventeen upwards, volunteered to join the WTC, and by the end of 1942 over a thousand Scottish women had done so. After joining they were sent to training centres where they received a month's training in the basics of forestry: felling, snedding,[2] sawing, barking, burning brushwood, measuring, hauling timber, working with horses and driving heavy vehicles. The camp at Shandford Lodge near Brechin in Angus trained about one hundred women a month, with some of them being judged competent enough to become trainers themselves.

Those women who stood the course were then sent out to camps, private estates and sawmills throughout Scotland to provide pit props, telegraph poles and railway sleepers for the war effort. A particular feature of life in the Scottish WTC was the purpose-built camps. The isolated nature of many of the forests meant that relatively few women lived in private billets.

JOINING-UP

One afternoon in June 1942, I was walking along Shandwick Place in Edinburgh when I saw in a window photographs of girls working in woods and I thought: 'That's for me.' So that is how on 1 July 1942 I was on my way to Meikleour Forestry Camp.   MARIE C. F. DICK (LATER MRS HENDERSON).

When the war broke out I was in a reserved occupation, working in the office of the North British Rubber Co. When Singapore fell there was no rubber, so our work came to an end. The office staff were all called up. I wanted to go into the WRNS but all I was offered were munitions or the Land Army so I told them I did not fancy either. Munitions were noisy and I did not like working with animals and cows, etc. They told me they were starting a new section of the Land Army to be called the Women's Timber Corps. Oh, says I, that will be better, trees are all right, so before long I was on my way to the glen, Innerleithen where I became WTC Member No 33 and started on a life that I came to enjoy.   BETTY CROLL.

I joined the corps in 1942 because things were beginning to get very black-looking and obviously the country was getting into a bit of a state and I was in an office and thought that I was needing to do something. My brother was in the Air Force and I felt my mother had enough on her plate without me being out of the country, so I first thought of the Land Army, but she wasn't happy about that and then eventually after another six months I went to my boss, Miss Gory, and said to her I felt I was needing to do something and thought then of the horticultural side of it ..., and Miss Gory she said: 'Well I'll go', so off she went and she came back and said: 'Well there are no vacancies in the horticultural side but they're starting the Timber Corps.' So I went along and presumably filled the forms up and came back, and then unfortunately three weeks later my brother was killed in the Air Force.

I was given six weeks' compassionate leave and at the end of that time I was due to go up.   ALISON MCLURE,
          (who had been working in a national insurance office in Edinburgh).

I was working in the printing department of Glasgow Corporation to pay for my [singing] lessons. So that was working very nicely until they sent around the form to say: 'Which service will you join?'

Now I had been for years attending meetings of the Peace Pledge Union, long before the war started. So I was an idealistic little pacifist and wrote to say that I was not joining any service. I don't think they believed me, of course. When you're only that age they think you're a nutter. Anyway then I got to thinking: 'They'll send me to something I hate!' And I thought to myself: 'What'll I do?' and so I decided to enquire around. I thought I was joining forestry. Although my family thought I was utterly mad. But I went down and saw these people, only to discover this was the Home Grown Timber Production Department.

I was pushing a pen on a Wednesday night. I was taken on a bus and dropped at the bottom of the Buchaille on Rannoch Moor on a January day in 1943. A foot of snow on the ground and I was just dumped there. And on the Friday I was shovelling ground on a river bed with a big navvy shovel.

MARGARET GRANT.

TRAINING AND WORK

I don't know if you know what happens to anybody who does this kind of thing. At least I don't know what happened to the other women, but as far as I was concerned I shut off completely. You're sore, you're tired, you're hungry. You're hungry, you're sore, you're tired. And so you don't think, couldn't think. You were only just kind of feeling everything. At least that's what happened to me. Now that was January. And one April morning, this was Glen Etive. It was so beautiful. Snow on the mountain tops, a turquoise blue skye with wee pink fluffy clouds. And I suddenly realised that I was a big healthy lump. About ten stone of muscle, and that life was wonderful. Life was really beautiful.

MARGARET GRANT.

After my month's training we were all sent to different forestry camps. I went to Dunphail, near Forres ... The camp there was for twenty girls. The work there was varied. I worked loading wood on to the tractor 'bogies'[3] then we drove to the station where we unloaded it and filled it on to the railway waggons. I sometimes was felling the trees and 'snedding' them: chopping off the branches with an axe, then the brushwood had to be burned.

NAN SMITH (LATER MRS BROWN),
(who had been a shop assistant in Edinburgh).

The training consisted of being taught how to lay-in[4] (fig.1), fell, cross-cut and burn the brushwood. After that the draggers, some with horses and some with tractors, hauled the logs to the place where they were loaded on to lorries and driven to the station. All this work was carried out by girls. The biggest logs for pit props were fourteen feet by eight inches and the smaller three feet by four inches. The trees which were too big to be made into props went to the sawmill where the girls worked too. Sometimes there were trees selected for telegraph poles and these were always selected and marked by the District Officer ... My

FIG. I
Laying-in.
Bonny
Macadam
Collection,
National
Museums of
Scotland.
60/15/12

next move was to Roughmount, another new camp about one and a half miles from Shandford and near the sawmill at Hilton. I was asked to go as forewoman and Morag Mackenzie was my 'ganger'. We were responsible for the work in the wood and for camp life. There were forty-one girls altogether. An office girl, cook, kitchen help and hut duties …

Before we went on piece work Morag and I had the experience of felling a big tree on the Glamis estate. Morag and I wanted to fell this big tree by ourselves but Bill Martin, foreman, made us have the help of two German POWs who were working in forestry, because we had to use a seven-foot cross-cut saw.

The stump or butt measured one metre across – quite the biggest tree we were ever likely to fell. Our piece work rates were nine pence or ten pence a tree. We employed an Italian POW. I say 'employed' as ten shillings was deducted from our pay. Sometimes we took down between sixty and seventy trees per day so it was worth our while paying Tony, as he was an excellent worker.

JEAN MACNAUGHTON,
(who had been a hairdresser in Glasgow).

The trees were cut very, very near ground level, not as you often see them today, about two feet above the ground. At the end of the month, we had a test and this was my result! A neatly enough 'V' cut as we were taught, but my trainer's remark: 'You'd think a mouse had been at it' fell on my ears, and very apt, as I viewed with her the tiny chips lying at the base. Of course the reason for that was, my having little strength as I had only been in an office up until then. I had no muscles built up – what difference at the end of the two years, when my muscles became like two bricks!

ALISON MCLURE,
(on training at Shandford in Angus and then at work on the Minto Esate in Peebleshire).

One day, watching a (male) driver trying to reverse an articulated lorry up to the sawmill, in fact, waiting to drop a load of bottoming from my tipper lorry, I was heard by Mr Allison to say I could do the thing better! In a way I was sorry I had done so, as from that minute on I was the pole-wagon driver: I then had to teach some other girls to drive the small vehicles, and also drive timber to several stations. Sometimes loads of pit props and sometimes big timber, needed for poles for desert warfare. From the sawmill I took loads of sawn wood, from small to very large planks. Once one got the knack of lifting, we were able to lift weights along with any man, as by that time our muscles were really something.

BONNY MACADAM,
(she had trained as a motor mechanic and obtained her PSV licence before the war).

I loved rafting. Standing up to the water in waders with a big hammer through your belt and a chain from the raft over your shoulder. You had things called dogs – a ring with a spike on it – and as the men came down with the horses, the men would drag the swingle tree into the water and then they would unloosen the load and push the logs towards you. And you would catch them, stop them, and then take another dog on to the chain and go bang, bang, bang, and then thread it on to the raft. Each log is attached by a bit of chain running through the rings of these dogs …

MARGARET GRANT

CAMP LIFE

The accommodation was in wooden huts, which were very comfortable so long as the wood-burning stove was functioning, but extremely cold as soon as the fire died out. It was round this stove that we dried our wet clothes.

It was quite a severe winter and the journey on the back of an open bogie was not something to look forward to on a dark winter's morning. I remember there was a loud bang and great fizzing noise beside my bed at 5.30 a.m. This was a bottle of lemonade which I had put there so as not to forget it in the morning. By 7 a.m. the whole thing was frozen solid.

The ablution hut too was a cold place – there were windows in it but these were up under the eaves and not glazed.   JEAN MACNAUGHTON's
(memories of camp life at Meikleour
in Perthshire).

The huts were very basic, very bare, just with rows of beds, you know, something about that size [pointing to her single bed], no, they were not as broad as that, otherwise I wouldn't sleep in another single bed as long as I live. You know, you were so you just used to lie in one position all the time. Mine was up beside the stove, we had one of these wood-burning stoves …

You went to bed with more clothes on sometimes than you did when you got up, it was so cold, but we managed. We didn't have any colds or anything, there was never anything wrong with me.

There were ablution sheds a wee bit further down [separate from the huts]. There were four or five basins in them. They had cold water, well you had to boil your water. In winter I used to use the water out of my hot water bottle for washing, a little cold but the coldness was off it, but as often as not the taps would be off as the tank would be full of dead leaves as it didn't get cleaned out often.

NAN MACLEAN,
(camp supervisor in Strathire, Perthshire).

We did have to rough it a bit at those early camps. There were no Tilley lamps, only paraffin (wick) ones which very often didn't work; so then it was candles, but we all thought it fun. No flush toilets at that time either, although at later camps there were. At Meikleour it was the 'pit', no doors just a piece of sacking; if you heard someone coming along the duckboards you shouted, one, two, or three.[5] At night we often had to chop wood for the boiler fire and *maybe* there would be hot water in two or three hours …   MARIE DICK,
(on Meikleour Camp).

THE UNIFORM

We were not given any uniform to begin with, having been told to take suitable working clothes and boots in our call-up papers. When in June 1942 the WTC was formed we were issued with a uniform similar to the WLA but with gabardine instead of corduroy breeches and a nice green beret instead of the 'pork pie' hat, khaki shirt and plain green tie, brown shoes and khaki stockings and a very warm top coat.[6] For work we were issued with dungarees, shirt, boots and oilskins (the last for working in the rain). The wages at that time were 37s a week. Deducted from that was 10s for hut rent and food and sixpence for uniform. I can't remember whether we had to give up clothing coupons or not.

JEAN MACNAUGHTON,
(on her first few months in the WTC).

FOOD

We had made up 'pieces'[7] at breakfast time, and we had a choice of pilchards in tomato sauce, or cheese, or jam and I sent [home] for a drum of malt which I never let anybody know was mine. We used malt extract on our 'pieces' for sweetness, and we stopped from twelve to half past twelve, half an hour for dinner, and the tea was boiled in billy-cans on site [the normal working day was from 8 a.m. to 5 p.m. with half an hour for lunch] (fig.2). Somebody made a fire and stuck two or three branches in and hung the billy-can on them. I loved it because I liked smoked tea but some of the girls, poor souls, you can imagine, coming from an office in Edinburgh for her first day in the woods, hands bleeding and heels, very down in the dumps, and she's handed a mug of tea and says, 'Oh that's lovely', until she tastes it!

And then we worked on till five and we got our meal at six when we went home. We had really and truly not bad food, it was very plain, in the camp we had a very very capable housekeeper ... we went home to sausage and mash, we had soup, meat and pudding and tea, or if we had our own (black-market) coffee.

BONNY MACADAM
(on life at Shandford Lodge training camp).

We made up our 'pieces' at breakfast to keep us going all day, and made tea in the dixie on a wood fire. I remember once we tried syrup tins to make it in. Sometimes we got a pie and we would put them on a shovel and on the fire to heat, often they tasted of smoke and paraffin, but we were always hungry.

MARIE C. F. DICK,
(who worked at Ethie, Glendoick, Meikleour and Roughmount; camps in Angus and Perthshire).

FIG. 2
Lunchtime in the woods. Bonny Macadam Collection, National Museums of Scotland. 60/15/17

Regular visits had to be made to the Food Office in Forfar to work out rations. I remember there was an excellent ration of cheese and although I had cheese sandwiches for lunch almost every day for four years I still like it. On Saturday afternoon in Brechin the butcher was visited and rations discussed with him.

JEAN MACNAUGHTON,
(on running the camp at Roughmount, Angus).

ENTERTAINMENT

Sunday night arrived and we were asked to congregate in the beautiful ballroom in the Lodge. Anyhow there we were, the Commandant searching for someone to play the piano and begin a sing-song. Silence reigned! Not a movement until I thought someone would get upset if no one volunteered to play or do something! I slowly got to my feet and walked to the piano in the corner, with my heart thudding, I could hear my heels hammering the floor involuntarily, despite the noise of the girls joining in the popular songs of the day. We had quite a night.

ALISON MCLURE,
(on her first few days at Shandford Lodge training camp).

Another of my jobs was to convey the girls to Brechin for a dance, or to Kirriemuir, as the buses were only suitable on a Saturday afternoon when we were free. Taking them there was easy, but when it came 'round-up time', trying to collect the correct number that I had taken there, *Well*!

BONNY MACADAM,
(trainer).

We went out for walks in the evening or if there was a local dance we went there. On a Saturday we used to go into Forres or sometimes to Elgin.

NAN SMITH,
(on life in Dunphail camp, near Forres, Morayshire).

We held dances in camp and invited the men from the Royal Signals at Montreachmont. Among them there was a pianist who had played with Henry Hall's Band and we had a piano and a gramophone (Morag and I bought it in Dundee for £3) so were all right for music.   JEAN MACNAUGHTON.

RISKS AND INJURIES

I saw a girl getting her fingers off. I was tailing on the big saw in the mill and throwing down short ends to her which she was pushing through a Liner or Petter – a cross-cut saw. Blethering the while. Suddenly she said: 'Look what I've done' and held up her fingers, which were spouting blood. So Johnny [Maxwell] decided that we all ought to do something only for a couple of weeks ...

Everybody had to do things like burn hag. When a tree is felled, it lies down and you've got to brush it, that's get all the branches off before it's cut and stacked. And you take them off with the axe. Now that often lies over the winter until the spring. Why, I don't know, but it's piled up in heaps and then it has to be burned; and you get showered with ticks. We used to have tick picking-off sessions on each other ...

I nearly drowned because the fellow who had just unloosed his load and floated it towards me, and his horse had started off to go up the track again, but he didn't notice that the hook on the swingle tree had caught on to the chain which was just under the water which was over my shoulder, and as the horse walked away this tightened and the whole load came towards me. When you're under water and there's timber above your head, you suddenly loose your sense of place, which way is up, or which way is out. However, luckily, the next man coming down hauled me out.   MARGARET GRANT.

I had a tree fall on my arm which I think is the cause of this [severe arthritis, especially in the shoulder] to this day. It came down and knocked me down and I fell across my knees. I went into Stirling Royal Infirmary and I was in there having it X-rayed when they brought in another fellow. He was the fellow who took my job over, but he was crushed and he was off for a while. I didn't break the shoulder but it has been so sore. Well I blame that anyway. Ever since, you know I've not any power in that hand you see. I wasnae off, I was straight back [to work] aye, it was sore but.   NAN MACLEAN.

The only time I was really upset was when I had to sned a large tree with huge overhanging branches. The foreman cut one or two, then I had to step in and do the rest. The bark which was smooth, was soaking, as it had poured heavily all night, and the axe skidded, struck a knot, swung round and hit my nose as I could not get my head up because of the other branches above it. I had of course to get to Hassendean Station, where a doctor was phoned for, but as he and the district nurse were out on call, it was an hour and a half before the nurse was able to be contacted. She cleaned the wound, and then Dr Pollock stitched it for me. I am so grateful to him as there is not a mark now, though the cut was jagged and I had two stitches put in.   ALISON MCLURE.

PARADES

We had two parades in 1943. The first one was in Edinburgh for the Timber Corps only. Afterwards we had tea at the City Chambers. The other one was for all the Services in Perth on June 5th. We had a Sergeant Major from the Black Watch up at the camp to drill us for the Perth parade. The poor man must have felt like giving up. One of the girls just could not get the hang of it, was out of step each time, but on the day of the parade we were complemented by an Army officer for our marching and smartness. Another gentleman paid for our tea at the Co-op which was greatly appreciated.   MARIE DICK.

AND AFTERWARDS

September 1944 they closed Glendoick camp. We were sent to different camps. About eight of us were sent to Meikleour, so I was back where I started. We were all sorry to leave Glendoick. Four of us met our future husbands while working. I was one of them …

   I have so many happy memories of my years as a lumberjill and friends from those days keep in touch and I met up with others at the reunions when the conversation was: 'Do you remember?' If we say we were lumberjills during the war, we are all too often met with a blank look but it would be nice to think we will not be forgotten.   MARIE DICK.

I missed the life, I missed it very much. I don't know, that sense of freedom. I must say the job I was in [after the war] it never felt as if I was bound in any way. You always felt that your time was your own and you made it and that was that. You missed the sort of camaraderie of the girls and that sort of thing.

   I wanted to do something for the war effort and the only thing I felt about my job was it shouldn't happen during the wartime. I would have enjoyed it so much more if there hadn't been a war on; but you felt that these lads were away fighting and here you were thoroughly enjoying yourself and still what was the use, you couldn't bring back the lads or anything like that, so you just had to make the best of it. NAN MACLEAN.

There were many glorious days when the scenery was absolutely beautiful. Glistening spiders' webs in the frost, trees stark, stiff and coated with frost rime, their branches a sheer picture to look at, with the wintry sun having the scene shimmering with light. Blue skies would suddenly darken and blacken towards the east. I would look up, thinking there would be a heavy downpour soon, if not thunder, but the Cheviots must have endured the storm since ten minutes or so later, there would not be a cloud to be seen ...

I came home to Edinburgh and I was off for quite a long time; and then went in to office work, and that was a nightmare. Every time it was a good day I wanted outside. ALISON MCLURE.

It's not just nostalgia that prompts me to write, for I loved every minute of my WTC life, while it was still happening, and the effects of this wonderful experience is with me still, and very strong ... After training, I was posted to Wallacetown camp, near Moniave, Dumfriesshire. This area is still my favourite place in the world, and I've gone back, at least once yearly, to enjoy, and yes, wallow in memory, and the lovely peace and beauty, which is utterly refreshing. War was ending and our camp closed. I was completely heartbroken, with literally physical pain, which I can, if I allow myself to, vividly recall. It was awful, leaving my heart behind. I went to Rothiemurchus, but in no way could I adjust to a new camp ... After my demob Mrs Simpson, the Chief Welfare Officer of the WTC, helped me to obtain a job, with Research Forestry, Assessment Party, based in Edinburgh; but travelling throughout Scotland. The four of us, who made up the party, were all ex-Timber Corps.

JESSIE MACLEAN

CONCLUSION

Most of the women who joined the WTC came from relatively sedentary backgrounds in towns and cities. When the corps started to be disbanded from the end of 1945 onwards, the majority were glad to return to their peacetime occupations, and perhaps the marriage and children which the war had forced them to postpone. Like the previous generation of women drafted into traditionally male occupations by the First World War, however, their wartime experiences gave them a feeling of independence and confidence in their own abilities which they might not otherwise have known.

ACKNOWLEDGEMENTS
I should like to thank the following for all their help in providing artefacts, documents and information: Betty Croll, Marie Dick, Margaret Grant, Affleck Gray, Bonny Macadam, Jessie MacLean, Nan MacLean, Alison McLure, Jean Macnaughton, Nan Smith.

ENDNOTES

1 Ministry of Supply/Women's Land Army Benevolent Fund (c.1945).

2 Snedding is the cutting of branches from the trunk of a felled tree.

3 A bogie is a low, heavy truck.

4 'Lay-in': putting a wedge shape into one side of the tree with the axe, before sawing from the other with the cut saw to ensure the tree falls away from those sawing it.

5 The number of minutes before they would be finished.

6 Nan MacLean referred to it as a 'bum-freezer'. They were short coats which came to just above the knees.

7 Lunchtime snack or sandwiches.

PRESENTING THE EVIDENCE: WOMEN'S HISTORY IN MILITARY MUSEUM DISPLAYS

Jane Hainsworth

The interpretation of women's history has only recently become a fashionable subject for inclusion in military history displays. The recognition by military curators of the need to reflect the role that women have played in their displays has been influenced by research into the 'hidden history of women' undertaken in academic institutions since the late 1960s. This has led to an attempt to redress the previous imbalance prevalent in military displays which portrayed military history as a man's subject with very limited appeal for the female visitor.

In practice the influence of this academic movement has signalled a departure away from the traditional approach of displaying medals, uniforms and armour collections in rows without any interpretation, towards an attempt to create more integrated social-history displays. This has meant widening the interpretation of the artefacts on display to include an analysis of the people who may have used and been affected by those artefacts and has allowed an opportunity to focus on how women have been involved in military development.

The challenge for curators in military museums when interpreting the history of female involvement in war is how to present a balanced yet inclusive view of the ways in which women have contributed to warfare, without providing a limited or negative stereotype of their work or ignoring large parts of their history.

In re-examining the contribution that women have made and in attempting to broaden the appeal of the galleries towards a female audience, curators have been forced to look again at the artefacts in their collection and ask more rigorous and imaginative questions of those objects. A piece of military equipment such as a shell, which at first sight may seem alien to female experience, may as a result of research prove to have been made or used by women. This enables a more integrated approach to the subject of military history and a broader appeal for both male and female visitors. Military Museums in the past have been in danger of thinking that it is necessary to display 'women's things' to appeal to female visitors. Certainly displaying embroidery or cooking implements can be interesting for women but it would be patronising and inaccurate to assume that this is all women want to see or are capable of empathising with. If these objects are all that is displayed to represent women's contribution, it distorts the reality of their experience and does not aid either sex in appreciating the more varied contribution women have made to the armed services or in wartime.

In the past selection of artefacts for display has therefore influenced the portrayal of the type of roles women have played. In many campaigns women did play passive roles, but this has not been the full extent of their involvement. Some military displays, in an attempt to include women, have been guilty of displaying the female contribution as solely that of cook, seamstress or camp follower with all the gender stereotypes which these roles imply.

By comparison, another traditional display technique employed in military museums was to highlight examples of 'exceptional' women who performed extraordinary roles beyond the experience of most women active in war. This can be used as an interesting way to present the contribution of individual women, but as the only inclusion of the women's story in a gallery it can appear as if the particular display is an additional rather than integral part of the gallery.

Curators must also remember to consider issues of ethnicity and class when approaching women's history. It is not possible to deal with a single female experience which can encompass the range of experiences of women of differing ethnic origin and social class across the centuries who have been involved in the development of British and Commonwealth armies and world war.

In interpreting and displaying the contribution women have made to military history in their displays, both the National Army Museum and the Imperial War Museum provide differing and yet equally valid opportunities for interpretation and interactive display. Both have overcome the temptation to portray women as solely camp followers or exceptional examples and have attempted an integrated approach in their displays.

The two museums have different mission statements. The National Army Museum tells the social history of the British Army in war and peace from 1485 to the present day. By comparison the Imperial War Museum presents the global history of conflict in the twentieth century. In providing opportunities for the interpretation of women's history, the National

FIG. 1
Mrs Skiddy with her husband, Waterloo Gallery (National Army Museum)

Army Museum's displays concentrate specifically on the contribution women have made to the armed services. The displays at the Imperial War Museum allow a more detailed examination of the female contribution to the domestic front during wartime.

The role of wife and mother during wartime is a central and necessary theme for inclusion in any display focusing on the contribution of women. While it is important to consider other roles undertaken in wartime, to ignore this central theme of women's history would be a distortion of reality.

To interpret and display this important role during the Waterloo campaign, the National Army Museum commissioned the artist, Gerry Embleton, to make wax figures of Mrs Skiddy (fig.1), a camp follower, carrying her husband on her back away from the battlefield of Corunna in 1812. Given that little clothing worn by the ranks for this campaign remains, the models provided an interesting opportunity to present this type of uniform in replica. Visitor surveys showed that the models were appreciated by both male and female visitors as a lively and informative way of presenting the role of a wife and camp follower and for providing a fresh approach to visual interpretation. However, Mrs Skiddy represents one particular class of women. The gallery lacks any treatment of the different campaign experienced by officers' wives, who lived, entertained and even participated in the war from houses in Portuguese cities and this detail would add more depth to the overall presentation of women in the gallery.

In the adjoining Victorian gallery wax figures of an Indian sepoy and his wife illustrate the development of the Commonwealth forces and the role of a colonial wife during this period. This is one of the few displays in the National Army Museum depicting the contribution of colonial women to the development of the Army. Equally, the Imperial War Museum also lacks specific displays relating to the involvement of ethnic women in war and Commonwealth military services. The Imperial War Museum has recently produced an educational pack which includes sound recordings, facsimile documents and video tapes detailing the contribution made by ethnic groups in World War Two which provides some background to this important part of female and military history. However much more research and interpretation into the contribution women from different ethnic cultures have made to war must be undertaken to correct the current bias in galleries towards the European female contribution.

The Imperial War Museum has focused on wives and mothers during World War Two by devoting a case to the display of ration books and women's clothes and clothing coupons to show how women were forced to economise on the Home Front. A more sinister and moving presentation is also interpreted in the World War Two Gallery. Using enlarged and close-up photographs the museum has portrayed the experience of female prisoners of war and refugees separated from and grieving for husbands and children.

An interesting contrast to these horrific photographs are the close-up head-and-shoulders photographs of the warders and wardresses of Belsen. The pictures presented are a fascinating yet shocking challenge to traditional gender stereotypes of women as war victims or patriotic symbols/matriarchs at home maintaining the home fires. It would be a valuable addition to the gallery to provide captions beside the photographs of these women describing them and their role at the camp to widen and challenge visitor perceptions. The role of women in wartime can be as ugly and violent as that of their male contemporaries.

One of the key themes which demonstrates how women have contributed to wartime is to focus on their contribution to economic production on the home front. Their employment in cottage industries and later factories created the resources which allowed campaigns to be planned and fought. Highlighting this work raises the positive profile of how women have increased production and puts military history in a social context which enables a greater examination of how artefacts relate to the people who made and were affected by their production and use. The use of audio-visual displays at the Imperial War Museum to show rows of female munitions workers at the production lines brings this story vividly to life and provides a valuable alternative medium to using a display case.

Both museums cover the history of the women's services in their displays. The acquisition of the Women's Royal Army Corps Museum collection in 1994 provided an ideal opportunity for the National Army Museum to interpret the development of the female services in their exhibition, 'The Right to Serve'. The exhibition examines the early forms of female support in the Civil Wars and Napoleonic Wars through to the development of the women's services up to the present day. This section includes a critique of the modern-day services, raising the question of whether women should be allowed to expand their status from non-combatant soldier to front-line fighter. The exhibition provides a wide scope for illustrating the variety of military roles women have performed and some of the struggles and dangers they have faced. A wide variety of display techniques and media are employed ranging from fine-art prints and recruitment posters to items of equipment, weapons and uniforms. The display is a useful forum extending the debate surrounding the nature of female soldiery in the present and also bringing to life the day-to-day experiences of women from a variety of backgrounds who have served with the army through the centuries.

Women have been widely portrayed in propaganda during wartime and this evidence in military museum displays allows for an interpretation

FIG. 2
One of the Varga girls, created by Alfred Vargas. (Imperial War Museum)

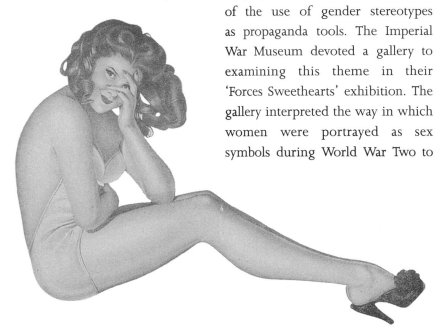

of the use of gender stereotypes as propaganda tools. The Imperial War Museum devoted a gallery to examining this theme in their 'Forces Sweethearts' exhibition. The gallery interpreted the way in which women were portrayed as sex symbols during World War Two to

encourage a nation at war. Pin-ups such as Betty Grable, the Varga girls (fig.2) and the cartoon strip heroine, Jane, were all exploited to their full potential to encourage troop morale. By comparison, illustrations of old ladies in bus queues depicted every-day situations on the posters, warning against the 'Hun' with slogans such as 'Careless talk costs lives'.

To encourage recruitment, posters of women and children watching distant marching troops reinforced the message 'Women of Britain say Go', whereas posters showing younger women cheerfully engaged in munitions work or in the Land Army encouraged women to sign up with appealing slogans such as 'Come into the factories!', 'Join the ATS' and 'My girl's a WOW!'. These posters are a visually appealing medium for display and provide an interesting study of the varied female stereotypes which were portrayed during the Second World War.

The interpretation of women's history in military museums has developed significantly since the 1960s. Such museums must continue to challenge the assumption that military history is a subject for male visitors and reinterpret their collections to display the full extent of female involvement in this subject. There is still much more work to be done before a complete story of the contribution women from different geographical and social backgrounds have made to war and military service is on permanent display in military museum galleries.

CHAPTER 6

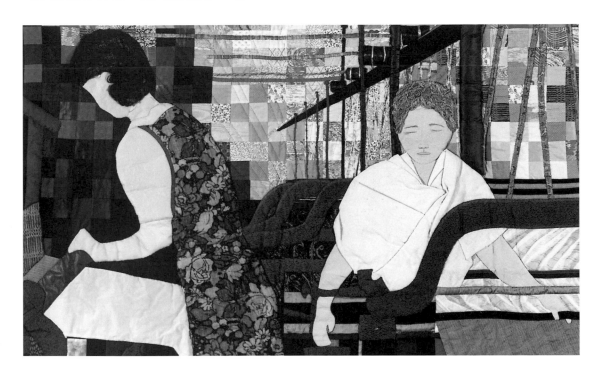

CONTEMPORARY COLLECTING AND WORKING OUTSIDE THE MUSEUM

IT'S A MAN'S WORLD?
A NEW TYNESIDE GALLERY   Catherine Ross

This paper is essentially a case study of one particular museum display completed in 1993 in Newcastle upon Tyne. Those who work in museums know that putting on a display or exhibition is a creative act involving choices, selections, the exercising or relinquishing of control over these selections, the balancing of intellectual ideas against dramatic effects etc. These are the choices and selections made by the people, the many people, involved in this particular display. Tackling the same subject today, the same people would almost certainly make different choices. I know I would. I also know all of you would have executed it differently. This, then, is one early-1990s approach to a museum display in which industry, technology and women all figure – although not necessarily in that order of precedence.

The main reason for looking at this particular case study in this particular conference is as one more illustration of that knotty old problem, comfortably familiar to us all, namely how to get women into a history traditionally dominated by men. It is, I would suggest, quite an interesting case study to look at because although it was undoubtedly important to bring in the female voices, it was equally important to do this while still doing justice to the north east's extremely strong sense of local pride and self-image, which – for better or worse – was bound up with a popular view of the past as a man's world.

Newcastle upon Tyne, like all strong regional cities, has a distinctive character and feel, born largely of its particular historic and economic circumstances. It has had a chameleon-like existence being, at various points in its history, military garrison, port, county town and shopping centre. But the part of its history that is closest to the surface in late twentieth-century Newcastle is the long last half of the nineteenth century when Newcastle became a classic industrial boom town, a surging success of carboniferous capitalism in a region dominated by four giant heavy industries: coal, iron and steel, shipbuilding and engineering. In the late twentieth century some of these industries have gone completely: the last coal was mined in Newcastle in the 1930s. Others are under sentence of death: for example, Swan Hunter, the Tyne's last shipyard. Nevertheless the nineteenth-century industries still loom large in Newcastle's twentieth-century sense of itself and its past. In many ways the dead industries are still a part of the living city: the working-class neighbourhoods which they created are still part of the geography of the city; the buildings associated with them – pubs with names like 'The Hydraulic Crane' – are not all demolished. And the culture that grew up in these urban neighbourhoods as a result of shared beliefs and experiences is still alive, despite the fact that the shared experiences of a settled industrial past have nowadays been overlaid by the experiences of a more savage, post-industrial present.

Another ingredient in Newcastle's particular mix of character and feel has been the north east's physical isolation from the rest of the country. This isolation, which still exists to a degree today, breeds real local pride and a sense of community but also enables what is in many ways an old-fashioned working-class culture to flourish. Austin Mitchell writing in the mid-1980s described the north east as 'a living museum', explaining that 'a way of life dying in the rest of the country is here perfectly preserved: its own language, a local culture, a real warmth and an in-built sense of superiority based on a clamorous inferiority complex'.[1] Many would disagree with the 'perfectly preserved' because the north east is much more vigorous and adaptable than that. However Mitchell's basic point that cultural values on Tyneside are essentially old-fashioned ones, largely undiluted by the late twentieth-century cultural meltdown, is still a fair one.

It is simplistic to say that a traditional working-class culture automatically produces a male-dominated view of the past, but the two are bound up together. Particularly when, as is the case on Tyneside, the industries at the root of the culture are not only large employers of men but also tend to cast men in a heroic role: the miners, the shipbuilders and the engineers – archetypes all. The Heroic Age of manufacturing industry on Tyneside was the period just before the First World War when Tyneside was transformed into one great arsenal and dockyard. One third of the male workforce was employed either directly or indirectly in the three big industries – coal, shipbuilding or engineering, which included armaments; and these industries brought not just jobs and prosperity to Tyneside, but also national prestige and international fame. Perhaps it is the status surrounding these industries as much as anything else that accounts for the unshakeable hold they seem to have on the popular imagination. Before the First World War Armstrong Whitworth's mammoth industrial complex at Elswick, the largest in Europe, was visited by kings and emperors. The launch of the liner *Mauretania* in 1907 drew newspaper reporters from around the world to Tyneside. Great ships were launched. Great guns were made. Great men came to admire them.

It is arguable that these great heroic industries of the early years of this century dominate Newcastle's view of its past to such a degree that their influence is felt not only in what came after them but also in what went before. By this I mean that they loom so large that not only do they over-shadow other parts of twentieth-century history but their shadow has also helped construct a selective view of Tyneside's pre-industrial past. For example, it is interesting to note how the figure of the Viking crops up so often and so prominently in accounts of the Tynesider's lineage. Why not a Roman soldier? Why not a Saxon monk? My view is that it's the combination of sea, military might and northern 'otherness' in the Viking which in some non-rational way echoes the self-confidence and pride of Newcastle's heavy industry round about 1900.

There was a good recent example of the Viking as Geordie ancestor at the 1992 Gateshead Garden Festival. British Gas's contribution to the festival was a large and lavishly produced pavilion, half museum, half walk-through experience, entitled 'Tyneside Heritage'. Its exterior was dominated by an elevated structure on which proudly stood four life-size figures – signalling the archetypes of Tyneside's past. There was a Viking carrying a sword, a sailor looking soulfully at the far horizon, a coalminer heaving a pickaxe and an engineer armed with a spanner: blood, sweat, tears, toil and industrial ingenuity. And, sad but inevitable to report, none of these four archetypes was a woman. However, despite this, the pavilion as a whole was not at all bad, and, more to the point for the poor museum curator, the figures were well made and did not deserve to go to waste. At the end of the festival Tyne and Wear Museums put in an offer and acquired the four figures, along with a few more that featured in the pavilion's interior scenes. We ended up with one Viking, three miners, one sailor, two engineers/shipbuilders, Lord Armstrong and two women, unspecified but probably wives because one was washing the back of a miner in the bath and the other was carrying a bucket of water.

My purpose in describing all this is not to wring my hands in distress or shake my fist in anger at the outrageous exclusion of women from Newcastle's history as played out in the popular imagination, but to point to it as a fact of life which curators had to work with. For better or worse, the pride in place felt in Newcastle was bound up with heavy industry, Vikings, miners, engineers and male inventors. Curators could not ignore this: how could we create a museum display that did justice to the other bits and at the same time acknowledge and indeed confirm and sustain Newcastle's existing sense of pride in its own history? That was the question with which the curators working on the 1993 display, 'Great City', were faced.

It was in some ways a question laced with irony, because museum curators of an earlier generation had played quite a strong part in constructing the 'it's a man's world' view of history. I've mentioned the worker and miners as heroes. Newcastle's history also boasts some real-life heroes: men from Tyneside who changed the world. The archetype here is George Stephenson, the rags-to-riches engineer who invented the steam engine and did indeed change the world. The chapter of self-help heroes who came after him is made up of George's son, Robert, who invented railway engineering; William Armstrong, who invented hydraulic machinery; Joseph Swan, who invented the light bulb, J. H. Holmes, who invented the light switch and Charles Parsons, who invented the marine turbine. Then of course there are the sporting heroes – from Jackie Milburn to Kevin Keegan – who, to be absolutely truthful, didn't change the world in quite the same way as the inventors and engineers, but who are treated on Tyneside as if they did. In many ways the TV detective Spender falls right smack in the middle of this male Geordie hero stereotype: tough, laconic, a rough diamond intensely proud of his roots. Interestingly, in a very early episode of the series, Spender insists on dragging his protesting daughters to, of all places, a museum. Why? To see a display on George Stephenson, because, as our hero is not ashamed to admit, George Stephenson is his hero.[2]

It is in promoting Tyneside's history as a series of biographies of famous men that museums have played their part. The Museum of Science and Engineering in Newcastle opened in the 1930s. It was the earliest provincial science museum in the country and had an overt mission to explore the local contribution to science and technology. One of the ways it has done this is to concentrate on local inventors, the clutch of local but nationally famous men – Stephenson, Armstrong, et al, – who are all dealt with more or less biographically in the gallery 'Pioneers of Tyneside Industry' which was one of the first galleries to open when the museum moved to its present home in the late 1970s. This gallery was followed by others which took wider approaches to their subjects – notably the shipbuilding gallery, 'From Dug Out to Dreadnought', however the picture of Tyneside history that the museum as a whole offered to visitors was still essentially a male-dominated one.

It was against this background that Tyne and Wear Museums decided to broaden out even further by introducing other subjects and approaches into the Museum of Science and Engineering. This process began in 1993 with the renaming of the building as the 'Newcastle Discovery' and the opening of 'Great City', a display looking at Newcastle from 1914 to the present day. This was the display which brought to the fore all those issues about balance and exclusions in existing histories and how we as curators could redress or counterbalance these without losing sight of the essential character of our place, the things that made Newcastle Newcastle. Inclusiveness was the thing we were generally aiming at: a history that included not just the industry and the pride it generated, but also the home life that fed off and into it; a history that included not just what happened in Newcastle, but also what people thought about what happened. We wanted a history that included women, children and old people as well as men of working age and we wanted a history that made the links between what happened on Tyneside to decisions and events that occurred elsewhere. It was life, the universe and everything, and I have written elsewhere about how we tried to bring some order to this vast canvas by adopting a three level focus: looking at the story of the city as a whole, looking at the life of neighbourhoods within the city, and looking at individuals and their experience of the limitations and opportunities the city offers them.[3]

The end result, I am pleased to say, comes across as far less clinically structured than this three-level approach suggests. Indeed some people have experienced 'Great City' as unstructured anarchy which, I have to admit, I am not as worried about as I probably should be since I do believe that permanent displays designed to last do well to be almost indigestibly rich; stimulating visually and intellectually, with lots of potential to be read in different ways by different visitors. Aiming for a display with the richness, variety and contradictions of a real city means accepting a degree of anarchy and loss of control over the final product. The hope is that, if this degree of anarchy is controlled with sensitivity, what one loses in precision of message is gained in stimulating visitors to think for themselves.

If I had to sum up the 'Great City' in museum terms I'd call it traditional, but with a post-modern twist. It's traditional in the sense that it's a chronological display where space equals time and visitors walk through from 1914 to the present day. Each of the seven period sections has a distinctive look, created through colours and design: thus in the 1940s visitors walk through a just-bombed living room, in the 1960s they walk through a science fiction interior based on the interior of Dr Who's Tardis. It's also traditional in the sense that it relies on text, albeit with a lot of sound, in the form of period music and broadcast oral history. The post-modern twist here is that the text is far more colloquial and impressionistic than museum text usually is. It's traditional in the sense that the display is packed full of objects, but the twist is that some of them are used in a less respectful way than traditional displays: being hidden away in drawers for people to discover in the 'Matchbox Museum' or displayed to take advantage of their kitsch or humorous qualities. 'Great City' is also not wholly traditional in that the glass case displays are almost outnumbered by the 'things to do', particularly for children who have their own area in each period section with jigsaws to put together, wheels of fortune to spin, clothes to dress up in, holes to peer through, mystery objects to feel, and roleplay games to follow. There are two roleplay games, one of which takes as its characters household pets: from Bob the Dog in 1914 to Gazza the Rabbit in the 1980s. Traditional though it may be, 'Great City' wants its visitors to have some fun.

So how did we work through our more serious aims, particularly the aim of getting women into the man's world? I want to look at one particular area where the women's cause was advanced and this was in the collecting carried out for the display, particularly of family photographs. An appeal was made for family photographs and a fair proportion of those offered are included in the display. Our interest in these amateur family photographs was partly to do with a general wish to involve as many people as possible in the process of putting the display together, and partly a wish to use some different images to the ones that usually featured in Tyneside's history. Newcastle has an exemplary local history library with a wonderful and well-used collection of photographs. The disadvantage of basing our work on these was not just that many had been seen before – Newcastle Libraries has been very active in publishing over the years – but also that they tended to reflect the interests of either civic departments or local papers, the sources of most of the library's collections. Amateur photographs offered a slightly different view of Newcastle's past both in terms of the actual images but also in a sense of the past as being about families and every-day life as much as great events and the official record.

Families became an important underlying thread in the display. As a trump card to play against the hero view of history, it was invaluable and it also seemed a particularly appropriate thing to emphasise on Tyneside where kinship and family ties remain strong in the culture, as much of the best writing about life on Tyneside, from Jack Common's *Kiddar's Luck*[4] to Sid Chaplin's *The Day of the Sardine*,[5] eloquently shows. In terms of increasing the presence of women and children in Newcastle's history, the extensive use in the display of family photographs did the job naturally without too much need for curators to exercise positive discrimination in their selections. We underlined the importance of families as much as possible in the text, and again, just doing this I felt helped the display to adopt a tone that counterbalanced the 'it's a man's world' view.

The second area of systematic collecting carried out for 'Great City' was that of oral history. This was to form the main component of those parts of the display that looked at our second 'level' – local communities and neighbourhoods. Each of our period sections focused in on a particular neighbourhood in Newcastle: for instance in the first period section, 1914 to 1926, we looked at Elswick, a classic example of a traditional urban community held together by the large industrial concern on its doorstep. In the present-day section we looked at Scotswood, a neighbourhood that has been unlucky enough to bear the brunt of all the urban problems that arrived in cities with the rise of unemployment in the 1970s and other more recent social changes. In order to get across to visitors some real impressions of what it was like to live in these parts of the city at those particular periods, it was decided that curators should stand back and let the inhabitants speak for themselves, which they do in the display through broadcast tapes. Each section gives the visitor a choice of four people to hear talking about their own particular memories.

These tapes are probably my favourite bit of 'Great City': living voices reach parts that written text cannot, and the sound of people talking makes the whole display come alive in ways that the objects, text and even the period music soundtrack cannot. More by chance and circumstances rather than design, the balance of these voices is female. For instance, the two sections mentioned above, Elswick and Scotswood, are dominated by women. The reason for this in the earlier Elswick section was simply that we could not locate any men who could talk about Elswick before the 1920s. In the case of the Scotswood section the choice of women was simply the fact that the best people to talk about Scotswood and what had happened to it in recent years were members of the Scotswood Community Project, a remarkable, largely women-led organisation which is moving mountains in its efforts to repair the damage done to their community. Interestingly, even when the voices were male, the subjects they tended to talk about were their homes rather than their work, since in many cases we were encouraging them to remember their childhood. For example, one of the most vivid interviews is with a retired shipbuilder who spoke in mouth-watering detail about the food his mother cooked in Walker just before the Second World War.

Although curators activated the collection of photographs and oral history, the presentation of this material in the display was largely a case of curators standing back and letting the content flow from the material itself. There were, however, several instances where curatorial intervention was more definite and it is worth pointing out one of these as relevant to this conference.

On the third of our levels, looking at individuals, we were trying to encourage people to think about diversity, difference and about how what you are as an individual affects your opportunities in and attitudes to life: for example, how a pensioner in Newcastle in the 1960s would probably have seen social change very differently from a teenager. In our first period section the differences we wanted to look at were gender ones, how men and women were affected by the First World War and its aftermath in different ways, how the choices and opportunities for women at that period were very different from the choices and opportunities most people now take for granted. For various reasons, not the least of which was that we had originally intended to use a video to illustrate this period but found that cost ruled it out, we devoted quite a lot of physical space to the position of women during this period – giving rise to some criticism that we had departed too far from Newcastle and strayed too much into national social history. I have no hesitation in justifying the amount of space we gave to the position of women around 1919 because of its importance in twentieth-century social history on any level, local or national. It was also, I feel, a useful thing to dwell on at the beginning of 'Great City' in that it provided a good, universally accessible way of explicitly introducing the notion of social change, the idea that things were not always the way they are nowadays. However, it is fair to say that by doing this we did create a picture of Tyneside around 1919, that was almost entirely a women's world: for example, the visitor sees a wall of local newspaper cuttings from 1919 all of which were selected to reflect the debates about women's role in that year: stories about these new-fangled flappers, the problems of munitions girls refusing to go back into domestic service, the debate over whether the wartime tram conductors should give up their jobs to the returning soldiers. We even promoted a female hero: Newcastle's first woman councillor, Mary Laverick, who was elected in 1919 and, in reply to a congratulatory remark on being Newcastle's first lady councillor, said, 'I object to being labelled as such. I am a Labour Party representative,' and insisted that she was 'in no way disconcerted at the prospect' of being the only woman in a council made up of sixty men.

As mentioned above, the British Gas's 'Tyneside Heritage' Pavilion at the Gateshead Garden Festival contained ten life-size sculpted figures, eight of which were figures of men, two of women. I now have to admit that 'Great City' contains six figures in all, of which five are women and only one is a man – and he, as a shell-shocked soldier returning from the war, is a pretty limp and pathetic figure. So have we failed to provide a more balanced view of history? Have we ended up by saying it's a woman's world instead of a man's world? I hope not. Newcastle's existing pride in place was something that we had to work with rather than against and we would have been foolhardy in the extreme to create a display about Newcastle that did not acknowledge the importance of shipbuilding, Newcastle United, the armaments industry and traditional male employment in the city's sense of its own identity. All of these have their place in 'Great City', and in the case of football, the thread runs all the way through quite explicitly from 1914 to today's new glory days under the undeniably heroic Kevin Keegan. What I hope we have done is to put all these aspects of Newcastle's twentieth-century history into a broader context so that the families, culture, opportunities and life choices that surrounded, flowed from and into these 'male' activities is seen more clearly. People will take what they want from the display and some will probably read it as a pretty conventional trot through the accepted main events: Armstrong Whitworth in the First World War, building the Tyne Bridge in the 1920s, Newcastle United in the 1950s, the Animals in the 1960s, male unemployment in the 1970s, youth crime in the 1980s. However, even those who choose to read the display selectively will, I hope, get some sense that the history of any industrial city is ultimately full of vigour and diversity, and that this diversity includes women, children, families, the young and the old, as well as men only.

ENDNOTES

1   Quoted in Robinson, F., (ed), 1988, p190.

2   'Spender', BBC Television series, starring Jimmy Nail, first shown 1992.

3   Ross, C., 1993.

4   Common, J., *Kiddar's Luck*, Turnstile Press, London, 1951.

5   Chaplin, S., *The Day of the Sardine*, Eyre and Spottiswoode, London, 1961.

'FASHION WORKS': A NEW DEVELOPMENT FOR TYNE AND WEAR MUSEUMS

Caroline Imlah

This paper was given prior to the opening in January 1995 of a new gallery about fashion in the north east: 'Fashion Works'.

This gallery signalled a new phase of development at the Newcastle Discovery Museum, Tyne and Wear's flagship museum complex. A whole new floor of the seven-storey Victorian building was opened up. 'Fashion Works', occupies 530 square metres. The development also includes 'A Soldier's Life' – the story of the Northumberland Hussars and the Fifteenth/Nineteenth King's Royal Hussars which opened in May 1995, and the 'Turbina' Gallery, displaying the world's first turbine-powered vessel, due to open in March 1996. This signifies a move away from the old Science and Engineering Museum to a more people-based approach.

The project 'Fashion Works' (original working title 'The Fashion House') was seen as something of a risk. Too lightweight perhaps, too expensive perhaps, too glamorous for the West End of working-class Newcastle?! But our approach was novel. Our aim was to capture the excitement and glamour of fashion, while at the same time showing the realities of a tough and competitive industry.

Tyne and Wear Museums is a county-wide network of thirteen galleries and museums, funded by five district councils, with a major grant from the Museums and Galleries Commission. After years of review and uncertainty we are at last proving ourselves with record visitor figures, and major new developments.

The History Department, established in 1990, consists of six staff – Principal Keeper of History, Keepers of Social History, of Maritime History and of Costume and Textiles, and two assistant keepers of social history. Four new permanent galleries, as well as a range of exhibitions, opened in 1994.

The costume and textile collection, some 8,000 items in all, covers male and female fashion from the early eighteenth century to the present day. The textiles are patchy – from Coptic textiles of the fourth century AD to a rare collection of Greek and Turkish embroideries. Designer fashion has little relevance here – the collection is solidly middle-class, sometimes – a bit too solid!

Until the past few years costume has been rather a poor relation, living on sufferance at the Laing Art Gallery, Newcastle. But in 1991 with a relaxation in the old fine art/decorative art hierarchy, and a new broader context for the display of art, which culminated in the award-winning new gallery 'Art on Tyneside', costume began to have a higher profile.

First there was the chance to prove ourselves with a major exhibition – 'Biba: The Label, The Lifestyle, The Look'. This exhibition in 1993 examined how one London boutique affected a whole generation of young women – Londoners and provincials alike. What was so extraordinary about Biba, as opposed to Quant, Bus Stop, or even Chelsea Girl, was the fact that people lived the dream – the co-ordinated eclectic lifestyle. Even before the exhibition opened, our 'Bring Out Your Biba' research campaign in 1991–1992 showed everyone that costume history could be more than simply posh frocks on parade. 'Get personal', was my message! Consumers were more important to interview, and involve, than design historians, so what we created was a lively, atmospheric, and emotional exhibition – a real experience of what Biba meant, and still means, to women growing up in the 1960s and 1970s. An important era in history, women's history, and fashion history.

Press coverage was pretty amazing. I think nearly every women's magazine and broadsheet covered Biba (and the exhibition). As intuition would have it – it was timed right for a 1970s revival. Going to the 'Clothes Show Live' at Earls Court in December 1992 had brought the media's attention to us – and so Biba's success was secured.[1]

A visitor survey during the exhibition had interesting results for a provincial art gallery. First, an astonishing eighty per cent were new or infrequent visitors – proof that there was a potential and, up till then, untapped market for fashion in museums. Thirty-nine per cent came from outside of the area (over half an hour's journey). And thirty per cent were aged between eighteen and twenty-five, a difficult audience to attract. Ninety-four per cent said they'd be interested in seeing more fashion-related exhibitions. Biba was the most popular exhibition the Laing has ever had – increasing attendances by a third – and it made a profit!

The experience gained from the Biba exhibition greatly affected my approach to my job, and how I wanted to plan a successful permanent costume gallery. The involvement of the public became crucial to every stage of the project; their views, their experiences and their memories bringing fashion history to life.

The subject of clothing and fashion is 'tailor-made' for Newcastle for several reasons:

    1. **The collection is large and varied, and only has some small visibility in 'Art on Tyneside' at the Laing, and 'Great City!' at The Newcastle Discovery Museum.**

2. **Fashion has a high profile in local schools, colleges and universities. The University of Northumbria at Newcastle runs two well-respected courses. Geordies are renowned for their own particular sense of style.**

3. **The clothing industry is a large employer on Tyneside. In 1985 clothing accounted for six per cent of the area's total manufacturing jobs. Retail jobs, which include a large proportion of clothing-related jobs, accounted for just over nine and a half per cent of the total employment figure.**

   Although 'Fashion Works' may be regarded as a risk, it should broaden the Newcastle Discovery Museum's visitor base. Many of the traditional heavy industries on display will now be balanced by reference to an industry in which women make up eighty per cent of the workforce.

4. **The gallery will have great appeal across all curricula in schools – from history, art, CDT, drama, literature, geography, science and maths.**

So, what did we plan to do?

Initially, the brief simply aimed to tell a chronological story of the clothing industry in the north east from the formation of guilds to the present day. Later, themes were pulled out to tell rather more important stories – 'Technology', 'Production', 'Retailing', 'Image Psychology', 'Recycling', 'Maintenance and Care of Clothes', and separate sections to look exclusively at menswear (which is poorly represented in the collection), and childrenswear. The introduction – 'Technology' – acts as a taster for the rest of the gallery. Here people are introduced to fibres, fabrics, dyes, methods of manufacture, and technology – giving them the skeleton of the story. This section is highly interactive – to give people the chance to examine different fibres and materials, to help them understand their properties, and hence their use.

A video based on a local firm shows the complex process behind the shop label, from concept to consumption, and the importance of everyone's role, not simply that of the designer. However, in a short three-minute film we may not achieve what we really want – but the research could always lead to something else in the future.

The next section, 'Production', was more difficult to prepare because of lack of time and resources – staff and money. This focuses on the people in the industry – the workforce. Throughout the gallery we have certain scenes to give atmosphere and emotion to what could be a rather dry, harsh tale. Here we have a scene based on Thomas Hood's *The Song of the Shirt*,[2] a poem written in 1843 dealing with the plight of an unfortunate needlewoman starving on piece-work.

This section looks at what life was like for Victorian women, when sewing skills were often the only means they had for earning a living. Much well-documented and published research has highlighted the scale of this problem in London and in the Midlands. We have attempted to find local examples to illustrate this tale, but on the whole northern employers were better than those further south.

Elaine Knox, of the University of Lancaster, is currently researching working women on Tyneside, as it seems they were 'invisible' in history: 'There have been more words written on the geological formation of the Northern Coalfield than on women's part in regional life. It would be pardonable to ask, "Were there any women on Tyneside?"'[3]

The regional economy depended, as is well known, on heavy industries – the railways, shipbuilding, foundries, engineering, and mining – employing a mainly male workforce. The relatively high wages earned by these men reinforced the separation of women from a waged economic role. Elaine Knox's research will go a long way to fill the gaps of women's lives in the history books of Tyneside. The 1871 Durham census showed 941 women to every 1,000 men – the lowest ratio in the country – with a correspondingly high marriage rate. In 1921 twenty-one per cent of women on Tyneside worked; nationally it was thirty-four per cent.

Jobs for women in the lighter industries on Tyneside – the potteries, the paper works and the hatmaking factories – declined this century. Lighter textile industries in the north east have found that they could not compete with the giants further south.

The fact is that, as in so many cases, official statistics look at male employment and unemployment in general. Women on Tyneside seem to have worked periodically, and in poorly-documented livings as slop workers, and by taking in laundry and sewing, or charring. Women on Tyneside, it seems, have preferred to adopt and approve of the Victorian domestic model of 'male breadwinner' and 'female homemaker'. At the moment it is difficult to say, let alone depict in a museum context, what the clothing industry was, or was not like on Tyneside.

Our third section, 'Retailing' shows where many of these women came to work later on in the 1930s. The story here starts with the development of department stores, like Bainbridge, the first in the world, now part of the John Lewis Partnership, and Fenwick, one of the most successful department-store chains. The families intermarried, and the firms are still behind any new retail development central to Newcastle. The chain stores like BHS and C & A came to Newcastle in 1932. Many women worked in retailing, as many men were unemployed. Today, despite a small population, Newcastle's

Northumberland Street is the busiest shopping street outside London's Oxford Street. Eldon Square is one of the most successful shopping malls in Europe. And Gateshead's Metro Centre is a magnet for Scandinavian tourists.

However, the gloss of success barely hides the truth – that much fashion is trash – and factory workers, homeworkers and shop assistants are still paid pathetic wages for 'women's work'.

The next section, 'Image', looks at fashion marketing, street 'tribes', and how certain areas of society, such as the visually impaired, or those with certain physical disabilities, deal with choosing clothes, and self-image.

At the crux of this gallery is participation from the public. A computer database will hold interviews with a wide spectrum of society, from Asian youths to blue-rinsed old ladies, goths to yuppies. A colour interactive will show how the visually impaired feel and experience colour. Crinolines and corsets will be displayed alongside aerobics videos and slimming fads – 'Standards for Beauty' will highlight the dangerous game of fashion.

In 1994 Newcastle, like everywhere else, was plastered with posters advertising the Wonderbra. The media batted this issue back and forth – did it demean women, patronise women, empower women? This unanswerable argument is the story of fashion in women's lives. Will we ever find an answer? 'Fashion Works' can at least ask the questions.

Our exhibition space has a running length of approximately thirty metres, with a central glazed case of twenty-four square metres. We will programme in three exhibitions a year, two initiated and one touring exhibition. Here we will examine themes and issues raised in the permanent gallery, and deal with subjects like ethnography and designer fashion, which lie outside this particular brief.

The first exhibition, 'The Strip Show' opened with 'Fashion Works' and ran until June 1995. It took a light-hearted look at the design and marketing of the football strip – topical for Newcastle United, and World Cup fever. This was followed by 'Chullus & Chumpis', a touring exhibition from Nottingham Castle Museum looking at contemporary Peruvian workwear. Next we intend to take a close look at the local firm, Jackson's the Tailor, a large employer in Tyne and Wear up until the 1970s, which will give us a chance to collect some oral history, and look at life behind the factory gates.

In the year 2000 we hope to present a major retrospective of Bruce Oldfield's work to celebrate his fiftieth birthday. He is a classic designer who learned much of his dressmaking skill from his foster mother in County Durham.

Whatever we achieve in the next few years – the generosity of the public is crucial. We couldn't do it without them, and I certainly need them on-side in 'Fashion Works'.

ENDNOTES

1 A presentation was made to the organisers of 'The Clothes Show Live', which resulted in the donation of a free stand, worth about £3,000 in sponsorship. We put on a mini-Biba exhibition, sold merchandise and distributed leaflets on the exhibition and its tour dates. This event caught Top Shop's eye, securing us £8,000 of sponsorship at the Last minute.

On 4 February 1993 'The Clothes Show' spent a day talking to staff and filming for transmission on the Sunday before the exhibition opened.

2 Thomas Hood's *The Song of the Shirt* is quoted in full in Walkley, C., 1981.

3 Elaine Knox's professional biography is in Coles, R. and Lancaster, B., 1992.

CONTEMPORARY COLLECTING AND RECORDING: ITS IMPORTANCE FOR WOMEN
Nick Lane

Celebrating an element of society, whatever its size or makeup, within a museum context is almost always a challenge and often proves to be controversial. Perhaps this in some way explains why many museums prefer to focus on society as a whole rather than examining elements within it. Take for example the relatively late scramble within museums to incorporate differing cultures and traditions in both their displays and collecting and recording activities. Add to that the inability of an even greater number of institutions to acknowledge the existence of a life outside their own middle-class horizons, and all of this leaves many museum collections much the poorer for their timidity – both now and for the future. My aims in this article are modest: to present examples from my own experience of how best to approach aspects of contemporary recording and to urge that this largely neglected area of museum work is pursued with greater vigour.

Looking at the role women play in British industry today, government figures reveal that of a total working population of 21.5 million, 10.7 million are women. In terms of manufacturing industry these figures translate into a workforce of just 4.3 million, of whom 1.25 million are women, or twenty-nine per cent.[1] For museums to translate these figures into something that reflects the role of women in modern industry is a daunting task. I believe the most effective way forward for museums in this field is the wholehearted adoption of a programme of contemporary collecting and recording – which will be acted on, rather than consigned to the filing cabinet. I deliberately add the word recording because, in my experience at least, the production of a photographic, video or sound tape record can come a poor second to the acquisition of artefacts. This is a sad irony, for the camera and tape recorder are the most important tools in any contemporary collecting project. The camera allows the curator to record the context from which objects are collected and if coupled with a tape recorder this combination offers a powerful source of alternative evidence to artefacts.

METHODOLOGY

The question soon arises of how best to undertake a project of contemporary recording. The example below illustrates the disadvantages of failing to adopt a structured and directed approach. At the same time, however, it serves as a useful reminder of the fate of much of British industry in the last decade and the immense task the Museum of London faced in trying to record too much with too little.

With the closure of much of the Port of London and the collapse of many of the capital's traditional trades and industries in the late 1970s and 1980s, the Museum of London was faced with the prospect of collecting what it could while it could, or allowing two hundred years of history to disappear. Such was the rate of change as the manufacturing base contracted in favour of service industries and property development that staff rarely, if ever, had the opportunity to plan or structure their collecting and recording activities. It was common to receive news that a factory was in the process of closing only a few days in advance; sometimes it was too late and likely museum artefacts had to be wrested away from the scrap merchant. Given the *ad hoc* manner which typified this rescue archaeology approach, it was rarely possible to construct a balanced view of London as a manufacturing centre – let alone take the time to structure such a programme. Consequently not only were whole sectors of industry overlooked – food processing, chemical production and new technology to give but three examples – but whole elements of London's manufacturing workforce were also largely omitted.

The following comments may help in the collecting and recording of industrial sites. For a record of any workplace to be as comprehensive as possible an attempt should be made to record every aspect of work – from the shopfloor to the general office to the canteen. Many photographic and/or video records of factories have suffered from concentrating on what they perceive as the *real work* – the shop floor – and ignoring the other elements that go to make up the work experience – the office, the canteen and the cleaners. It is this very process that excludes the representation of women in the workplace. This, furthermore, can create a view of the factory as a male preserve, particularly if the women are employed in activities not associated with shopfloor work, as is often the case. It is important, therefore, to attempt to record all aspects of the workplace.

There are always constraints that need to be acknowledged in trying to achieve a complete and balanced record. For example, certain individuals will not be photographed, just as some will decline to be interviewed. People who have little interest in their job may have difficulty in understanding your interest in their work, and their ability to help may therefore be limited. Other people may be nervous or shy and unwilling to co-operate.

Not unnaturally, there is rarely enough time thoroughly to collect from and record an industrial environment. It can take a considerable amount of time to build up the necessary rapport that is needed for an interview or a set of photographs to be successful.

The most effective way in which to record the experiences of women in the workplace is through project work. Realistic targets must be set; any attempt globally to record women in industry will be likely to produce sketchy results. The answer then is to focus on one trade, or one workplace, for which the results are bound to be more comprehensive.

USING CONTEMPORARY EVIDENCE IN DISPLAYS

Applying contemporary evidence can sometimes prove to be a little more hazardous than when dealing with matters past, although there are safety measures that can be adopted in order to represent people fairly.

1 **We should always strive for a balance and be aware of sexual, ethnic and age differences. Some would say that this is to discriminate in a positive fashion however, balance is the ultimate objective. This should be applied to all elements of a potential display: selection of images, selection of artefacts, the selection of sound recordings and text. The process should begin at an early stage, in particular when determining who to involve in the oral history/photographic recording.**

2 **Adopt a checklist and refer to it; constantly question how balanced your approach is.**

3 **Research thoroughly, especially with the aid and advice of focus/ community groups. The more involvement that can be achieved with groups representing those you are trying to reach, the better.**

This represents but one approach, and there are always alternatives. The most obvious of these is to pay lip-service to the issue of contemporary collecting, and then do nothing. Passive collecting could be one way, for this is actually a form of not collecting. There is no such thing as passive collecting where contemporary collecting and recording is concerned. The only way in which successfully to undertake a programme of contemporary collecting is to do so *proactively*.

It is important to grasp exactly what it means to ignore contemporary collecting. First and foremost, it results in a lack of evidence for the future; if the objective is to record the role of women in the workplace in the 1990s, then this will be achieved only if someone makes the attempt. Failure to accept this challenge will also deny others a future perspective on how we view ourselves. Unfortunately it appears that too many curators seem to be stricken by an inertia born of the fear of being seen to discriminate or be pilloried for following a 'flawed' methodology. Rather they seem content to leave it all to the sociologist or social anthropologist, forgetting that academics generally depend on quite different sources of evidence from museums. Ultimately I believe that it is this body of contemporary evidence that we all should be striving to collect for the people and historians of tomorrow. Something, surely, has to be better than nothing.

ENDNOTES

1   'Employees in Employment in Great Britain,' reproduced in *Employment Gazette*, May, 1994. These figures are published monthly by the Employment Department based on an enquiry to employers on a sample basis. Additional information is available from the Labour Force Survey, which is published quarterly.

'PIECES OF HISTORY': QUILTS AND BANNERS CELEBRATING WOMEN'S LIVES AND ACHIEVEMENTS

Deborah Cherry

This paper is not so much about women in industry, but about women's industry, energy and enthusiasm, and how when called upon, it can be mobilised and used with great effect and benefit to all, in the cause of womankind.

This is the story of how Preston women made history, how their self-esteem soared with every stitch, and how the success and experience of co-ordinating 'Pieces of History', the award-winning community arts project, has convinced me of the need in the UK for an education resource that will celebrate and promote women's history and present-day achievements in schools and in the community, in creative and innovative ways. The challenge awaits us, the work ahead exciting and new, my aim to 'tell all' and inspire.

In September 1992 the call went out to all Preston women to pick up their needle and thread and help make history: commemorative quilts and banners celebrating the lives and achievements of Preston women, past and present, from the Suffragettes and the Mill Girl, to the Dick, Kerr Ladies Football Team,[1] women that lived in the Maudland area and Preston Women of Today.

The project was organised for Preston Well Women Centre, as their contribution to the 1992 Preston Guild celebrations. This is a once-every-twenty-years event, celebrating the town, its industry, art and culture. At a time when the whole of Preston was blowing its trumpet, I felt we should be blowing ours, loudly!

The design skills of fine art students from the University of Central Lancashire and illustrator Katherine Walker were enlisted, and the invaluable practical support of Claire Nicholson and the Quilters' Guild. Soon about a hundred women, many of whom hadn't picked up a needle in years, were meeting regularly at St Walburge's Parish Centre and at each other's homes, and working with great zeal on what began as five pieces but – due to public demand – grew to seven: five quilts and two banners that toured as the 'Pieces of History' Exhibition.

Given the central role women played in the Lancashire cotton industry, a tribute was long overdue. The Mill Girl Quilt (Fig. 1), designed by Georgina Riley, celebrates women who worked at Horrockses Centenary Mill, Preston. Founded in 1791, it was one of the largest and oldest cotton mills in our once thriving cotton town. Horrockses cotton was world-famous, our Fabric

Appeal, contributed to by people all over Lancashire, who gave sheets, pillowcases, dresses and dolly bundles, incorporated into the quilt, making it an even more personal tribute.

Responding to our call, many of the now elderly women who had worked at Horrockses contacted me, very keen to help, but with failing eyesight unable to sew. Encouraged instead to talk about their cotton-mill days, their valuable testimony was included in the exhibition, which deliberately set out to highlight aspects of mill life, particularly as it related to women's experience, that had not perhaps been highlighted before. For example, the Cotton Queen competitions, held annually throughout the 1930s to promote the cotton industry. Organised by the *Daily Dispatch*, the competition was open to all mills who would submit photographs of their most attractive female workers to the newspaper, and the winner chosen by public ballot.

FIG. I
'The Mill Girl
Quilt'. Designed
by Georgina Riley.
By permission of
the National
Museum of
Labour History

Margaret Hull (née Farnworth), a former weaver, came forward with treasured memories and memorabilia, of her time as Cotton Queen for Preston in 1936. The exhibition included the pink lace gloves she wore at her coronation, the sash and brooch she was awarded, and a special souvenir supplement that appeared in the *Daily Dispatch* to commemorate the Crowning of the Cotton Queen of All England finals at Blackpool Tower. Photographs showed Margaret carrying out official duties, such as modelling outfits at trade fairs, crowning Rose Queens and presenting trophies – one to the 'Van Man of the Year' at Preston's Steam Laundry – while stills from a film entitled *Cotton Queen* in which she and other Cotton Queens were featured along with Stanley Holloway, recorded Margaret's moment of screen stardom.

Agnes Hindle, also a former weaver at Horrockses, described the day Wilfred Pickles visited the mill and interviewed her for a recording of his radio show 'Have a Go':

> **They came for me one day and asked me would I like to go into the canteen as Wilfred Pickles wanted to interview me. So I go in and it was about holidays, and well I'd been to Butlins for first time that year and it was shocking. Well I told him it was; I didn't wrap anything up. They had their own jam pots on table; rationing was still on. But do you know it was ten guineas. It was**

supposed to be three Grand Gala Weeks. It was no different from anything else and the food was awful, awful. So I told Wilfred the truth … I remember listening to it, but he cut a bit out of what I said about Butlins.[2]

The focus of the next quilt was the Maudland area, where many women worked in the mills. Designed by Jane Anderson, this quilt celebrates women who lived in this very old part of the town, whose houses were demolished in the 1970s. As in many other traditional working-class areas, women worked within and in many cases outside of the home to provide or supplement the family income. They looked after immediate and often extended family members and by necessity were dab hands at 'making do'. They were strong-minded, hard-working, cheerful and resilient, tied by bonds of friendship and community. These qualities were picked up by Jane Anderson, who explained:

I have made the figures of the women large and solid-looking and have placed them centrally to emphasise their strength and importance in the community … The two women look confident and relaxed, engrossed in their doorstep conversation … I used this image to convey that special feeling of companionship that can develop between women when they live and work together in their day-to-day lives.[3]

The design for the quilt celebrating Preston Women of Today (fig.2) was by Rachel Lander. Made up of rows of footwear from slippers to stilettos, what quickly became known as the 'Shoes Quilt' constituted the main fundraising element of the project.

The Guild Mayor and Mayoress, Harold and Enid Parker, launched the quilt on International Women's Day in 1993. For a three-month period the quilt was at venues throughout the town, and passers-by invited to add a stitch to a shoe of their choice, give a donation and sign their name in a History Book to be kept with the quilts for future Preston Guilds. Staffed by volunteers sporting 'I'm Making History' badges and sashes, over 2,000 people took part and £1,700 was raised. 'Would you like to go down in history, Sir/Madam?' How could they refuse?!

The quilt celebrating the Dick, Kerr Ladies Football Team who in 1921 became the undefeated British champions, is by Jillian Bradley. Dick, Kerr's tram factory was one of the largest employers in Preston, its women's football team, world-famous. The quilt records some of the team's achievements as they played in Europe, Canada and against men's teams in America. Thanks to Gail Newsham, former players from the 1930s, 1940s and 1950s were reunited during the Guild celebrations, for the first time in over thirty years. The autographs of many have been embroidered on to the quilt.

The project captured the imagination of press and public alike, with features in *History Today* magazine, specialist craft and needlework magazines, and coverage on local and national TV and radio. Following a feature on 'Woman's Hour' (BBC Radio 4), we received letters from women all over the country asking how they could be involved. Another piece was clearly needed; a double-sided Friendship Quilt made up of embroidered patches enabling women both in the UK and abroad to take part. 'I'm Making History' sewing kits were sold to raise money for the Centre and, following the lead of Preston women, women worldwide seized their chance to go down in history.

Katherine Walker designed one of two banners made in tribute to Edith Rigby and the Preston Suffragettes: a modern interpretation of a banner adopted by the local Women's Social and Political Union (WSPU) (fig.3), the latter little known about until we recovered its history. The original banner featured a painting by local artist Patti Mayor entitled 'A Portrait of a Half-Timer'. The subject was Annie Lund, aged eleven, who spent half of each day working at Horrockses mill and the other half at school. Annie was given sixpence for sitting. The banner carried the inscription 'Preston Lasses Mun Hev the Vote!', and was paraded at a Suffragette rally in Hyde Park in 1907 where, according to Edith Rigby's niece and biographer Phoebe Hesketh, Patti was complimented on her work by George Bernard Shaw.

For those working on our banner, a Banner Workshop was held. Hosted by Thalia Campbell, organiser of the '100 Years of Women's Banners' Exhibition. The day consisted of an illustrated talk on the history of women's banners and a practical skill-sharing session, during which sample banners were examined and advice given. About forty women attended from as far afield as Surrey, Leeds and Manchester.

Schoolchildren too were involved, girls from Moor Park High School, who made the second tribute to the Preston WSPU. Following a Banner Day at the school, during which they learned about the part local women played in the Suffragette movement and were given practical guidance on appliqué and quilting, the girls depicted in fabric their impressions of those courageous women.

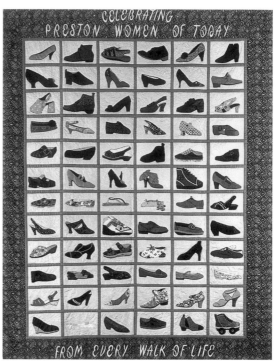

FIG. 2
'Shoes quilt' designed by Rachel Lander. By permission of the National Museum of Labour HIstory

FIG. 3
Banner in tribute to
Edith Rigby and the
Preston Suffragettes.
Designed by
Katherine Walker.
By permission of the
National Museum of
Labour HIstory

On 23 July, the anniversary of Edith Rigby's death, about two hundred women from Lancashire, Bristol, Leeds and London, many dressed as Suffragettes, took part in our March of the Women to herald the launch of the 'Pieces of History' Exhibition at the Harris Art Gallery.[5] Parading through Preston with banners and placards aloft, they arrived at the Harris to find access denied. In the ensuing drama, eight Suffragettes managed to elude a 'police' cordon and, emerging triumphant on the Harris balcony, to the delight of the cheering crowd below, they proceeded to chain themselves to the railings in protest. Scuffles broke out and several 'arrests' were made.

'Pieces of History' celebrated women's lives and achievements in the most positive, public and effective way possible; making women's history visible in a way that generated interest, good humour and support. The project was inclusive rather than exclusive; men as well as women played a part.

By bringing together artists, craftspeople and women in the community to work for a common cause, harnessing all that energy, enthusiasm, skill and experience, and with a clear strategy, clever marketing and creative ideas, the project succeeded. Not only was public awareness increased dramatically, but the self-esteem of the women and schoolgirls involved, their belief in themselves and their capabilities increased a hundredfold. Having literally made history, there is nothing they can't now do!

Like the Suffragettes before us, we knew the value of publicity and used every method of advertising to promote our cause: a slogan was coined, posters and leaflets printed and a range of 'I'm Making History' merchandise produced in the glorious colours of purple, white and green: sashes and sweatshirts, stickers and badges – to be worn at all times and with pride – sold to increase awareness and raise money for the Well Women Centre and the war chest.

As part of our strategy to publicise widely, regular press releases were sent out, presentations given wherever and whenever possible to local groups and organisations and everyone involved encouraged to seize every opportunity to 'tell all' about it both here and abroad. A Quilters' Guild member, for example, spoke about the project at the Great American Quilt Festival and sold forty sewing kits to eager supporters.

Ours was a well-orchestrated campaign, and for me a personal crusade to tell the world, not only about the achievements of Preston women, but about the achievements, capabilities, and potential of women, full stop.

My crusade continues. As co-ordinator of 'Pieces of History', I have been invited to California to spend some time with the National Women's History Project (NWHP), an educational resource that has been promoting women's history to great effect for almost fifteen years.[6] Having felt for a long time that a lot more could and should be done in this country to celebrate and increase awareness about women's lives and achievements in creative and innovative ways, both in schools and in the community, I am very keen to seize this marvellous opportunity to find out more, exchange information and ideas and apply what I learn on my return.

Funding permitting, a series of illustrated talks on 'Pieces of History', will be given and contacts established with teachers, youth and community workers, women's organisations, artists, craftspeople and others involved in promoting women's history and present day achievements in creative ways, with the possibility of working on joint projects in the future. The findings will be included in a study to assess the feasibility of setting up a similar project in Lancashire, which would be a prototype for projects throughout the country.

Provisionally called the 'Lancashire Women's Heritage Project', the resource would seek to encourage the working together of academics, groups like WHAM and Women's History Network, writers, artists and craftspeople to work with women of all ages and social and ethnic backgrounds. Projects and curricular-linked educational activities would be set up which would celebrate and increase awareness of women's lives and achievements, in schools and in the community, in creative and innovative ways: through literature, performance, film and photography, all the arts at our disposal. Projects that would draw on and enhance the experience, skills and expertise of all those involved, increasing their confidence and self-esteem, not just for the life of the project but for long after.

There is a wealth of talent, energy and enthusiasm out there, women re-tired or otherwise that would love to share their experiences, go into schools, get involved, a ready-made resource just waiting to be tapped, and tapped while it still can be. Women like Margaret Hull, the Cotton Queen, won't be there for ever. We must enlist their help in passing these stories on and providing role models for girls to show them just what women can achieve.

Through quilts and banners, a commemorative March of the Women and a photo-call, schoolchildren involved in 'Pieces of History' learned about the Suffragettes and the achievements of other local women. There must be

Edith Rigbys in every town; why aren't children learning about them? Because, teachers tell me, the information isn't there, the resources aren't available. They need to be and the world needs to know. We have a far better chance of achieving this if we set up an educational resource as described above. The approach needs to be co-ordinated, creative and populist, and practised in the skills of marketing and publicity.

Can it be done? Of course it can! It *has* to be done. Such a resource is vital, and as 'Pieces of History' and the work of the National Women's History Project have shown, this kind of project can be enormously successful at increasing awareness about women's lives and achievements. What it needs is funding, serious funding, either by the state or by commercial sponsorship.

The 'Pieces of History' Exhibition is testimony to the hundreds of hours of hard work, determination, tremendous enthusiasm and commitment shown by the many women who picked up their needle and thread in response to our call. They have played an important part in ensuring their own, their mothers' and their grandmothers' rightful place in Preston's history.[7]

ACKNOWLEDGEMENTS

To Claire Nicholson and Richard English for helping to make dreams become reality.

ENDNOTES

1 Dick, Kerr are the surnames of two men who founded the Preston-based tram and later munitions factory, to which the Dick, Kerr Ladies' Football Team were attached: W. B. Dick and John Kerr. For more information see Newsham, G. F., 1994.

2 Taped interview with Angus Hindle, a former weaver at Horrockses, by Deborah Cherry. Transcript included in the 'Pieces of History' Exhibition.

3 Statement by quilt designer Jane Anderson included in the 'Pieces of History' Exhibition.

4 Despite my 'Desperately Seeking Suffragette Banner' appeal, the whereabouts of the banner remain unknown. I have however managed to locate Patti Mayor's painting, last seen on exhibition in the 1950s, at Preston's Harris Museum and Art Gallery.

5 This particular 'spectacle of women' was hastily arranged when plans were dashed to have a Suffragette abseil from the balcony of St Walburge's church, scattering leaflets as she fell.

6 National Women's History Project, 7738 Bell Road, Windsor, California, 95492.

7 Copies of the *Pieces of History Final Report* by Deborah Cherry are available for reference at the Fawcett Library, London; Lancashire County Record Office, Preston; and the Harris Reference Library, Preston. An 'I'm Making History' badge is included in the National Badge Collection, British Museum, London. The 'Pieces of History' Exhibition and 'Stitch-In' were sponsored by the Miller Arcade, Preston. The project was supported by: the Quilters' Guild, Preston Leisure Services, North West Arts, Lancashire County Council, the University of Central Lancashire's Women's Unit and Fashion and Fine Art Department, TGWU, Moor Park High School, St Walburge's Church, *Everywoman*, Albert Hartley's Mill, Standfast Mill, Beckfoot Mill, Ainsworth Finishing Company, Dorma, Needlecrafts, Madeira Threads, Perry Down, Vantona, Ashleigh Polythene Company Ltd, Preston Tourist Information Centre, Asda, Sainsbury's and Samlesbury Hall.

DISCOVERING WOMEN'S HISTORY IN LONDON'S DOCKLANDS

Eve Hostettler

Our work in a small museum on the Isle of Dogs in the East End of London in the 1980s was directed both by an awareness of the need to present women in the history of the local community and by the support and involvement of local women themselves. This paper addresses three aspects of the museum's work: how our interest in women's history developed; what was discovered and how it was presented and made accessible; and how local women have been involved in the processes of discovery and representation.

AN AWARENESS OF WOMEN'S HISTORY

In 1980 two people were employed to work on a community history project on the Isle of Dogs, which is part of London's Docklands. The Isle of Dogs is known locally, and referred to here, as 'the Island'. The two workers were myself and Bernard Canavan, both historians from a 'people's history' background with experience in the fields of adult education and working-class history. In the fifteen years of the project's existence, we worked with local people to create a small museum about the history of the traditional community. During the same period, the Island underwent massive redevelopment in order to become a new business and financial centre for London.

In 1980, life on the Isle of Dogs had reached a turning point. The West India and Millwall Docks had closed. The London Docklands Development Corporation was being set up. The future was uncertain, and in the meantime the environment was dominated by post-war council estates and the boarded-up sites of abandoned riverside factories. The derelict dock area was shut off behind walls and fences and there was widespread unemployment and insecurity among the local population.

The late 1970s had been a period of rapid and far-reaching change. Until then, the local docks and related services, such as transport and storage, had provided work for many hundreds of local people. The sights, sounds and smells of ships and cargoes had filled the air. Many local families had been associated with dock work for several generations. No one living on the Island could be unaware of the docks.

By 1980, this was all in the past, but the change was so recent that local life was still dominated by the effects of dock closure. In the pubs and clubs where ex-dockworkers spent their leisure time, among the cab-drivers, school-keepers and entrepreneurs which dock-workers had become, the rights and wrongs of closure were still fiercely debated. Public and private concern about unemployment was expressed mainly in terms of the male unemployed. Men were dominant in local politics. There was a sense that the Island *was* the docks and that the docks were a male domain. Their closure was seen as a disaster for the Island and Islanders, as in many ways it was.

Our project was to recover the history of the community in all its aspects. The docks were very much to the fore, but the deserted factories, the housing estates, the schools, churches and pubs all bore witness to other features of local life. It was clear that the Island story must encompass more than the story of the docks and the culture of dock work. In particular, the role of women in the local economy and culture seemed to be largely ignored in every-day discourse, yet clearly, they had a role. Part of our project work would be to fill this silence, and as it turned out, local women themselves would make a major contribution.

WOMEN, WORK AND COMMUNITY ON THE ISLE OF DOGS

We proceeded by a combination of conventional research and the personal contributions of local people, overcoming on the way our own ignorance and the indifference with which, as strangers, we were at first regarded. Here is an outline of what, over the years, we discovered about women's working lives on the Isle of Dogs, and what sources we used.

Census reports and enumerators' books revealed the growth of Island population in the nineteenth century, from a few dozen in 1800 to over 21,000 in 1901. From street directories and maps it was possible to chart the expansion of trades and industries and the development of roads, houses, factories, shipyards, churches, schools and pubs during the same period. From the birthplaces of residents recorded in the census enumerators' books, it was evident that people had come to the Island throughout the century, individually or in families, from all over the United Kingdom, attracted by the prospect of finding work in this developing industrial part of East London. We found through life-history interviews that these migrations were traditional for many families. Stories, told originally by grandmothers, were retold in the late twentieth century by women in their 80s, of the tedious journey from some northern town, the late-night arrival in a strange place, the muddy streets, the help provided by new neighbours or the long walks sometimes undertaken back to Kent or Essex or East Anglia. Sometimes these stories were linked to faded studio portraits or personal papers such as birth and marriage certificates. A few people had undertaken serious research and could chart the movements of their ancestors in great detail.

The occupations recorded in the census up to the last quarter of the nineteenth century were predominantly male trades in the docks, shipyards and engineering works. Many married women were not recorded as having an occupation, though some appeared as laundresses, charwomen, nurses and dressmakers. During this period many employers and managers of local firms lived on the Island, and their households included single girls and women employed as domestic servants. The low numbers of young unmarried women in working-class homes is probably an indication that they were employed as living-in domestic servants in other parts of London; there was little regular work available locally for women. Street directories revealed a few women with their own businesses, keeping shops or public houses. In newspapers and magazines, reports of the developing Island provided glimpses of other activities like the casual buying and selling of seasonal items such as watercress and shrimps. In recorded interviews, people recalled grandmothers who had taken in washing, scrubbed out ships, taken lodgers, attended at childbirth and laid out the dead. The extent of this kind of casual work is impossible to quantify from official sources, but examples often crop up in qualitative, personal sources such as reminiscence and letters. A complete set of log books from the 1870s had survived in one local school;[1] these provided evidence that women who had migrated to the Island from rural areas close to London, often returned to their home villages, with their children, for the summer months, during the pea-picking, fruit-picking, corn-harvesting and hop-picking seasons. Only the last-named survived as a regular annual working holiday in the twentieth century.

During the last three decades of the nineteenth century, the Island's ship-building yards closed or were converted to ship repair, and new factories were built on vacant riverside sites. The population continued to grow through in-migration as people from all over the British Isles moved into London in search of work. There was also a counter-flow out of the area. Skilled shipbuilders and engineers, thrown out of work by the closure of the yards, moved away, sometimes returning to their old homes in the north. Employers, managers and those skilled workers that remained, moved away from the increasingly crowded streets to live in more pleasant suburbs. In the 1980s an American post-graduate student analysed the occupations of household heads, as recorded in the census.[2] His tables showed that by 1901 the Island had lost its heterogeneous mix and had become almost uniformly working-class with a predominance of unskilled and semi-skilled workers. Employment was characteristically low-paid or seasonal, or both.

This change reduced the local demand for domestic servants, but opportunities for women's employment were opening up in other areas.

Manufacturing investment was attracted to the Island by the easy access to the river for transport and by the supply of cheap labour, all close to the expanding London markets. Two key sectors providing employment for both men and women, were packaging – ropes, cables, sacks, tarpaulins, kegs, drums, boxes, tubes, etc, and food processing, with three major firms established here – McDougall's for flour, Morton's for sweets and confectionery, and Maconochie's for pickles and jams.

While the traditional buying and selling, laying out, cleaning, and other ways of earning small amounts, continued particularly among the older women and widows, there were now opportunities for regular employment for women and girls in the new factories. Evidence for this comes from business histories (published as newspaper reports or centenary booklets), a few autobiographies, old photographs, the census and reminiscence. The middle-class women who came to the Island and founded St Mildred's Settlement in 1897 described the factory workers in one of their Annual Reports, noting with some dismay their rough aprons, hair in curlers, feet wrapped in sacking on snowy days, and worst of all, their fondness for drinking sprees![3]

The factory women worked long hours in unpleasant and sometimes dangerous conditions. Some we talked to remembered their first jobs most vividly, and described working with hot, stinking glue, opening barrels of pickling cauliflowers alive with caterpillars and handling pigs' bladders soaked in freezing brine.

But factory work meant that single women could now live at home after leaving school, instead of going into service, and that both single and married women could contribute to the family income. Early twentieth century studio portraits show the factory girls in their best clothes, looking graciously Edwardian apart from their work-worn hands! A little could be put by from meagre wages towards marriage, and now young women were more likely to marry locally and settle down near their families, continuing to work until their first child. Close kinship networks developed, in which women linked by family and marriage helped each other in numerous small but vital ways. Again, reminiscence, linked to photographs, provides a great deal of evidence for this.

During World War One, Island women became munitions workers, metalworkers and engineers, or as rare photographic evidence shows, even handling cargoes in the docks. Support within families and between neighbours became even more important in this time of recurring domestic crises and bereavement.

Factory work, and other means of casual employment, continued in the inter-war years. The New Survey of London records show many households on the Isle of Dogs where young women were earning more than their fathers and where clearly their earnings were contributing to the comfort and well-being of the family. The extent to which married women worked on a regular basis is harder to determine. Except in households where several adult children were working, most married women took what opportunity they could of earning even a few extra pence in the time-honoured ways – cleaning, taking in washing, lodgers, dressmaking, giving piano lessons, selling home-made ice-cream or toffee, lending money, taking goods to the pawnshop for those too proud to go themselves, and of course, the annual hop-picking. Some worked in factories if relatives or neighbours could mind their children, though the prevailing ethic was that it was a 'disgrace' for married women to work. In fact I have often been assured that 'married women *never* worked', in spite being able to provide copious evidence to the contrary!

New social trends, already discernible in the 1930s, accelerated during and after the Second World War. Better education encouraged more girls to aspire to office work on leaving school, and there were plenty of new opportunities, not least in the expanding Civil Service. There were jobs for older married women there too. Equally, the creation of the welfare state, while taking over some of the traditional neighbourhood roles of older married women, also provided them with new roles, as 'dinner ladies', school cleaners and home-helps. The war had made it more acceptable for married women to work, and the 'twilight shift' was introduced in local factories so that married women could leave their children to the care of fathers in the evening while they did a few hours at the mill. This development mirrored a national post-war trend towards more married women working part-time.

These changes were a mixed blessing as far as the 'Ladies' of St Mildred's were concerned. Their Annual Report for the 1950s noted approvingly the pretty dresses and nice hairstyles of the modern factory girls, but spoke despairingly of the working mothers, who were too busy to find time for a quiet chat, and who appeared to neglect their housework to sit and watch television (bought on hire purchase) in the evenings. Factory work continued to be a major source of local employment for women and girls into the 1970s, but it was on the decline. There was no drama, as with the closure of the docks, but gradually, one after another, over a period of two decades, Island factories closed their doors and the firms moved away. Changing technology, changing markets, changing transport needs, all contributed to these moves. The effect locally was decline in local job opportunities for men as well as women. Meanwhile, the wider social changes of the post-war years were undermining traditional community structures and fundamentally altering women's roles in the home and the neighbourhood.

The developments of the 1980s eventually brought some gain in employment terms, with opportunities for women in both waged work and self employment in the expanding service sector – office cleaning, retail and catering, and in clerical and secretarial work. When the Island's first superstore opened in 1983, this was hailed with relief not only for the shopping facility but for the jobs it created for local women.

RECOVERY, ACCESS AND INVOLVEMENT

In the process of working with local people to recover the history of their local community, we accumulated thousands of photographs, and a quantity of printed ephemera, as well as many written and tape-recorded life stories. Operating on the principle that what came from the community should be returned to it, these collections were made accessible to the public. This was done in a variety of ways – through local history classes, outings, workshops, travelling exhibitions, a monthly newsletter, publications, school projects and by putting the whole photograph collection on open access. Our first travelling exhibition was 'Island Women', and all our exhibitions had their first showing in the local superstore. Our very first history outing was to an Island firm, a rope works, which had relocated to the south of England. There we collected photographs, artefacts and reminiscence, but just as important was that some of the women who had worked there and who came on the outing, had their memories reaffirmed. After that visit the old rope walk, grass-grown and neglected, became the focus of a group activity. The grass was removed and the rails of the rope-making machines exposed; the rope walk eventually became a landscaped garden, with a heritage information board to explain its original purpose.

From the start of the project in 1980, women have been in the forefront of recovering and preserving all aspects of their local history. The first (and only!) person to respond to our initial request for information was a woman, who later became an active volunteer and Chairwoman of our Board of Trustees. The first person to bring in a school photograph from the 1930s, with the names of all the children still clear in her memory, was a woman. Women have been in the majority in our classes and workshops, undertaking archive research, constructing domestic interiors, rediscovering how to make rag rugs and spending many hours making a series of beautiful wall-hangings. Most of our long-term active volunteers have been women – they collate the newsletter for posting, organise local deliveries, sell publications and maintain local exhibitions of photographs in shops and launderettes.

In asserting the importance of women's history in a male-dominated culture, we filled a need, closed a gap, put a voice where there had been silence and redressed an imbalance. We also tapped a pool of resources and energy and drew on a vital and vivid source of living history.

ENDNOTES

1   St Edmund's School Log books in a private collection.

2   *Life and Labor in the Isle of Dogs: The Origins and Evolution of an East London Working-Class Community, 1800-1980.* PhD Thesis by Thomas J. Cole, University of Oklahoma, 1984. A copy is deposited in the Local Studies Archive, Tower Hamlets Central Library.

3   St Mildred's Settlement: founded in 1897 as a base from which volunteers could work on the Isle of Dogs, the Settlement provided spiritual and material support for the women and girls who were employed in the workshops and factories and who lived in the surrounding streets. Activities included clubs for boys and girls and young people, country holidays, lunch-hour services in the factories, and health visiting. The Settlement flourished in this way until after the Second World War. Since then the need for welfare support has been increasingly met by the social services, and St Mildred's House was converted into flats for parish workers attached to the Church of England on the Island.

ENDPIECE

WOMEN IN INDUSTRY AND TECHNOLOGY

WHAM,
THE FIRST TEN YEARS

The 'Guerilla Girls' or 'a Gentle Group of Academics
and Museum Workers'   Sue Kirby   305

THE 'GUERILLA GIRLS'[1] OR A 'GENTLE GROUP OF ACADEMICS AND MUSEUM WORKERS'[2]

Sue Kirby

THE ORIGINS OF THE GROUP

In 1983 a number of Social History Curators Group committee members proposed that the group should organise a study day with the theme of 'Women's History and Museums'. In March of that year four women from the committee met to draw up a programme for such an event. The idea of a meeting focusing on 'Women's History' was replaced with plans for a conference which would, first, examine the representation of women in museum and gallery collecting and interpretation (not just historical collections but scientific and art collections too), and second, discuss the needs and expectations of women, both those working in and those using museums.

The first day of the conference related to the first aim, with ten collections workshops followed by six sessions outlining techniques and strategies. The second day concentrated on the role of women in the museums profession and included contributions from members of Women in Libraries, trade unions and the Greater London Council.

Over eighty people attended the conference, which was held at Woolton Hall, Manchester on 7 and 8 April 1984. At the final session of the conference it was agreed that a 'Women and Museums' group should be set up as an autonomous body. It was agreed that the new group should be organised on a regional basis and to this end a number of regional co-ordinators were co-opted.

The Manchester conference inspired these co-ordinators to arrange meetings in their regions, first off the mark being the north west, which met on 9 June 1984 in Lancaster and immediately started work on a travelling exhibition on women and industry. In July the regional co-ordinators and other interested people met in Leicester and formally took the decision to set up an independent organisation, 'Women, Heritage and Museums'. The conference proceedings were published that August.

Proposals for future WHAM activities put forward at Manchester included: organisation of further conferences and workshops; co-ordination of sub-groups to work on specific issues, including classifications and collections registers; setting up of a job-sharing register; application of pressure on museums and galleries to provide better coverage of women's history and achievements in displays; publication of a newsletter and production of touring exhibitions.

The plenary session agreed on the need for a regular conference and meetings, a newsletter and a job-sharing register. The point was made that WHAM should aim to support all women concerned with museums, including volunteers and those in low-paid jobs supporting collections staff. WHAM's aims and objectives adopted in 1984 (with one added at the Bristol conference, 1988) are to: promote positive images of women through museum collecting, exhibitions and activities; encourage informed museum practice through training seminars, resource lists etc, in relation to women's contribution in society; publicise museums as places where women's heritage can be studied and enjoyed; provide a wider forum for exchange of ideas and sharing of information on women's heritage; campaign for equal employment in museums and related fields; initiate debate and respond to relevant issues through the press and professional organisations etc; combat racism and discrimination on grounds of disability, age or sexual orientation, as these issues affect women, whether as museum workers, users or as women represented by museums.

ACHIEVEMENTS
So what has WHAM managed to achieve in its first ten years?

The group has, firstly, attracted members from both within and outside the profession. Links have been made with people from many other countries in all continents except Antarctica. Right from the start, the group tried to attract museum users as well as professional museum workers and to make links with the academic world.

Second, a large number of meetings and visits on subjects across the range of museums — for example women in the arts and crafts movement, women and archaeology, women and weapons, women and science — have been held, mostly organised through the group's regional networks, of which there are eight at present.

The Group has also run five conferences since Manchester. The first, 'Working for Women's Heritage', held at Brighton in 1985, attracted seventy delegates who explored in greater depth *how* women's heritage could be interpreted, with a special look at the use of film. 'Opening Doors: Women's Access to Museums', held at Bristol in 1988, saw the invasion of this usually rather staid museum by 800 toddlers and their carers who enjoyed such delights as the archaeology sandpit, (paper) plate painting and story-telling. There were thirteen organisers and sixty delegates to the more formal day which followed to look at issues around motherhood, childcare and employment.

'Interpreting Women's History', held at Edinburgh in 1990, was attended by between thirty and forty people who heard about Harlow New Town, analysed museum labels, listened to some of the Springburn mothers and had a great welcome at both the People's Palace in Glasgow and the newly-opened 'People's Story' in Edinburgh. There was also a presentation on some proudly feminist contemporary art. Sadly the conference planned for 1992 in north Wales had to be cancelled. However a small but enthusiastic band did get together in Cardiff in May 1993 to hear papers on wartime tin-plate making and the Crawshay family of Cyfartha Castle, Merthyr Tydfil. 'Women in Industry and Technology, Current Research and the Museum Experience', at the Museum of London, on 20 and 21 May 1994, attracted 150 delegates for our tenth-anniversary conference.

An important tool in the exchange of information and publicising of events has been the twenty-three Newsletters published, with regional groups also going into print in recent years with local bulletins. There have also been four editions of the resources list, which has grown from an A5 pamphlet to a 118-page ring-bound book.

From 1984 to 1994, WHAM members and supporters have undertaken or contributed to many exhibitions which explore women's heritage. To pick out just a few: 'Fit Work for Women', researched by north-west WHAM, produced and toured by NWMAGS (the North Western Museum and Art Gallery Service, now the North West Museums Service), on the road between 1986 and 1989; the Kaleidoscope initiative on Merseyside (November 1989); 'The People's Story' in Edinburgh (1989) – one of the first long-term displays to give equal weight to both 'his' and 'her' story; 'The Purple, White and Green' (1993) – at long last a proper airing for the wonderful WSPU collection held by the Museum of London.

The group also encouraged the setting-up of creches at annual study weekends (the first being at SHCG in 1983) and better childcare facilities within museums (for example Coventry). New initiatives such as Snibston show child-friendly designs have been taken on board. There have been special features on children in museums in newsletters 8 and 9 (reports on the Bristol Conference), 17, 18 and 19.

The group has fostered new ways of working, for example sharing tasks and working co-operatively. The guiding principle has been to build confidence and skills among members. WHAM has also been one of the first groups to tackle equal opportunities issues, for example racism at a 1986 meeting; racism awareness training at WHAM's 1991 AGM; and disability.

WHAM has, indeed, been a key player in getting the Museums Association (MA) to consider the 'equal opportunities' implications of all aspects of museum policy, practice and provision. Prompted by the group, it carried out a survey in 1985 and held a meeting on 'Women, Careers and Museums' in February 1988.

The following sessions have been held at MA conferences: Plymouth 1987: *Racism*; Belfast 1988: *Irish women's history*; York 1989 (with MAGDA, the Museum and Galleries Disability Association): *Disability and race*; Glasgow 1990: *Classification*; Newcastle 1991: *Getting the balance right – towards a fairer interpretation of gender*; Liverpool 1993: *Flexible working*.

WHAM was instrumental in the setting-up in 1989 of the Equal Opportunities Working Party, which has produced the MA Briefing on Equal Opportunities, a handy document full of useful references and practical advice.

'COULD DO BETTER'

Turning to the debit side, what have our failures been? What have we not been able to achieve?

Membership is now growing once again but is not as large as we hoped it would be. A long-standing problem is people not renewing. There is a hard core of long-term members, but possibly not enough to ensure continuity. The group's regionally-based organisation has encouraged participation at grass-roots level but has also led to great difficulties, what Rachel Hasted described in 1988 as the 'tyranny of structurelessness'. In our desire to avoid conventional structures where a small committee does all the work, we formed an organisation which was unable to respond quickly or strongly enough to national issues. Regional activity has been patchy, with some groups faltering when one or two people leave the region. However the new constitution adopted on 12 June 1989 has given a stronger national structure.

One of the original projects was to be a Directory of Collections relating to Women's History. This has proved too difficult and costly to undertake. Recently London south east WHAM attempted a survey of the national museums, but there were insufficient volunteers to undertake the work. In any case enough had been done to show how difficult it would be to get consistent responses.

A national posters project, proposed as cheaper and more effective than a national touring exhibition, did not materialise, nor has the newsletter been as regular as members, not least the committee and newsletter co-ordinator!, would like. The regions have shared editing and production, a way of working which has meant varying standards. However, production standards have improved over the years.

The group probably reflects the museums profession as a whole in being largely white and middle-class. We need to take the issues of race and class on board with greater commitment. Sometimes political naïveté and a failure to network have been a sticking point. For example, WHAM failed to organise sufficiently in preparation for the AGM of the MA in Glasgow in 1990 and a subsequent ballot of members, when MA constitutional changes proposed by the Equal Opportunities Working Party failed to get the required majority.

CONFERENCE 1994

What have been the main themes to emerge from this conference?

1. **A lot of research is there – but it is taking a long time to filter into displays, particularly long-term displays. WHAM needs to keep its links with the academic world and women outside museums. Members should keep networking so we know what work has been done. Our job is to turn research into representation. This needs more careful examination of the process which translates historical research into museum display.**

2. **There is still a tendency to accept artefacts, visual and oral evidence as objective. We need to *interrogate* all evidence and encourage our visitors to do the same; make it clear when we do not have the evidence and provide a context when we do. Involving the public in their content and design increases the likelihood of inclusive displays, as initiatives in Newcastle and Preston show.**

3. **The conference's concentration on *industry* is indicative of the fact that former industrial sites are providing the opportunities in the museum world – funding, development etc.**

    It also reflects a growing interest in women's contribution to the industrial labour market, but work both inside and outside of the home must be shown as equally valid and WHAM is working to achieve this balance.

4. **Women's skills in oral communication need to be constantly improved, both regarding presentation of papers and communication with staff and with the Public.**

We are in a very different environment from that current at the time of the first conference. At Manchester we were addressed by a member of the Equal Opportunities Unit of the Greater London Council. The GLC is now history and many Equal Opportunities Officers have lost their jobs. People, including museum employees, now work in a climate of frequent change. Museum workers are constantly having budgets cut, the threat of redundancy has become commonplace and some (including WHAM members) have actually lost their jobs.

Women, whether working in museums or elsewhere, are at the mercy of the economic climate. At the end of the 1980s we were told that with the shortage of school leavers, employers were desperate for women workers. It seemed that a 'golden age' of woman-friendly work practices was about to dawn – creches, career breaks etc. In 1994 a report from the Institute of Management revealed that women were not reaching the top jobs in industry. Media discussion has dismissed this as only the concern of whinging, middle-class women. We are told our real concern should be the worklessness of many of the men in contemporary Britain.

The year 1994 was the Year of the Family. As far as politicians and popular press were concerned, all problems could be laid at the door of single mothers. There is nothing new here, of course, as Diane Atkinson[3] showed in her paper on the sweated trades. A hundred years ago those campaigning against sweated labour were quick to condemn the women, often widowed or deserted, who involved their children in work. More often this aspect caused more concern than the nature of the work itself or the poverty which forced the women to take it up.

To summarise, in many ways it is more difficult for WHAM to achieve its objectives now than it was ten years ago.

THE FUTURE

The final discussion session of the 1994 conference threw up a number of different views on and approaches to the group's work. In particular, the negative image of the group in some quarters and its name and style were discussed in some depth. Some of the main points are summarised below:

1. **WHAM is bound to meet resistance – it is challenging real vested interests. A professional, active body is vital.**

2. **Women, Heritage and Museums has no ready-made audience. As women, we are not part of a homogeneous group. Black, White, middle-class, working-class, heterosexual or homosexual, married or single, mothers or child-free, it is a truism that different women have different perspectives.**

3. **At the AGM it was agreed to hold at least two high-profile meetings a year, with direct reference to members' work.**

4. WHAM members encompass a wide range of individuals and groups working with women's history. The organisation should encourage and provide the means for members to establish informal links, to share information and to offer support.

5. Links with other organisations, including those outside museums, should be strengthened, for example by the organisation of joint meetings.

6. Individual members and the group as a whole should find out what is going on in European museums. Awareness of current practice in European museums and the establishment of contacts should be an aim for the future.

To conclude with Rachel Hasted's words from her 1991 article discussing images of Black people in advertising and packaging between 1880 and 1990: '"Women", as a category, embraces a diversity of experience which requires infinite care to represent. Only equality of resources with those employed in representing the category "Men" will actually be sufficient to attempt it.'

So deploy whatever strategies suit you and your circumstances and get out there and fight for those resources!

ENDNOTES

1   Gaby Porter's description of the group during discussion at the Women in Industry and Technology Conference, Museum of London, 21 May 1994.

2   Description of the group in an article on WHAM in the *Yorkshire Post*, 10 April 1985.

3   Atkinson, D., (this volume).

APPENDICES

APPENDICES

LIST OF CONTRIBUTORS

Lindsay Allason-Jones is Archaeological Museums Officer at the University of Newcastle.

Dr. Diane Atkinson formerly worked at the Interpretation Unit, Museum of London and recently completed a PhD in the politics of female homework in Spitalfields, east London, 1880-1910.

Anita Ballin is Education Officer at the Imperial War Museum, London.

Margaret Brooks is Keeper of the Sound Archive at the Imperial War Museum, London.

Beverley Butler is Lecturer in Museum Theory at University College, London.

Taja Čepič is Senior Curator at Mestni Muzej (City Museum) Ljubljana, Slovenia.

Deborah Cherry is Director of 'Women First' in Preston.

Jill Cook is an Assistant Keeper in the Department of Prehistoric and Romano British Antiquities at the British Museum.

Nina Crummy is the Archaeological Archive Manager at the Museum of London.

Anna Davin is an Editor of *History Workshop Journal*, a Research Fellow at Middlesex University and teaches on the Women's History MA at Royal Holloway College, University of London.

Amanda Devonshire is Curator and Administrator at Chertsey Museum in Surrey.

Sharon Gater is Research Assistant at the Wedgwood Museum, Barlaston, Staffordshire.

Dr Jane Geddes is Lecturer in History of Art, University of Aberdeen.

Jane Hainsworth was formerly Public Relations Officer at the National Army Museum, Chelsea, London.

Vivienne Holgate is Keeper of Archaeology at Verulamium Museum, St Albans.

Dr Katrina Honeyman is Senior Lecturer in Economoics and Social History at the University of Leeds.

Eve Hostettler is Co-ordinator of the Island History Trust in London, Docklands.

Caroline Imlah is the Keeper of Costumes and Textiles, Tyne and Wear Museums, Newcastle.

Catherine Johns is an Assistant Keeper in the Department of Prehistoric and Romano British Antiquities at the British Museum.

Su Jones is Lecturer in Social Anthropology and Sociology at Fircroft College, Selly Oak in Birmingham, and a post-graduate student in the Cultural Studies Department, Birmingham University.

Dorothy Kidd is Ethnological Archive Curator at the National Museum of Scotland.

Sue Kirby is Curator of Welwyn Hatfield Museum Service at Mill Green Museum and Mill, Hatfield.

Nick Lane is an Assistant Curator at the Grange Museum of Community History in Neasden, London.

Stephanie Pinter-Bellows is an osteoarchaeologist.

Rosemary Preece is Curator and Visitor Services Manager at the National Coal Mining Museum for England.

Frances Pritchard is Curator of Textiles at the Whitworth Art Gallery, University of Manchester.

Dr Catherine Ross is Head of Department, Later London History and Collections at the Museum of London.

Dr Pamela Sharpe is a Lecturer in Social and Economic History in Department of Historical Studies, University of Bristol.

Judith Stevenson is an Assistant Curator in the Department of Early London History and Collections at the Museum of London.

Dr Marie-Louise Stig Sørensen is a University Lecturer in Archaeology at Cambridge University.

Andrea Taziker is a post-graduate research student at the University of Birmingham.

Rosemary Weinstein is Curator, Post-medieval Collections in the Department of Early London History and Collections, Museum of London.

Sue Werner is Education Officer at Forge Mill Needle Museum in Redditch.

Linda Wigley was formerly Curator at Trowbridge Museum, Wiltshire and is now Development Manager at the Bath Royal Literary and Scientific Institution.

Barbara Wood is an Assistant Curator in the Department of Early London History and Collections at the Museum of London.

GENERAL SOURCES FOR PART ONE

M. Anderson and K. Winkworth, 'Museum and Gender: An Australian Critique', *Museum*, 171, pp147-51, 1991.

T. Bennett, *The Birth of the Museum: History, Theory, Politics*, Routledge, London, 1995.

B. J. Butler, 'The Museum of Women's Art: Towards a Culture of Difference, in Art in Museums', S. M. Pearce, (ed.), *New Research in Museums*, vol. 5, Athlone Press, 1995.

Madalena Braz Texeira, 'From Strength to Strength: A Short History of Museums and Women in Portugal', *Museum*, 171, pp126-28, 1991.

M. S. Campbell, 'Beyond Individuals', *Museum News*, 69, pp37-40, July-August, 1990.

A. Cummings, 'The Role of Women in Caribbean Museum Development: Where are we Now?', *Museum*, 171, pp140-43, 1991.

E. des Portes and A. Raffin, 'Women in ICOM', *Museum*, 171, pp129-32, 1991.

T. Dublin, N. Grey Osterud and J. Parr (eds), 'Special Issue on Public History', *Gender and History*, 1994.

J. R. Glaser, 'The Impact of Women on Museums', *Museum*, 171, pp180-82, 1991.

J. R. Glaser and A. A. Zenetou, (eds) *Gender Perspectives: Essays on Women in Museums*, Smithsonian Institution Press, 1994.

A. Higonnet, 'A New Centre: The National Museum of Women in the Arts', in Sherman and Rogoff (eds), *Museum Culture*, Routledge, London, 1994.

D. Horne, *The Great Museum*, Pluto Press, 1984.

S. Jones, and S. Pay, 'The Legacy of Eve', in *The Politics of the Past*, P. Gatherole, and D. Lowenthal, (eds), Unwin Hyman, 1990.

S. Jones, *Presenting the Past: Towards a Feminist Critique of Museum Practice*, WHAM, 14, 1990.

S. Jones, 'The Female Perspective', *Museums Journal*, Feb., pp24-27, 1991.

G. Kavanagh. 'Objects as Evidence' in *History Curatorship*, Leicester University Press.

S. Kirby and J. Leggett, 'WHAM Weekend', *Museums Journal*, October, 1990.

L. Knowles, 'The Career Position of Women in Museums', *Museums Journal*, September, 1988.

J. Leggett, 'Women in Museums – Past, Present and Future', in *WHAM Conference Proceedings*, 1984.

P. Mainardi, 'Museums and Revisionism', *Australian Journal of Art*, 7, pp4-15, 1988.

E. P. Mayo, 'A New View?', *Museum News*, 69, July-August 1990.

B. Melosh and C. Simmons, 'Exhibiting Women's History' in *Presenting the Past: Essays on History and the Public*, S. Benson, S. Brier and Rosenweig (eds), 1986.

Museum, 171, Special Issue, Focus on Women, 1991.

Museum News, 69, Four-article anthology, 'Making a Difference: Women in Museums', July-August, 1990.

Museums Journal, Special Issue on Women and Museums, 1988.

S. M. Pearce (ed.), *Interpreting Objects and Collections: A Reader** (This reader has articles re. gendered collecting), Routledge, London, 1994.

G. Porter, 'Gender Bias: Representations of Work in History Museums', Proceedings of the Annual Study Weekend, 'Bias in Museums', A. Carruthers (ed.), in *Museum Professionals Transactions* 22, 1986.

G. Porter, 'Putting Your House in Order: Representations of women in domestic life', in *The Museum Time Machine*, R. Lumley (ed.), Reaktion Books, London, 1988.

G. Porter, 'How are women represented in British History Museums?', *Museums*, 171, pp159-62, 1991.

D. R. Prince, 'Women in Museums', *Museums Journal*, Sept., pp55-60, 1988.

Putnam Miller (ed.), *Reclaiming the Past: Landmarks in Women's History*, 1992.

I. Rogoff, *From Ruins to Debris: The Feminisation of Fascism in German History Museums*, 1994.

D. Sherman and I. Rogoff (eds), *Museum Culture*, Routledge, New York, 1994.

J. Sellers, 'Managing Museums with Women in Mind', *Feminist Arts News*, 3, p6, 1991.

Skjoth, 'Focus on Women', *Museum*, 171, 1991.

K. Sturtevant, *Feminist Walking Tours*, Chicago Review Press, 1990.

K. Taylor, 'Risking It: Women as Museum Leaders', *Museum News*, 63, Feb., pp20-32, 1985.

K. Taylor, 'To Create Credibility', *Museum News*, 69, July-August, pp41-42, 1985.

K. Taylor, 'Pioneering Efforts of Early Museum Women' in J. R. Glaser and A. A. Zenetou (eds), *Gender Perspectives: Essays on Women in Museums*, Smithsonian Insitution Press. Washington and London, pp11-27, 1994.

R. Tong, *Feminist Thought: A comprehensive introduction*, Routledge, London, 1989.

T. Trucco, 'Where are all the women museum directors?', *Art News*, 76, Feb., pp52-7, 1976.

M. Tucker, 'From Theory to Practice: Correcting Inequalities' in J. R. Glaser and A. A. Zenetou (eds), *Gender Perspectives: Essays on Women in Museums*, Smithsonian Insitution Press. Washington and London, pp51-54, 1994.

M. Tucker, 'Common Ground', *Museum News*, 69, July-August, pp44-6, 1990.

D. Tuminaro and A. Hawkings, 'You've Come A Long Way...', *Museum News*, 50, June, pp27-35, 1972.

P. Ullberg and J. H. Wos, 'The right preparation and the right attitude', *Museum News*, 63, Feb., pp33-36, 1985.

P. West, 'Gender Politics and the "Invention of Tradition": The Museumization of Louisa May Alcott's Orchard House', in *Gender and History*, Vol 6, No 3, Nov., T. Dublin, O. Grey, N. Sterud and J. Parr (eds), Oxford UK and Cambridge, USA, pp456-468, 1994.

S. Wilkinson et al, 'Soldering On', *Museums Journal*, November, pp22-8, 1991.

Women's Changing Roles in Museums, Conference Proceedings, E. Cochran-Hicks (ed.), 1986.

WORK PATTERNS

P. Blyton, *Changes in Work Time*, Crome Helm Publishing, London, 1985.

P. Hewitt, *About Time: The revolution in work and family life*, Rivers Orram Press, London, 1993.

P. Leighton and Syrett, *New Work Patterns: Putting Policy into Practice*, Pitman Publishing, London, 1989

WOMEN'S HISTORY/FEMINISM

C. Battersby, *Gender and Genius: Towards a Feminist Aesthetics*, Women's Press, London, 1989.

D. Beddoe, *Discovering Women's History: A Practical Manual*, Pandora, London, 1993.

H. Cixous, 'The Laugh of Medusa', in Elaine Marks and Isabelle de Courtivron (eds) *New French Feminisms*, pp245-264, Schoken Books, New York, 1981.

H. Cixous, 'Sorties', in Elaine Marks and Isabelle de Courtivron (eds), *New French Feminisms*, pp90-98, Schoken Books, New York, 1971.

S. de Beauvoir, *The Second Sex*, Penguin, Harmondsworth, 1972.

M. Daly, *Gyn/Ecology*, Beacon Press, Boston, 1978.

A. Davies, *Women, Race and Class*, Women's Press, London, 1981.

A. Dworkin, *Pornography*, Perigree Books, New York, 1981.

S. Firestone, *The Dialectic of Sex*, Bantam Books, New York, 1970.

B. Friedan, *The Feminine Mystique*, Penguin, Harmondsworth, 1982.

G. Greer, *The Female Eunoch*, Paladin, London, 1970.

S. Griffin, *Women and Nature*, Women's Press, London, 1978.

E. Grosz, *Sexual Subversions: Three French Feminists*, 1989.

D. Haraway, *Primate Visions: Gender, Race, and Nature in the World of Modern Science*, Routledge, New York, 1989.

D. Haraway, *Simians, Cyborgs, and Women: The Re-invention of Nature*, Routledge, New York, 1991.

L. Irigaray, *Speculum of the Other Woman*, trans., Gillian C. Gill, Cornell University Press, New York, 1985.

L. Irigaray, *Je, Tous, Nous: Toward a Culture of Difference*, Trans., Alison Martin, Cornell University Press, New York, 1993.

J. Kristeva, 'Woman's Time', *Signs: Journal of Women in Culture and Society*: 7(1), pp13-35, 1981.

G. Lerner, *The Majority Finds its Past*, New York, 1979.

A. Lorde, 'An Open Letter to Mary Daley', in Cherrie Moraga and Gloria Anzaldua (eds), *This Bridge Called My Back: Writings of Radical Women of Color*, Persephone Press, Watertown, Mass, 1979.

C. MacKinnon, *Feminism, Marxism, Method and State*, 1982.

K. Millet, *Sexual Politics*, Virago, London, 1970.

J. Mitchell, *Women: The Longest Revolution*, MacMillan, London, 1966.

L. Mulvey, *Visual Pleasure and Narrative Cinema*, 1975.

S. Ortner, 'Is female to male as nature is to culture?', in *Woman, Culture and Society*, M. Rosaldo and L. Lamphere (eds), pp67-87, Stamford University Press, Stamford, 1974.

C. Paglia, *Sexual Personae: Art and Decadence from Nefertiti to Emily Dickenson*, 1990.

S. Rowbotham, *Woman's Consciousness Man's World*, Penguin, London, 1973.

S. Rowbotham, *Search and Subject, Threading Circumstance*, Penguin, London, 1974.

D. Spender, *Women of Ideas and What Men Have Done to Them: From Aphra Behn to Adrienne Rich*, Routledge, London, 1982.

R. Tong, *Feminist Thought: A Comprehensive Introduction*, Routledge, London, 1989.

A. Walker, *In Search of Our Mother's Gardens*, 1983.

N. Wolf, *The Beauty Myth*, Vintage Press, London, 1990.

N. Wolf, *Fire With Fire*, Vintage Press, London, 1993.

V. Woolf, *A Room of One's Own and Three Guineas*, (ed.) and intro. Morag Shiach, Oxford University Press, 1992.

V. Woolf, *A Woman's Essay*, (ed.) Rachel Bowlby, Penguin, London, 1993.

M. Yamada, *Asian Pacific Women and Feminism*, Routledge, New York, 1981.

BIBLIOGRAPHY FOR PART TWO

Part Two CHAPTER 1

Women in Prehistory

J-F. Alaux, 'Gravure féminine sur plaquette calcaire du Magdalénien supérieur de la grotte de Courbet' (commune de Penne-Tarn), *Bulletin de la Société Préhistorique Française*, 69, pp109-112, 1972.

K. Arnold, R. Gilchrist, P. Graves and S. Taylor, 'Women and Archaeology', in *Archaeology Review from Cambridge*, vol. 7.1, 'Women in Archaeology', Spring 1988, pp2-8, 1988.

N. M. Ashton, J Cook, S. G. Lewis and J. Rose, *High Lodge. Excavations by G. de G. Sieveking 1962-68 and J. Cook, 1988*. British Museum Press, London, 1992.

K. A. Behrensmeyer, 'Taphonomy and hunting' in M. H. Nitecki and D. V. Nitecki (eds), *The Evolution of Human Hunting*, pp423-50, Plenum Press, New York, 1987.

T. Bennet, *The Birth of the Museum: History, Theory, Politics*, Routledge, London, 1995.

L. R. Binford, *Bones: Ancient Men and Modern Myths*, Academic Press, New York, 1981.

L. R. Binford, 'Human ancestors: changing views of their behavior', *Journal of Anthropological Archaeology*, 4, pp292-327, 1985.

L. R. Binford, 'Elephant hunters at Torralba' in M. H. Nitecki and D. V. Nitecki, *The Evolution of Human Hunting*, pp47-105, Plenum Press, New York, 1987.

B. Bodenhorn, 'Gendered Spaces, Public Places: Public and Private Revisited on the North Slope of Alaska', in *Landscapes, Politics and Perspective*, Barbara Bender (ed.), Berg Publishers, Oxford, 1993.

J. A. Brown, *Palaeolithic Man in Northwest Middlesex*, Macmillan & Co., London, 1887.

J. Brown, 'A Note on the Division of Labour by Sex', *American Anthropologist*, 72, pp1073-78, 1970.

H. T. Bunn, 'Archaeological evidence for meat-eating by Plio-Leistocene hominids from Koobi-Fora and Olduvai Gorge', *Nature*, 291, pp574-77, 1981.

H. T. Bunn, 'Patterns of skeletal representation and hominid subsistence activities at Olduvai Gorge, Tanzania, and Koobi-Fora, Kenya', *Journal of Human Evolution*, 15, pp673-90, 1986.

H. T. Bunn and E. M. Kroll, 'Systematic butchery by Plio-Pleistocene hominids at Olduvai Gorge, Tanzania', *Current Anthropology*, 27, pp431-52, 1986.

H. T. Bunn, J. W. K. Harris, G. L. Isaac, Z. Kaufula, E. M. Kroll, K. Schick, N. Toth and A. K. Behrensmeyer, 'FxJj50: an early Pleistocene site in northern Kenya', *World Archaeology*, 12, pp109-36, 1980.

V. G. Childe, *Prehistoric Communities of the British Isles*, W. and R. Chambers, London, 1940.

D. V. Clarke, T. G. Cowie and F. Foxon, *Symbols of Power at the Time of Stonehenge*, National Museum of Antiquities of Scotland, Edinburgh, HMSO, 1985.

B. and J. Coles, *Sweet Track to Glastonbury. The Somerset Levels in Prehistory*, Thames & Hudson Ltd, London, 1986.

M. W. Conkey, 'Contexts of action, contexts for power: Material culture and gender in the Magdalenian' in *Engendering Archaeology: Women and Prehistory*, J. M. Gero and M. W. Conkey (eds), pp 57-92, Basil Blackwell, Oxford, 1991.

M. W. Conkey and J. Spector, 'Archaeology and the Study of Gender', in *Advances in Archaeological Method and Theory*, M. B. Schiffer (ed.), vol. 7, 1984.

J. Cook and N. M. Ashton, 'High Lodge, Mildenhall', *Current Archaeology*, 123, pp133-138, 1991.

J. Cook and A-C. Welté, '*A newly discovered female engraving from Courbet*' (Penne-Tarn), France, *Proceedings of the Prehistoric Society*, 58, pp29-35, 1992.

J. Cook and A-C. Welté, 'La grotte du Courbet' (Tarn): sa contribution dans l'histoire de l'homme fossile et de l'art paléolithique, *Bulletin de la Société Préhistorique Ariège-Pyrénées*. In press.

J. Cotton, 'Illuminating the Twilight Zone? Displaying prehistory at the Museum of London', Proceedings from the Society of Museum Archaeologists Conference, London, *Representing Archaeology in Museums* (forthcoming), 1995.

J. Cotton and B. Wood, *Retrieving Prehistories at the Museum of London: A gallery case study* in *Public Audiences and Archaeological Displays*, Paulette McManus (ed.), UCL,

Institute of Archaeology occasional paper, (forthcoming).

H. Coxall, 'Museum Text as Mediated Message', *WHAM! Women Heritage and Museums Newsletter*, No. 14, pp15-21, October 1990.

B. Cunliffe, *Iron Age Communities in Britain*, Routledge & Kegan Paul, London, Henley and Boston, 1994.

B. Cunliffe, *The Oxford Illustrated Prehistory of Europe*, BCA by arrangement with Oxford University Press, Oxford, 1994.

F. Dahlberg, *Woman the Gatherer*, Yale University Press, New Haven and London, 1981.

P. Darasse and **S. Guffroy**, 'Le Magdalénien supérieur de l'abri de Fontalès près Saint-Antonin' (Tarn-et-Garonne), *L'Anthropologie*, 64, pp1-35, 1960.

T. Darvill, *Prehistoric Britain*, B. T. Batsford, Ltd, London, 1987.

R. Dawkins, *The Selfish Gene*, Oxford University Press, Oxford, 1976.

P. de L'Isle, 'Sur les fouilles faites dans un gisement ossifère de l'Age du Renne à Bruniquel' (Tarn-et-Garonne), *Compte rendu des séances hebdomadaires de l'Académie des Sciences de Paris*, 64, pp628-29, 1867.

H. Delporte, *L'Image de la Femme dans l'Art Préhistorique*, Picard, Paris, 1993.

M-A. Dobres, 'Feminist Archaeology and Inquiries into gender relations: some thoughts on universals, origin stories and alternating paradigms', in *Archaeological Review from Cambridge*, vol. 7.1, 'Women in Archaeology', pp31-44, Spring 1988.

J-P. Duhard, 'The shape of Pleistocene Women'. *Antiquity*, 65, pp552-61, 1991.

M. Ehrenberg, *Women in Prehistory*, British Museum Press, London, 1989.

E. Fee, 'Is feminism a threat to scientific objectivity?' *International Journal of Women's Studies*, 4, pp378-92, 1981.

C. Gamble, *Time Walkers: The prehistory of global colonisation*, Harmondsworth, Penguin, 1993.

E. Gamble, *The Evolution of Woman*, The Knickerbocker Press (G. P. Putnam Sons), New York and London, 1894.

P. Gathercole, 'Introduction', in *The Politics of the Past*, P. Gathercole and D. Lowenthal (eds), Unwin Hyman, London, 1990.

J. M. Gero, 'Socio-Politics of Archaeology and the

Woman-at-home Ideology' in *American Antiquity*, vol. 50, pp342-50, 1985.

J. M. Gero, 'Genderlithics: women's roles in stone tool production' in J. M. Gero and M. W. Conkey (eds), *Engendering Archaeology*, pp3-30, B. Blackwell Ltd, Oxford, 1991.

J. M. Gero and M. W. Conkey, 'Tensions and pluralities' in J. M. Gero and M. W. Conkey (eds), *Engendering Archaeology*, pp163-93, B. Blackwell Ltd, Oxford, 1991.

J. M. Gero and M. W. Conkey, *Engendering Archeology: Women and Prehistory*. Blackwell Ltd, Oxford, 1991.

K. Gough, 'The origin of the family' in R. A. Reiter (ed.), *Towards an Anthropology of Women*, pp51-76, Monthly Review Press, New York and London, 1975.

S. Green and E. Walker, *Early Modern Hunters in Wales*, National Museum of Wales, 1991.

M. Gross and M. B. Averill, 'Evolution and patriarchal myths of scarcity and competition', in S. Harding and M. B. Hintikka (eds), *Discovering Reality*, pp71-95, D. Reidel, London, 1983.

M. Hall, 'Potteries Pot-holes', *Museums Journal*, vol. 94, no. 3, p22, 1994.

M. Hall, 'A Rewarding Display', *Museums Journal*, vol. 94, no.10, pp18-19, October 1994.

S. Harding, *The Science Question in Feminism*, Open University Press, Milton Keynes, 1986.

I. Hodder, *The Present Past. An Introduction to Anthropology for Archaeologists*, B. T. Batsford Ltd, London, 1982.

B. Hubbard, 'Have only men evolved?' in S. Harding and M. B. Hintikka (eds), *Discovering Reality*, pp45-69, D. Reidel, London, 1983.

L. Hurcombe, 'Our own engendered species', *Antiquity*, vol. 69, no. 262, March 1995.

G. L. Isaac, 'The activities of early African hominids' in G. L. Isaac and G. McCown (eds), *Human Origins* pp483-514, W. A. Benjamin, Menlo Park, California, 1976.

G. L. Isaac, *Olorgesailie*, University of Chicago Press, Chicago, 1977.

S. James, *Exploring the World of the Celts*, Thames & Hudson Ltd, London, 1993.

S. James, 'Drawing Inferences; visual reconstructions in theory and practice', in *The Archaeology of Visual Representation*, Clive Gamble and Brian Molyneaux, Routledge, (forthcoming).

L. L. Johnson, 'A history of flint knapping experimentation 1838-1976', *Current Anthropology*, 19, 2, pp337-72, 1978.

S. Jones, 'Presenting the Past: towards a feminist critique of museums practice', *WHAM! Women Heritage and Museums Newsletter*, no. 14, pp22-7, October 1990.

S. Jones and S. Pay, 'The Legacy of Eve', in *The Politics of the Past*, P. Gathercole and D. Lowenthal (eds), Unwin Hyman, London, 1990.

V. Kanel and P. Tamir, 'Different Labels – Different Learnings', *Curator*, 34/1, 1991.

C. Knight, *Blood Relations, Menstruation and the Origins of Culture*, Yale University Press, New Haven and London, 1991.

A. Kuper, *The Chosen Primate. Human Nature and Cultural Diversity*, Harvard University Press, Cambridge, Massachusetts and London, 1994.

E. Ladier, 'La Vénus du Courbet', *L'Anthropologie*, 96, 2-3, pp349-56, 1988.

E. Ladier and A-C. Welté, *Bijoux de la Préhistoire. La Parure magdalénienne dans la vallée de l'Aveyron*, Accord, Toulouse, 1994.

M. Landau, *Narratives of Human Evolution*, Yale University Press, New Haven and London, 1991.

J. Lautier and J. Bessac, 'La Grotte de la Magdeleine des Albis à Penne' (Tarn), *Travaux et Recherches*, 13, pp75-86, 1976.

M. D. Leakey, *Olduvai Gorge volume 3: Excavations in Beds I and II, 1960-63*, Cambridge University Press, Cambridge, 1971.

M. D. Leakey and R. L. Hay, 'Pliocene footprints in the Laetolil Beds at Laetolil, northern Tanzania', *Nature*, 278, pp317-23, 1979.

M. D. Leakey and R. E. F. Leakey (eds), *The Fossil Hominids and their Context, 1968-78*, Koobi-Fora Research Project I, Clarendon Press, Oxford, 1978.

M. P. Leone, 'Method as Message: Interpreting the Past with the Public', *Museum News*, vol. 62, no. 1, pp35-41, October 1983.

A. Leroi-Gourhan and M. Brèzillon, *Fouilles de Pincevent: essai d'analyse ethnographique magdalénien*. 2 vols. CNRS, Paris. (Gallia Préhistoire supplément 7), 1972.

H. Longino and H. Doell, 'Body, bias and behaviour: a comparative analysis of reasoning in two areas of biological science, *Signs*, 9, 2, pp206-27, 1983.

I. Longworth and J. Cherry, (eds), *Archaeology in Britain since 1945*, British Museum Press, London, 1986.

D. Lowenthal, 'Bias: Making the most of an incurable

malady', in *Bias in Museums*, 'Museums Professionals Group Transactions', Annette Carruthers (ed.), no. 22, 1987.

D. Mania and T. Weber, *Bilzingsleben III, Homo erectus - seine Kultur und Umwelt*, VEB Deutscher Verlag der Wissenschaften, Berlin, 1986.

J. V. S. Megaw and D. D. A. Simpson, *Introduction to British Prehistory*, Leicester University Press, Leicester, 1981.

N. Merriman, *Prehistoric London*, Museum of London, HMSO, London, 1990.

N. Merriman, *Beyond the Glass Case, The Past, The Heritage and The Public in Britain*, Leicester University Press, Leicester, 1991.

A. Morrison, *Early Man in Britain and Ireland*, Croom Helm, London, 1980.

Museums Journal, 'Openings' p22, *Museums Journal*, February 1994.

S. P. Needham and M. L. S. Sørensen, 'Runnymede Refuse Tip: A Consideration of Midden Deposits and their formation', in *The Archaeology of Context in the Neolithic and Bronze Age*. J. C. Barrett and I. A. Kinnes (eds), University of Sheffield, Sheffield, 1988.

L. Nixon, 'Gender bias in archaeology' in L. J. Archer, S. Fischler & M. Wyke (eds), *Women in Ancient Societies* pp1-23, The Macmillan Press Ltd, Basingstoke, 1994.

K. P. Oakley (sixth edn. 1972), *Man the Toolmaker*, British Museum (Natural History), London, 1949.

K. P. Oakley, 'Tools makyth Man', *Antiquity*, 31, pp199-209, 1957.

R. Owen, 'Description of the cavern of Bruniquel and its organic contents', *Philosophical Transactions of the Royal Society*, pp159, 517-33, 535-57, 1869.

S. Pearce, *The Bronze Age metalwork of South Western Britain*, British Archaeological Reports, Oxford, 1983.

S. Pearce, *Archaeological Curatorship*, Leicester University Press, Leicester, 1990.

J. Pfeiffer, *The Emergence of Man*, Harper and Row, New York, 1978.

R. Potts, *Early Hominid Activities at Olduvai*, Aldine de Gruyter, New York, 1988.

D. Prince and R. T. Schadler-Hall, 'The Image of the Museum: a case study of Kingston upon Hull', *Museums Journal*, 85 (2), pp39-45, 1985.

P. C. Rice, 'Prehistoric Venuses: symbols of motherhood or womanhood?' *Journal of Anthropological Research*, pp102-14, 1980.

M. B. Roberts, *Excavation of the Lower Palaeolithic site at Amey's Eartham Pit, Boxgrove, West Sussex: a preliminary report*, Proceedings of the Prehistoric Society, 52, pp215-45, 1986.

D. A. Roe, 'Precise moments in remote time', *World Archaeology*, 12, pp107-08, 1980.

W. Roebroeks and T. Van Kolfschoten, 'The earliest occupation of Europe: a short chronology', *Antiquity*, 68, pp489-503, 1994.

M. Rowlands, 'The archaeological interpretation of prehistoric metalworking', *World Archaeology*, vol 3, pp210-24, 1971.

K. D. Schick and N. Toth, *Making Silent Stones Speak*, Simon and Schuster, New York, 1993.

A. Sieveking, *A Catalogue of Paleolithic Art in the British Museum*, British Museum Press, London, 1987.

D. Shanks and C. Tilley (eds), *Ideology, Power and Prehistory*, Cambridge University Press, Cambridge, 1984.

N. Shoemaker, 'The Natural History of Gender', in *Gender and History*, vol. 6, no. 3, pp320-33, November 1994.

S. Slocum, 'Woman the Gatherer: male bias in anthropology' in R. A. Reiter (ed.), *Towards an Anthropology of Women*, pp37-50, Monthly Review Press, New York and London, 1975

W. G. Smith, *Man the Primeval Savage*, Edward Stanford, London, 1894.

J. D. Spector, 'What this awl means: towards a feminist archaeology' in J. M. Gero and M. W. Conkey (eds), *Engendering Archaeology*, pp388-406, B. Blackwell Ltd, Oxford, 1991.

N. Stern, 'The structure of the Lower Pleistocene archaeological record, A case study from the KoobiFora Formation', *Current Anthropology*, 34, 3, pp201-25, 1993.

M. L. Stig Sørensen, 'Is there a Feminist Contribution to Archaeology?', in *Archaeological Review from Cambridge*, vol. 7.1, *Women in Archaeology*, pp9-20, Spring 1988.

J. Stonehouse, *Idols to Incubators, Reproduction theory through the ages*, Scarlet Press, London, 1994.

C. Stringer and C. Gamble, *In Search of the Neanderthal, Solving the Puzzle of Human Origins*, Thames & Hudson Ltd, London, 1994.

N. Tanner and A. Zihlman, 'Women in evolution. Part 1: innovation and selection in human origins', *Signs*, 1, 3, pp104-19, 1976.

R. Tong, *Feminist Thought: A Comprehensive Introduction*, Routledge, London, 1994.

E. Trinkhaus, 'Bodies, brawn, brains and noses: human ancestors and human predation', in M. H. Nitecki and D. V. Nitecki (ed.), *The Evolution of Human Hunting*, pp107-45, Plenum Press, New York and London, 1987.

Tucker, in J. R. Glaser & Zeneton, (eds), *Gender Perspectives: Essays on Woman in Museums*, p51, Smithsonian Institue Press, Washington and London, 1991.

M. Twain, *Extracts from Adam's Diary*. Harper and Brothers, p109, New York and London, 1904.

M. Twain, *Extracts from Eve's Diary*. Harper and Brothers, New York and London, 1906.

P. Vergo, 'The Reticent Object', in *The New Museology*, Peter Vergo (ed.), Reaktion Books Ltd, London, 1989.

K. Walsh, *The Representation of the Past. Museums and heritage in the post-modern world*, Routledge, London and New York, 1992.

S. L. Washburn, 'Tools and human evolution', *Scientific American*, pp104-19, 203, 1960.

S. L. Washburn and C. S. Lancaster, 'The evolution of hunting' in R. B. Lee and I. DeVore (eds), *Man the Hunter*, pp293-303, Aldine Publishing Co, Chicago, 1968.

P. West, 'Gender Politics and the "Invention of Tradition": The Museumization of Louisa May Alcott's Orchard House', in *Gender and History*, Vol. 6, No. 3, pp456-68, T. Dublin, O. Grey, N. Sterud and J. Parr (eds), Oxford UK and Cambridge USA, November 1994.

P. E. Wheeler, 'The thermoregulatory advantages of large body size for hominids foraging in savannal environments', *Journal of Human Evolution*, 23, 4, pp351-62, 1992a.

P. E. Wheeler, 'The influence of the loss of functional body hair on the water budgets of early hominids', *Journal of Human Evolution*, 23, 5, pp379-88, 1992b.

P. E. Wheeler, 'The thermoregulatory advantages of heat storage and shade-seeking behaviour to hominids foraging in equatorial savannal environments', *Journal of Human Evolution*, 26, 6, pp339-50, 1994.

V. Woolf, *A Room of One's Own and Three Guineas*, (ed.), and intro Morag Shiach, Oxford University Press, 1992.

J. Wymer, *The Palaeolithic Age*, Croom Helm, London, 1982.

A. Zihlman, 'Women in evolution. Part 2: Subsistence and social organisation among early hominids', *Signs*, 4, 1, pp4-20, 1978.

A. Zihlman, 'Women as shapers of the human adaptation' in F. Dahlberg (ed.), *Woman the Gatherer*, pp75-120, Yale University Press, New Haven and London, 1981.

UNPUBLISHED WORK

Unpublished visitor research, Museum of London, 1992.

USEFUL GENERAL SOURCES

Series under general editorship of Dr Stephen Johnson at **English Heritage**, produced jointly by B. T. Batsford Ltd and English Heritage, London. Many relevant titles include the following:

Parker Pearson, 1993 Michael Parker Pearson, *Bronze Age Britain*.

Malone, 1989 Caroline Malone, *Avebury*.

Pryor, 1991 Francis Pryor, *Flag Fenn: Prehistoric Fenland Centre*.

Bewley, 1994 Robert Bewley, *Prehistoric Settlements*.

Shire Archaeology Series, Published by Shire Publications Ltd, Aylesbury, Bucks.

Includes general period booklets, such as:

Wymer, 1991 John Wymer, *Mesolithic Britain*.

Site type booklets, such as:

Holgate, 1991 Robin Holgate, *Prehistoric Flint Mines*.

and object based booklets, such as:

Gibson, 1986 Alex Gibson, *Neolithic and Early Bronze Age Pottery*.

MUSEUMS WITH RECENT DISPLAYS

Brighton Museum, Chelmsford Museum, Castle Museum, Colchester, Hull and East Riding Museum, Museum of the Iron Age, Andover. Museum of London. Red House Museum, Christchurch. Tolson Memorial Museum, Huddersfield. Tullie House Museum, Carlisle.

Part Two CHAPTER 2

Fragmentary Evidence from Roman Britain

L. Allason-Jones, *Women in Roman Britain*, British Museum Publications, London, 1989.

L. Allason-Jones, 'Roman and native interaction in Northumberland' in *Roman Frontier Studies 1989*, Valerie A. Maxfield and Michael J. Dobson (eds), Exeter University Press, Exeter, 1991.

L. Allason-Jones and R. Miket, *The Catalogue of Small Finds from South Shields Roman Fort*, Society of Antiquaries of Newcastle upon Tyne, 1984.

K. Ambrosiani, 'Viking Age combs, combmaking and combmakers', *Stockholm Studies in Archaeology*, 2, 1981.

E. Birley, J. Charlton and P. Hedley, 'Excavations at Housesteads in 1932' in *Archaeologia Aeliana*, 4th series, vol. 10, pp82-96, 1933.

A. K. Bowman, *Life and Letters on the Roman Frontier: Vindolanda and its people*, British Museum Publications, London, 1994.

K. Bradley, 'Child labour in the Roman world' in *Historical Reflections*, vol. 7, pp311-30, 1985.

R. G. Collingwood and R. P. Wright, *The Roman Inscriptions of Britain*, Clarendon Press, Oxford, 1965.

N. Crummy, 'Bone-working at Colchester', in *Britannia*, 12, pp277-85, 1981.

N. Crummy, 'The Roman small finds from excavations in Colchester 1971-9', *Colchester Archaeological Report*, 2, Colchester Archaeological Trust Ltd, Colchester, 1983.

N. Crummy, 'The Roman small finds from the Culver Street site', in *Excavations at Culver Street, the Gilberd School, and other sites in Colchester 1971-85*, by Philip Crummy, *Colchester Archaeological Report*, 6, Colchester Archaeological Trust Ltd, Colchester, 1992a.

N. Crummy, 'The Roman small finds from the Gilberd School site', in *Excavations at Culver Street, the Gilberd School, and other sites in Colchester 1971-85*, by Philip Crummy, *Colchester Archaeological Report*, 6, Colchester Archaeological Trust Ltd, Colchester, 1992b.

N. Crummy et al, *Small finds from the suburbs and city defences*, Winchester City Museums, publication 6, forthcoming.

B. Cunliffe, *The Temple of Sulis Minerva at Bath , The Finds from the Sacred Spring*, vol. 2, Oxford University Committee for Archaeology, Oxford, 1988.

M. d'Avino, *The Women of Pompeii*, Loffredo, Naples, 1967.

E. Diehl, *Inscriptiones Latinae Christianae Veteres*, Berlin, 1925-31.

W. Drack and R. Fellmann, *Die Römer in der Schweiz*, Konrad Theiss, Stuttgart, 1988.

C. Espérandieu, 1911, *Recueil Général des Bas-Reliefs, Statues et Bustes de la Gaule Romaine* (10 vols), republished Gregg Press Incorporated, New Jersey, 1965.

H. R. Fairclough trs., Horace Satires, Loeb, London, 1978.

J. G. Frazer trs., Ovid Fasti, Loeb, London, 1931.

S. S. Frere, *Verulamium Excavations 1*, Reports of the Research Committee of the Society of Antiquaries of London, no. 28, 1972.

P. Galloway and M. Newcomer, 'The craft of comb-making: an experimental enquiry', in *Bulletin* (Institute of Archaeology), 18, pp73-90, 1981.

C. J. Going, 'The Mansio and other sites in the south-eastern sector of Caesaromagus: the Roman pottery', *Chelmsford Archaeological Trust Report*, 3.2, *CBA Research Report*, 62, the Council for British Archaeology, London, 1987.

R. Graves trs., Suetonius, *The Twelve Caesars*, Penguin, London, 1957.

S. Greep, 'A model sword from Bucklersbury House, London', in *Transactions of the London and Middlesex Archaeological Society*, 32, pp103-6, 1981.

A. Huebner, *Corpus Inscriptionum Latinarum*, Berlin, 1863.

M. Hutton and E. H. Warmington trs., Tacitus Germania, Loeb, London, 1970.

Juvenal, *The Sixteen Satires*, translated by Peter Green, Penguin Books, Harmondsworth, 1967.

W. C. A. Ker trs., Martial Epigrams, Loeb, London, 1919.

P. Krueger and A. Watson (eds), T. Mommsen, 1817-1903 trs., *The Digest of Justinian*, Philadelphia, 1985.

J. Liversidge, *Britain in the Roman Empire*, Sphere Books Ltd, London, 1973.

D. Magie trs., *Scriptores Historiae Augustae*, Loeb, London, 1922.

Martial, *Epigrams*, translated by James Michie, Penguin Books, Harmondsworth, 1972.

A. McWhirr, L. Viner and C. Wells, *Romano-British Cemeteries at Cirencester*, Cirencester Excavation Committee, Cirencester, 1982.

J. H. Mozley trs., Ovid *Ars Amatoria*, Loeb, London, 1969.

R. Niblett, *Roman Hertfordshire*, The Dovecote Press Ltd, Stanbridge, Wimbourne, Dorest, 1995.

P. Nixon trs., Plautus *Mostellaria III*, Loeb, London, 1924.

D. P. S. Peacock, *Pottery in the Roman World: an Ethnoarchaeological Approach*, Longman, Harlow, 1982.

A. Pitt-Rivers, *Excavations in Cranborne Chase*, 1, 1887.

G. G. Ramsey trs., Juvenal *Satires*, Loeb, London, 1979.

E. Schmid, 'Beindrechsler, Hornschnitzer und Leimsieder im römischen Augst', in *Provincialia*, Festschrift für Rudolf Laur-Belart, 1968.

Tacitus *Annals*, translated by Michael Grant, Penguin Books, Harmondsworth, 1971.

O. Temkin trs., Soranus *Gynaecology*, Baltimore, 1956.

J. M. C. Toynbee, *Art in Roman Britain*, Phaidon, London, 1962.

S. Treggiari, 'Jobs for Women' in *American Journal of Ancient History*, vol. 1, 2, pp76-104, 1976.

C. Van Driel Murray, 'Gender in Question' in *Theoretical Roman Archaeology: Second Conference proceedings*. P. Rush, (ed.), Worldwide Archaeology Aldershot, 1995.

L. P. Wenham, *The Romano-British Cemetery at Trentholme Drive*, York, HMSO, London, 1968.

J. P. Wild, 'The Textiles from Verulamium', in *Excavations in Verulam Hills Field, St Albans*, I. E. Anthony, Hertfordshire Archaeology vol. 1, 1968, pp9-50, 1968.

J. A. Zienkiewicz, *The Legionary Fortress Baths at Caerleon*, II The Finds, Cadw: Welsh Historic Monuments, Cardiff, 1986.

Part Two CHAPTER 3

Apprentices, Wives and Widows

A. Abram, 'Women Traders in Medieval London', *Economic Journal*, 26, pp276-85, 1916.

E. Amt, (ed.), *Women's Lives in Medieval Europe: a sourcebook*, Routledge, 1993.

B. S. Anderson and J. P. Zinsser, *A History of their own. Women in Europe from Prehistory to the Present*', Vol. I. Penguin, 1988.

J. A. D. Anderson, 'Arthrosis and its Relation to Work', *Scandinavian Journal of Work Health*, 10, pp429-33, 1984.

J. Lawrence Angel et al, 'Life Stresses of the Free Black Community as Represented by the First African Baptist Church, Philadelphia, 1823-1841', *American Journal of Physical Anthropology*, 74, pp213-29, 1987.

D. Baker, (ed.), *Medieval Women*, Blackwell, 1978.

C. B. Barron, 'The "Golden Age" of Women in Medieval London', in *Medieval Women in Southern England*, Reading Medieval Studies, 25, pp35-58, 1989.

C. B. Barron, 'Introduction to: The widows World in Later Medieval London', in C. B. Barron and A. F. Sutton (eds), *Medieval London Widows 1300-1500*, Hambledon Press, London and Rio Grande. pxiii-xxxiv, 1994a.

C. B. Barron, 'Johanna Hill (d. 1441) and Johanna Sturdy (d.c. 1480), bell-founders' in C. B. Barron and A. F. Sutton (eds), *Medievel London Widows*, 1300-1500. Hambledon Press, pp.99-112, 1994b.

C. B. Barron and A. F. Sutton, (eds), *Medieval London Widows 1300-1500*, Hambledon Press, London and Rio Grande, 1994.

I. K. Ben-Amos, 'Women Apprentices in the Trades and Crafts of Early Modern Bristol', *Continuity and Change*, 6, 1991.

J. Bennett, 'The Village Ale-Wife: Women and Brewing in 14th Century England', in Barbara Hanawalt (ed.), *Women and Work in Pre-Industrial Europe*, Bloomington, Indiana University Press, 1986.

J. Bennett, 'Medievalism and Feminism', *Speculum*, 68, 1993.

H. S. Bennett, *The Pastons and their England. Studies in an Age of Transition*, Cambridge University, 1968.

J. M. Bennett, *Women in the Medieval English Countryside. Gender and Household in Brigstock before the Plague*, Oxford University Press, New York, 1987.

J. M. Bennett, 'History that stands still: women's work in the European past', *Feminist Studies*, 14, 1988.

J. M. Bennett, 'Medieval Women, Modern Women: Across the Great Divide', in David Aers (ed.), *Culture and History 1350-1600: Essays on English Communities, Identities and Writing*, Harvester Wheatsheaf, London, 1992.

M. Berg, 1985 *The Age of Manufactures 1700-1820. Industry, Innovation and Work in Britain*, 1985, 2nd Edition, Routledge, London, 1994.

M. Berg, 'Technological and organisational change during the industrial revolution: new questions', unpublished contribution to *Towards a new history of* *industrialisation in Britain*, a session organised by the Women's Committee of the Economic History Society for the Society's Annual Conference, University of Nottingham, 8-10 April, 1994.

M. **Berg**, 'What difference did women's work make to the Industrial Revolution?', *History Workshop Journal*, 35, 1993.

M. **Berg**, 'Women's work and the Industrial Revolution', *Refresh*, 12, 1991.

M. **Berg**, 'Women's work, mechanisation and the early phase of industrialisation in England' in *On Work, Historical, Comparative and Theoretical Approaches*, R. E. Pahl (ed.), Blackwell, Oxford, 1988.

H. **Bird**, 'When the body takes the strain', *New Scientist*, pp49-52, 7 July, 1990.

J. **Boulton**, 'London widowhood revisited: the decline of female remarriage in the seventeenth and early eighteenth centuries', *Community and Change*, 3, 1990.

P. S. **Bridges**, 'Changes in activities with the shift to agriculture in the southeastern United States', *Current Anthropology*, 30, pp385-94, 1989.

C. **Brooke**, *The Medieval Idea of Marriage*, Oxford University Press, 1989.

M. **Budny and D. Tweddle**, 'The Maaseik embroideries', *Anglo-Saxon England*, 13, pp65-96, 1984.

S. **Cahn**, *Industry of Devotion. The Transformation of Women's Work in England, 1500-1660*, Columbia University Press, New York, 1987.

L. **Charles and L. Duffin**, (eds), *Women and Work in Pre-Industrial England*, London, 1985.

A. **Clark**, *Working Life of Women in the Seventeenth Century*, (listed 1919), reprinted Routledge and Keegan Paul, London, Boston, 1982.

H. **Cleere and D. Crosley**, *The Iron Industry of the Weald*, Leicester, 1985.

G. **Cohen**, *Le Théâtre en France au Moyen Age*, vol. I, pl. 33, Paris. The manuscript is Arras Bib. MS 675, 1928.

M. N. **Cohen,** *Health and the Rise of Civilization*, Yale University Press, New Haven, Connecticut, 1989.

H. **Colvin**, (ed.), *The King's Works*, vol.1, pp222-4, HMSO, London, 1963.

H. C. **Coote and J. R. D. Tyssen**, *Ordinances of Some Secular Guilds in London*, Trans. London and Middlesex Archaeological Society, IV, pp32-5, 1871.

P. J. **Corfield and D. Keene**, *Work in Towns 850-1850*, Leicester University Press, Leicester, 1990.

H. H. **Cotterell**, *Old Pewter, its Makers and Marks*, Batsford, London, 1929.

T. **Cox**, *Jehan Fouquet*, p. xxiv, 71, 1931.

M. K. **Dale**, *Women in the Textile Industries and Trade of Fifteenth Century England*, MA Thesis, University of London, 1928.

M. K. **Dale**, 'The London Silkwomen of the Fifteenth Century', *Economic History Review*, 1st series vol. 4, pp324-335, 1932-34.

A. **Dasnoy**, 'Henri Bles' in *Etudes d'Histoire et d'Archaeologie Namuroises, dédiées a Ferdinand Courtoy*, vol. II, pp619-26, 1952.

J. **de Vries**, 'Between purchasing power and the world of goods: understanding the household economy in early modern Europe', in *Consumption and the World of Goods*, John Brewer and Roy Porter (eds), Routledge, London, 1993.

E. **Dixon**, 'Craftswomen in the Livre des Métiers', *Economic Journal*, 5, pp209-28, 1895.

D. **Doyle**, 'Clinical aspects of osteoarthrosis', in *Copeman's textbook of the theumatic diseases*, J. T. Scott (ed.), pp846-73, 1986.

P. **Dronke**, *Women Writers in the Middle Ages*, Cambridge University Press, 1984.

O. **Dutour**, 'Enthesopathies (Lesions of Muscular Insertions) as Indicators of the Activities of Neolithic Saharan Populations', *American Journal of Physical Anthropology*, 71, pp221-24, 1985.

P. **Earle**, 'The female labour market in London in the late seventeenth and early eighteenth century', *Economic History Review*, 2nd series vol XLII no. 3, August 1919, pp328-353, 1989.

G. **Elphick**, *Sussex Bells and Belfries*, Chichester, 1970.

E. **Ennen**, (ed.), *The Medieval Woman*, translated by Edmund Jephcott, Blackwell, 1984.

M. **Erler and M. Kowaleski**, (eds), *Women and Power in the Middle Ages*, University of Georgia Press, 1988.

C. **Fell**, *Women in Anglo-Saxon England and the impact of 1066*, British Museum Publications, 1984.

M. **Fitch**, 'The London makers of Opus Anglicanum', *Transactions of the London and Middlesex Archaeological Society*, 27, pp288-96, 1976.

F. A. **Foster**, (ed.), 'The Northern Passion', *Early English Text Society*, orig. series, no. 145, pp168-73, 1913. The Harleian text is B. L. Harley Ms 4198, f76.

F. A. **Foster**, (ed.), 'The Northern Passion', *Early English Text Society*, orig. series, no. 147, pp164-5, 1916.

B. E. Frederickson et al, 'The natural history of spondylolysis and spondylolisthesis', *Journal of Bone and Joint Surgery (A)*, 66, pp699-705, 1984.

J. Geddes, 'The Blacksmith's Life, Wife and Work 1250-1450, Tools and Trades', *The Journal of the Tools and Trades History Society*, Vol. 1, pp15-38, 1983.

J. Geddes, 'The Iron Industry', in *English Medieval Industries*, John Blair, Nigel Ramsey (eds), pp167-188, Hambledon Press, London, 1991.

R. Gilchrist, *Gender and Material Culture: The Archaeology of Religious Women*, Routledge, London, 1993.

P. Glanville, *Silver in England*, Unwin Hyman Ltd, London, 1987.

P. Glanville and J. Faulds-Goldsborough, *Women Silversmiths 1685-1845. Works from the Collection of the National Museum of Women in the Arts*, co-published, Thames and Hudson Ltd, London and the National Museum of Women in the Arts, Washington, DC, 1990.

P. J. P. Goldberg, 'Female labour, service and marriage in northern towns during the later Middle Ages', *Northern History*, 22, pp18-38, 1986.

P. J. P. Goldberg, 'Women in fifteenth-century townlife' in J. A. F. Thomson (ed.), *Towns and Townspeople in the fifteenth century*, pp107-128, Alan Sutton Publishing Ltd, Stroud, 1988.

P. J. P. Goldberg, 'Marriage, migration, and servanthood: the York Cause Paper evidence', in *Women is a Worthy Wight. Women in English Society, c.1200-1500*, P. J. P. Goldberg (ed.), Alan Sutton Publishing Ltd, Stroud and Wolfeboro Falls, 1992a.

P. J. P. Goldberg, *Women, Work and Life Cycle in a Medieval Economy: Women in York and Yorkshire c.1300-1520*, Clarendon Press, Oxford, 1992b.

N. M. Hadler, 'Industrial rheumatology, Clinical investigations into the influence of patterns of usage on pattern of regional musculo-skeletal disease', *Arthritis and rheumatism*, 20, pp1019-25, 1977.

N. M. Hadler et al, 'Hand structure and function in an industrial setting: influence of three patterns of stereotyped repetitive usage', *Arthritis and Rheumatism*, 21, pp210-20, 1978.

N. M. Hadler et al, 'The Variable of Usage in the Epidemiology of Osteoarthrosis', in *Epidemiology of Osteoarthritis*, J. G. Peyron (ed.), Symposium Paris, June 1980.

B. A. Hanawalt, *The Ties that Bound: Peasant Families in Medieval England*, New York and Oxford, 1986a.

B. A. Hanawalt, (ed.), *Women and Work in Pre-industrial Europe*, Indiana University Press, Bloomington, 1986B.

B. A. Hanawalt, *Growing up in Medieval London: The experience of childhood in history*, Oxford University Press, 1993.

W. O. Hassell, (ed.), The Holkam Bible Picture Book, London, p28, f31b. The manuscript is B. L. Add MS 47682, 1954.

J. Hatcher and T. C. Barker, *A History of British Pewter*, Longman, Aberdeen, 1974.

I. Hershkovitz et al, 'Ohalo II Man – Unusual Findings in the Anterior Rib Cage and Shoulder Girdle of a 19,000-year-old Specimen', *International Journal of Osteoarchaeology*, 3, pp177-88, 1993.

B. Hill, 'The marriage age of women and the demographers', *History Workshop Journal*, 28, 1989a.

B. Hill, *Women, Work and Sexual Politics in Eighteenth Century England*, Basil Blackwell, Oxford, 1989b.

R. H. Hilton, 'Women in the Village', in R. H. Hilton *The English Peasantry in the Later Middle Ages. The Ford Lectures for 1973 and Related Studies*, pp95-112, Clarendon Press, Oxford, 1975.

R. H. Hilton, 'Women Traders in Medieval England', in R. H. Hilton *Class, Conflict and the Crisis of Feudalism*, 1985.

M. Hoffman, *The Warp-Weighted Loom*, Studia Norvegica, Oslo, 1964.

M. Hoffman, 'Clothworkers Pewter', *Journal of the Pewter Society 1*, Spring, pp24-30, 1977.

K. Honeyman and J. Goodman, 'Women's work, gender conflict and labour markets in Europe 1500-1900', *Economic History Review*, XLIV, 1991.

M. C. Howell, 'Women, the family economy and the structures of market production in cities of northern Europe during the late middle ages', in *Women and Work in Pre-industrial Europe*, Barbara A. Hanawalt (ed.), Indiana University Press, Bloomington, 1986a.

M. C. Howell, *Women, Production, and Patriarchy in Late Medieval cities*, University of Chicago Press, Chicago and London, 1986b.

P. Hudson, 'Introduction' unpublished contribution to *Towards a new history of industrialisation in Britain*; a session organised by the Women's Committee of the Economic History Society for the Society's Annual Conference, University of Nottingham, 8-10 April, 1994.

P. Hudson and W. R. Lee, (eds), *Women's Work and the Family Economy in Historical Perspective*, Manchester University Press, Manchester, 1990.

O. Hufton, 'Women in history: early modern Europe', *Past and Present*, 101, 1983.

J. Humphries, *Industrialisation and the making of gender*, unpublished paper presented to the Women's Committee session at the Annual Conference of the Economic History Society, University of Nottingham, 8-10 April, 1994.

J. Jesch, *Women in the Viking Age*, Boydell Press, Woodbridge, Suffolk, 1991.

S. Jones, 'The female perspective', *Museums Journal*, 91 (2), pp24-7, 1991.

R. Jurmain, 'Degenerative changes in peripheral joints as indications of mechanical stress: opportunities and limitations', *International Journal of Osteoarchaeology*, 1, pp247-52, 1991.

D. Keene, 'Tanners' Widows, 1300-1500', in Caroline Barron and Anne Sutton (eds), *Medieval London Widows 1300-1500*, pp1-28, Hambledon Press, 1994.

J. Olsen Kelley and J. Lawrence Angel, 'Life Stresses of Slavery', *American Journal of Physical Anthropology*, 74, pp199-211, 1987.

J. H. Kellgren and J. S. Lawrence, 'Osteoarthrosis and disc degeneration in an urban population', *Annals of Rheumatic Diseases*, 17, pp388-97, 1958.

K. A. R. Kennedy, 'Morphological Variations in Ulnar Supinator Crests and Fossae as Identifying Markers of Occupational Stress', *Journal of Forensic Sciences*, 28, pp871-76, 1983.

D. Kent, 'Ubiquitous but invisible: female domestic servants in mid-eighteenth century London', *History Workshop Journal*, 28, 1989.

D. King, 'Embroidery and textiles', in *Age of Chivalry: Art in Plantegenet England 1200-1400*, J. Alexander and P. Binski (eds), Royal Academy of Arts and Weidenfeld and Nicolson, London, 1987.

M. Klein Ehrminger, *The Cathedral of Strasburg*, 1970.

M. Kowaleski, 'Women's Work in a Market Town: Exeter in the Late Fourteenth Century' in B. Hanawalt (ed.) *Women and Work in Pre-Industrial Europe*, Bloomington, Indiana University Press, 1986.

M. Kowaleski and J. M. Bennett, 'Crafts, Guilds and Women in the Middle Ages: Fifty years after M. K. Dale' in J. M. Bennett, E. A. Clarke, J. F. O'Barr, B. A.

Vilen and S. Westphal-Wihl (eds), 'Working Together in the Middle Ages: Perspectives on Women's Communities', *Signs*, 14, 1989.

P. Kriedte, H. Medick, and J. Schlumbohm, *Industrialisation before Industrialisation*, Cambridge University Press, Cambridge, 1991.

Vladimir Krejci and **Peter Koch**, *Muscle and Tendon Injuries in Athletes*, Georg Thieme, Stuttgart, 1979.

M. W. Labage, *Women in Medieval Life: A Small Sound of the Trumpet*, London, 1986.

K. E. Lacey, 'Women and work in fourteenth and fifteenth century London', in L. Charles and L. Duffin (eds), *Women and Work in Pre-Industrial England*, London, pp24-82, 1985.

K. Lacey, 'The production of "Narrow Ware" by silkwomen in fourteenth and fifteenth century England', *Textile History*, 18 (2), pp187-204, 1987.

F. Lachaud, 'Embroidery for the court of Edward I (1272-1307)', *Nottingham Medieval Studies*, 37, pp33-52, 1993.

Ping Lai and **Nancy Lovell**, 'Skeletal Markers of Occupational Stress in the Fur Trade: A Case Study from a Hudson's Bay Company Fur Trade Post', *International Journal of Osteoarchaeology*, 2, pp221-34, 1992.

W. Arbuthnot Lane, 'The anatomy and physiology of the shoemaker', *Journal of Anatomy and Physiology*, 22, pp593-628, 1888.

L. E. Lanyon et al, 'Mechanically adaptive bone remodelling', *Journal of Biomechanics*, 15, pp141-54, 1982.

L. E. Lanyon and C. T. Rubin, 'Static vs. dynamic loads as an influence on bone remodelling', *Journal of Biomechanics*, 17, pp897-905, 1984.

G. T. Lapsley, 'The Account Roll of a Fifteenth-Century Ironmaster', *English Historical Review*, xiv, pp509-29, 1899.

J. S. Lawrence, **R. De Graaff** and **V. A. Laine**, *The Epidemiology of Chronic Rheumatism*, Blackwell, Oxford, 1962.

J. Lown, *Gender and Clan during Industrialisation: a Study of the Harstead Silk Industry in Essex 1825-1900*, Phd Thesis, University of Essex, 1984.

L. Lindberg and **L. G. Danielsson**, 'The Relation between Labor and Cosarthrosis', *Clinical Orthopaedics and Related Research*, 19, 1984.

M. D. Lockshin et al, 'Rheumatism in Mining Communities in Marion County, West Virginia', *American Journal of Epidemiology*, 90, 1, 1969.

R. W. Malcolmson, *Life and Labour in England 1700-1780*, Hutchinson, London, 1981.

C. Merbs, *Patterns of Activity-Induced Pathology in a Canadian Inuit Population*, National Museums of Canada, Ottawa, 1983.

C. Middleton, 'The familiar fate of the Famulae: gender divisions in the history of wage labour' in *On Work. Historical, Comparative and Theoretical Approaches*, R. E. Pahl (ed.), Blackwell, Oxford, 1988.

T. Molleson, 'Seed preparation in the Mesolithic: the oesteological evidence', *Antiquity*, 63, pp356-62, 1989.

T. Molleson et al, *The SpitalFields Project Volume 2: the anthropology – The Middling Sort*, CBA Research Report 86, Council for British Archaeology, York, 1993.

G. Nuki, *The Aetippathogenesis of Osteoarthrosis*, Pitman Medical, London, 1980.

D. E. O'Connor and J. Haselock, 'The Stained and Painted Glass', in *A History of York Minster*, G. E. Aylmer and R. Cant (eds), pp350-55, Oxford, 1977.

D. J. Ortner, 'Description and Classification of Degenerative Bone Changes in the Distal Joint Surfaces of the Humerus', *American Journal of Physical Anthropology*, 28, pp139-56, 1968.

D. J. Ortner and **W. Putschar**, *Identification of Pathological Conditions in Human Skeletal Remains*, Smithsonian Institution Press, Washington DC, p419, 1981.

G. R. Owen, 'Wynflaed's wardrobe', *Anglo-Saxon England*, 8, pp195-222, 1979.

D. W. Owsley et al, 'Demography and Pathology of an Urban Slave Population from New Orleans', *American Journal of Physical Anthropology*, 74, pp185-97, 1987.

B. S. Pande and I. Singh, 'One-sided dominance in the upper limbs of human foetuses as evidenced by asymmetry in muscle and bone weight', *Journal of Anatomy*, 109, pp457-59, 1971.

S. A. C. Penn, 'Female Wage Earners in Later Fourteenth Century England', *Agricultural History Review*, 35, 1987.

E. Power, *Medieval English Nunneries c.1275-1535*, Cambridge University Press, 1922.

E. Power, *Medieval People*, London, 1924

E. Power, *Medieval Women*, M. M. Postan (ed.), Cambridge University Press, 1975.

M. Prior, (ed.), *Women in English Society 1500-1800*, Methuen and Co, London, 1985 rev. ed., Routledge, London, New York, 1985.

M. Prior, (ed.), 'Women in the Urban Economy' in *Women in English Society 1500-1800*, (ed), M. Prior, pp93-117, 1985.

S. Rappaport, (ed.), *Worlds within Worlds: Structure of Life in Sixteenth Century London*, Cambridge University Press, Cambridge, 1989.

T. Rathbun, 'Health and Disease at a South Carolina Plantation: 1840-1870', *American Journal of Physical Anthropology*, 74, pp239-53, 1987.

D. Resnick and G. Niwayama, *Diagnosis of Bone and Joint Disorders*, Vol. 2, W. B. Saunders, Philadelphia, 1981.

M. Roberts, 'Sickles and Scythes: Women's Work and Men's Work at Harvest Time', *History Workshop*, 7, 1979.

M. Roberts, '"Words they are women, and deeds they are men": Images of work and gender in early modern England', in Lindsey Charles and Lorna Duffin (eds), *Women and Work in Pre-industrial England*, Croom Helm, London 1985.

M. Roberts, 'Women and work in sixteenth-century English towns' in *Work in Towns 850-1850*, Penelope J. Corfield and Derek Keene (eds), Leicester University Press, Leicester, 1990.

J. Rogers, I. Watt and P. Dieppe, 'Composition of visual and radiographic detection of bone changes at the knee joint', *British Medical Journal*, 300, pp367-68, 1990.

J. T. Rosenthal, (ed.), *Medieval Women and the Sources of Medieval History*, Georgia University Press, 1990.

E. Sairanen, L. Brushaber and M. Kaskinen, 'Felling Work, Low Back Pain and Osteoarthritis', *Scandinavian Journal of Work and Environmental Health*, 7, pp18-30, 1981.

L. F. Salzman, 'Women', in *English Life in the Middle Ages*, Chapter XII, pp249-265, Oxford University Press, London, 1926.

L. F. Salzman, *Building in England*, Oxford, rev. edn. 1967, p337, 1952.

H. R. Schubert, *History of the British Iron and Steel Industry*, London. pp156-60, 1957.

A. H. Schultz, 'Proportions, variability and asymmetries of the long bones of the limbs and the clavicles in man and apes', *Human Biology*, 9, pp281-328, 1937.

E. Sellers, (ed.), 'York Memorandum Book', *Surtees Society*, CXX, after 1397, p93, 1912.

C. C. Seltzer, 'Anthropometry and arthritis', *Medicine*, 22, pp163-203, 1943.

P. Sharpe, 'Literally spinsters; a new interpretation of local economy and demography in Colyton in the seventeenth and eighteenth century', *Economic History Review*, 44, 1991.

R. R. Sharpe, (ed.), *Calendar of Wills Proved and Enrolled in the Court of Husting*, London. 67, pp63, 1871.

R. R. Sharpe, (ed.), *Calendar of Letter-Books ... of the City of London ... Letter-Book L*, 11 vols, pp165-7, 1899-1912.

E. Shorter, 'Women's work: what difference did capitalism make?' *Theory and Society*, 3, pp513-528, 1976.

S. Shulamith, *The Fourth Estate: A History of Women in the Middle Ages*', Methuen, 1983.

K. D. M. Snell, *Annals of the Labouring Poor. Social Change and Agrarian England 1660-1900*, Cambridge University Press, Cambridge, 1985.

K. Staniland, *Medieval Craftsmen: Embroiderers*, British Museum Press, London, 1991.

F. M. Stenton, *Anglo-Saxon England*, Oxford University Press, Oxford, 1943.

A. Stirland, 'A Possible Correlation between Os Acromiale and Occupation in the Burials from the Mary Rose', *Proceedings of the 5th European Meeting of the Paleopathology Association, Sienna, Italy, 1984*, pp327-34, 1987.

A. Stirland, 'Diagnosis of occupationally related paleopathology: Can it be done?', in *Human Paleopathology – Current Syntheses and Future Options*, D. Ortner and A. Aufderheide (eds), pp40-50, Smithsonian Institution Press, Washington DC, 1991.

S. M. Stuard, (ed.), *Women in Medieval Society*, University of Pennsylvania Press, 1976.

A. Sutton, 'Alice Claver: Silkwoman of London and maker of mantle laces for Richard III and Queen Anne', *The Ricardian*, 5, pp243-47, 1980.

A. Sutton, 'Alice Claver, silkwoman (d.1489)' in C. Barron, and A. Sutton, (eds), *Medieval London Widows 1300-1500*, pp129-142, Hambledon Press, 1994.

H. Swanson, *Medieval Artisans. An Urban Class in Late Medieval England*, Oxford, 1989.

J. A. Tainter, 'Behaviour and status in a Middle Woodland mortuary population from the Illinois Valley', *American Antiquity*, 45, pp308-13, 1980.

Theophilus, *On Divers Arts*, translated and with an introduction by J. G. Hawthorne and C. S. Smith, pp165-79, New York, 1979.

A. H. Thomas and P. E. Jones, (eds), *Calendar of Plea and Memoranda Rolls, 1323-64*, 6 vols, vol. 1, p274, Cambridge, 1926.

S. Thomspon, *Women Religious. The Founding of English Nunneries after the Norman Conquest*', Oxford University Press, 1991.

E. Trinkaus, 'Squatting among the Neanderthals: a problem in the behavioural interpretation of skeletal morphology', *Journal of Archaeological Science*, 2, pp327-51, 1975.

R. F. Tylecote, *A History of Metallurgy*, p71, London, 1976.

D. H. Ubelaker, 'Skeletal evidence of kneeling in prehistoric Ecuador', *American Journal of Physical Anthropology*, 51, pp679-86, 1979.

E. Uitz, *Women in the Medieval Town*, London, 1990.

D. Valenze, 'The art of women and the business of men: women's work and the diary industry c.1740-1840', *Past and Present*, 30, 1991.

E. Veale, 'Matilda Penne, skinner (d.1392/3)' in C. Barron and A. Sutton (eds), *Medieval London Widows 1300-1500*, pp47-54, Hambledon Press, 1994.

A. Vickery, 'Golden age to separate spheres? A review of the categories and chronology of English women's history', *History Workshop Journal*, 36, 1993.

H. A. Waldron, 'Variations in the Rates of Spondylolysis in Early Populations', *International Journal of Osteoarchaeology*, 1, pp63-65, 1991.

H. A. Waldron, 'The health of the adults', in *The SpitalFields Project, Volume 2: the anthropology – The Middling Sort*, T. Molleson et al (eds), pp67-87, CBA Research Report 86, Council for British Archaeology, York, 1993.

J. C. Ward, *English Noblewomen in the Later Middle Ages*, Longman, 1992.

G. Warner, (ed.), *Queen Mary's Psalter*, London, pp28, 256. The manuscript is BL Royal MS 2 B VII, f252b, 1912.

L. Weatherill, 'A possession of one's own: women and consumer behaviour in England 1660-1740', *Journal of British Studies*, 25, 1986.

C. Welch, *History of the Worshipful Company of Pewterers of the City of London* (2 vols), Blades, East and Bladcs, London, 1902.

C. Welch, History of the Cutlers' Company of London, vol.1, pp249-59, 1916.

M. Wensky, 'Women's guilds in Cologne in the later Middle Ages', Journal of European Economic History, vol. 11, 3, pp631-50, 1982.

S. Wright, 'Churchmaids, Huswyfes and Hucksters': the employment of women in Tudor and Stuart Salisbury' in Lindsey Charles and Lorna Duffin (eds), Women and Work in Pre-Industrial England, Croom Helm, London, 1985.

OTHER SOURCES

The Bulletin of the Wealden Iron Research Group (WIRGS).

Journal of the Pewter Society. (1977-continuing).

Medieval Women in Southern England. Reading Medievel Studies. 1989.

Wealdon Iron Research Group. Contact: The Secretary, Wealdon Iron Resarch Group, 8 Woodview Crescent, Hildenborough, Tonbridge, Kent.

Part Two CHAPTER 4

From the Pit to the Office

150 Jahre Österrechische Tabak Regie 1784-1934, Wien, 1934.

II. statisticni letopis mesta Ljubljane za leto 1939 Mestne obcine ljubljanske-statisticni odsek, Ljubljana, 1940.

S. Allen and L. Walkowitz, Homeworking: Myths and Realities, Macmillan Education, London 1987.

R. Andrejka, Najstarejse ljubljanske industrije, Kronika slovenskih mest, I, 1934.

R. Andrejka, Razvoj ljubljanskih industij 1859-1869, Kronika VI, 1939.

W. Avery, Old Redditch: Being an Early History of the Town, Redditch Indicator, 1887.

G. J. Barnsby, Birmingham Working People, Integrated Publishing Service, Wolverhampton, 1989.

G. J. Barnsby, Social Conditions in the Black Country 1800-1900, Integrated Publishing Services, Wolverhampton, 1980.

E. R. S. Bartleet, History of a Needle, Hudson & Sons, Birmingham, 1890.

J. Benson, British Coalminers in the Nineteenth Century: A Social History, Gill and Macmillan, Dublin, 1980.

J. Benson, (ed.), The Working Class in England 1875-1914, Croom Helm, London, 1974.

J. Benson, **R. G. Neville**, and **C. H. Thompson**, Bibliography of the British Coal Industry: Secondary Literature, Parliamentary and Departmental Papers, Mineral Maps and Plans and a Guide to Sources, Oxford University Press, Oxford, 1981.

M. Berg, The Age of Manufacturers 1700-1820, Fontana, London, 1985.

E. Boyle, The Irish Flowerers, Ulster Folk Museum, 1971.

A. Buck, Thomas Lester, his lace and the East Midlands Industry, Ruth Bean, Bedford, 1981.

A-M. Bullock, Lace and Lace-Making, Batsford, London, 1981.

E. Cadbury, Women's Work and Wages, Fircroft College Study.

T. Čepič, Ljubljanska tobacna tovarna skozi cas, Ljubljana, 1991.

C. Channer and **A. Buck**, In the cause of English Lace, Ruth Bean, Bedford, 1991.

Children's Employment Commission, First Report of the Commissioners: Mines, HMSO, London, 1842.

Children's Employment Commission, Appendix to First Report of Commissioners: Mines; I: Reports and Evidence from Sub-Commissioners, HMSO, London, 1842.

Children's Employment Commission, Ibid.; II: Report and Evidence from Sub-Commissioners, HMSO, London, 1842.

R. Church, The History of the British Coal Industry; III, 1830-1913: Victorian Pre-Eminence, Clarendon Press, Oxford, 1986.

C. Chinn, They Worked All Their Lives: Women of the Urban Poor in England 1880-1939, Manchester University Press, 1988.

M. Cilensek, Nase skodljive rastline v sliki in besedi, Druzba Sv, Mohorja v Celovcu, 1892.

S. Cohn, The Process of Occupational Sex-Typing: The Feminization of Clerical Labour in Great Britain, Temple University Press, Philadelphia, 1985.

T. Davy, 'Women Shorthand Typists in London 1900-39' in Leonie Davidoff and Belinda Westover (eds), Our Work, Our Lives, Our Words: Women's History and Women's Work, Macmillan Education, Basingstoke, 1986.

J. de Mann, The Cloth Industry in the West of England 1640-1880, Oxford, 1971.

N. Dennis, **F. Henriques**, **and C. Slaughter**, *Coal is our Life*, 1956, reprinted Tavistock Publications, London, 1969.

C. Dickens, 'Needles' *Household Words: A Weekly Journal*, Vol. IV, 27, Sept-13 March, No. 79-103, London, 1852.

C. Dyhouse, *Feminism and the Family: England 1880-1039*, Basil Blackwell, Oxford, 1989.

P. Earnshaw, *A Dictionary of Lace*, Shire Publications, Princes Risborough, 1982.

H. Faber, Tabakwarenkunde, Fachbuchverlag, Leipzig, 1958.

W. Felkin, *History of the machine-wrought hosiery and lace manufactures*, 1867, David and Charles: Newton Abbott, 1967.

J. Fischer, 'Cas vesolniga socialnega punta se bliza', Socialna in politicna zgodovina delavskega gibanja v Ljubljani od zacetkov do 1889, Republiska konferenca ZSMS, Ljubljana, 1983.

J. Fischer, Delavke Tobacne tovarne v Ljubljani 1871-1914, Prispevki za zgodovino delavskega gibanja, XXIV, 1-2, 1984.

S. Gater, 'Alfred and Louise Powell – an Introduction', *Proceedings of the Wedgwood Society*, No. 11, 1982.

F. Gestrin, Oris gospodarstva na Slovenskem v prvem obdobju kapitalizma (do leta 1918), Kronika, XVII, 3, 1969.

Gospodarska statistika Slovenije v luci poklicne statistike in delavskega zavarovanja, Socialno ekonomski institut, zbirka studij st. 5, Geografski institut na univerzi kralja Aleksandra v Ljubljani, Ljubljana, 1939.

Z. Halls, *Nottingham Lace*, (City of Nottingham Museums and Libraries 1964); second edn, 1973.

Hansard's Parliamentary Debates, *Third Series: Commencing with the Accession of William IV; LXIII: 3 May to 16 June*, London, 1842.

W. T. Hemming, *The Needle Region and Its Resources*, Redditch Indicator, 1877.

M. Hiley, *Victorian Working Women: Portraits from Life*, The Gordon Fraser Gallery Ltd, London, 1979.

J. Hopewell, *Pillow Lace and Bobbins*, (Shire Album 9: Princes Risborough), 1975.

D. Hudson, *Munby, Man of Two Worlds*, John Murray, London, 1972.

J. G. Jenkins, *Getting Yesterday Right. Interpreting the Heritage of Wales*, University of Wales Press, Cardiff, 1992.

A. V. John, (ed.), *Unequal Opportunities: Women's Employment in England 1800-1918*, Basil Blackwell, Oxford, 1986.

A. V. John, 'Colliery legislation and its consequences: 1842 and the women miners of Lancashire', *Bulletin of the John Rylands University Library of Manchester*, 61, no. 1, pp78-114, 1978.

A. V. John, *By the Sweat of their Brow: Women Workers at Victorian Coal Mines*, 1980, reprinted Routledge & Kegan Paul, London, 1984.

A. V. John, *Coalmining Women*, Cambridge University Press, Cambridge, 1984.

R. W. Johnston, 'Early Telegraph Days', *St Martin's Le Grand*, 1984.

E. Kohn, H. Huber, R. Reiter and Mosser, Die Sozialgeschichte, Die Arbeits und Lebensverältnisse der Bescheftigten des Unternehnmens, Austria Tabak. Europa verlag, 1986.

S. Kremensek, Ljubljansko naselje Zelena jama kot etnoloski problemi, Ljubljana, 1970.

S. Kremensek, Nacin zivljenja Slovencev 20, stoletja, Zasnova preucevanja, dosedanje raziskave in problemi, Ljubljana, 1980.

F. Kresai, Delavstvo med gospodarsko krizo na Slovenskem, Prispevki za zgodovino delavskega gibanja, X, 1-2, 1970.

J. Lavric, Prerez gospodarskega polozaja leta 1938, Ljubljana, 1938.

S. M. Levey, *Lace: a history*, Victoria and Albert Museum, London, 1983.

S. M. Levey, 'Straight Lace', *Museums Journal*, November 1995, vol. 95, no. 11, pp. 34-5, 1985.

J. Lewis, *The Politics of Motherhood*, Croom Helm, London, 1980.

B. Lindsay, *Irish Lace: its origin and history*, Hodges, Figgis & Co., Dublin, 1886.

A. Longfield, *Irish lace*, Irish Heritage Series, Dublin, 1978.

B. J. Lough, *The Working Class in Britain 1850-1939*, Longman, London, 1989.

Luton Museum and Art Gallery, *Pillow Lace in the East Midlands*, 1958.

A. Melik, O poklicni sestavi prebivalstva v mestih v Sloveniji, Tehnika in gospodarstvo, III, 1936/37.

A. E. Morrall, *A Short Description of Needlemaking*, Express Printing, Redditch, 1886.

M. T. Morrall, *A History and Description of Needlemaking*, A. Hobson, Ashton under Lyne, 1852.

J. Morris, *Women Workers and the Sweated Trade: The Origins of Minimum Wage Legislation*, Gower Publishing, Aldershot, 1986.

A. J. Munby, Manuscript Diaries, Trinity College, Cambridge.

N. O'Cléirigh, 'Limerick Lace', Irish Arts Review, Dublin, 1988.

B. Palliser, The History of Lace, Sampson, Low & Co., London, 1875.

Parliamentary Papers, House of Commons Library.

J. Peatman, 'The Abbeydale Industrial Hamlet: History and Restoration', Industrial Archaeology Review XI 2, pp141-54, Spring 1989.

I. Pinchbeck, Women Workers and the Industrial Revolution 1750-1850, 1930, reprinted, Virago, London, 1981.

A. Podbregar, Dosedanji in perspektivni razvoj Tobacne tovarne v Ljubljani, Rokopis, Zbirka Tobacne Ljubljana.

A. Podbregar, Ustanovitev Tobacne tovarne. Rokopis, Zbirka Tobacne Ljubljana.

K. Ponting, The Woollen Industry of South-West England, Adams and Dart, 1971.

K. Ponting, A History of the West of England Cloth Industry, Macdonald, 1957.

K. Rogers, Warp and Weft – The Somerset and Wiltshire Woollen Industry, Barracuda Books, 1986.

K. Rogers, Wiltshire and Somerset Woollen Mills, Pasold Research Fund Ltd, 1976.

J. Sarsby, Missuses and Mouldrunners – An Oral History of Women Pottery-Workers at Work and at Home. Open University Press, Milton Keynes; Philadelphia, 1988.

J. Schmiechen, Sweated Industries and the Sweated Trades: The London Clothing Trades, 1860-1914, Croom Helm, London, 1984.

I. Slokar, Zacetki tobacne industrije v Ljubljani, Kronika, IX, 1, 1961.

J. Sorn, Razvoj industrije med obema vojnama, Kronika, VII, 1, 1959.

Splosni pregled dravske banovine, Ljubljana 1939.

Spominski zbornik Slovenije, Ljubljana 1939.

M. Stiplovsek, Prispevki za zgodovino sindikalnega gibanja na Slovenskem 1868-1945, Zalozba Obzorja, Maribor, 1989.

H. G. Swift, A History of Postal Agitation, Pearson, London, 1900.

J. Tagg, The Burden of Representation: Essays on Photographies and Histories, Macmillan, London, 1988.

P. Thane (ed.), The Origins of British Social Policy, Croom Helm, London, 1995.

S. Timmins (ed.), Birmingham and the Midland Hardware District, 1866, reprinted Class Library of Industrial Classics, No. 7, London, 1967.

S. Timmins (ed.), 'The Workshops of the World: The Metropolis of Needlemaking', The Working Man; a Weekly Record of Social and Industrial Progress, vol. 1, no. 9, Saturday 3 March 1866, reprinted Greenwood, New York, 1970.

V. Valencic, Ljubljanska industrija od 16. stoletja do prve svetovne vojne, Katalog k razstavi Zgodovinskega arhiva Ljubljana, Ljubljana, 1973.

A. Vogelnik, Donesek k stanovanjskemu vprasanju Ljubljane, Tehnika in gospodarstvo, V, 11-12, 1939.

A. Vogelnik, Ugotovitev zivljenskih stroskov slovenske delavske in namescenske druzine, Tehnika in gospodarstvo, V, 11-12, 1939.

I. Vriser, Razvoj prebivalstva na obmocju Ljubljane, Ljubljana, 1956.

C. Walkley, The Ghost in the Looking Glass, Peter Owen, London, 1981.

P. Wardle, Victorian Lace, 1968; revised second edn Ruth Bean, Bedford, 1982.

D. Warwick and G. Littlejohn, Coal, Capital and Culture, Routledge, London, 1992.

Wedgwood Museum Manuscripts, Transcripts of the letters of Josiah Wedgwood I, vols. I-XV

F. Windischer Gradivo za statistiko trgovine, obrta in industrije v Sloveniji, Uredil dr. Izdala Zbornica za trgovino, obrt in industrijo v Ljubljani, 1929.

H. J. Yallop, The History of the Honiton Lace Industry, Exeter University Press, 1992.

Yugoslav Tobaccos, Federal Chamber of Foreign Trade, Beograd, 1960.

Zgodovina Ljubljane- prispevki za monografijo, Kronika, Ljubljana, 1984.

Zgodovina Slovencev, Cankarjeva zalozba, Ljubljana, 1979.

Zgodovinski arhiv Ljubljana, LJU, fond Tobacne tovarne Ljubljana.

SITE SPECIFIC MATERIAL
Abbeydale Industrial Hamlet, Sheffield

Abbeydale Industrial Hamlet (Guidebook) – Sheffield City Museums, 1981.

Beamish, The North of England Open Air Museum. (A brief guide).

Beamish, *Time to Return*, Publicity Leaflet, 1992.

Beamish, *Washday*, Information Sheet 4, 1987.

Big Pit Mining Museum, Blaenafon, *Big Pit. Pwll Mawr. The Big Pit Story*, (Guidebook) Big Pit Mining Museum, Blaenafon, 1992.

The Black Country Museum, *Recreating the heart of an industrial community*, Publicity Leaflet, 1993.

The Black Country Museum, *Colour Guidebook* (28 pages), published by Pitkin Pictorials, 1992.

Bo'ness & Kinneil Railway, *A Window to the Past*, Publicity Leaflet, Bo'ness Heritage Trust/Scottish Railway Preservation Society, 1993.

Killhope Lead Mining Museum, Leaflet given with entrance ticket.

Morwellham Quay, Young Explorers Activity Guide, published by Morwellham Quay Trust, 1990. Part of Resource Pack for Teachers (£4.95).

Morwellham Quay, *Morwellham Quay in the Tamar Valley*, Frank Booker. DART Publication 78, Jarrold & Sons, Norwich, 1983.

Scottish Maritime Museum, Irvine, Ayrshire Tourist Board Publicity Leaflet – *History and Heritage in Ayrshire*, Ayrshire Tourist Board, 1993.

Scottish Mining Museum, Newtongrange Information Sheet No. 1, *Wullie Drysdale. A Miner and his family: 1900*, by E. D. Hyde, Scottish Mining Museum, 1986.

Woodhorn Colliery Museum, Publicity Leaflet, Wansbeck District Council, 1993.

Yorkshire Mining Museum, *Victorian Workers*, Information Sheets 1-5, 1992.

ADDITIONAL REFERENCES (All available at the British Library)

Counting House , *Shorthand World*, *St Ethelburga*, *Phonetic Journal* – published, Bath, *The Telegraphist*, *City Press*, *Fraser's Magazine*, *Phonographer & Typist*, *Quarterly Journal of the National Phonographic Society*, *Typist's Review*, *Women's Employment*, *Women's Industrial News*, *Potteries Examiner*.

Part Two CHAPTER 5

The Industry of War

P. **Adam-Smith**, *Australian Woman at War*, Nelson, Melbourne, 1984.

I. A. **Andrews**, *Economic Effects of the War upon Women and Children in Great Britain* (Carnegie Endowment for International Peace: Preliminary economic studies of the war), Oxford University Press, London, 1918.

V. **Bamfield**, *On the Strength: The Story of the British Army Wife*, Knight, 1974.

M. **Barrow**, *Women, 1870-1928: a select guide to printed and archival sources in the United Kingdom*, Mansell Publishing, London, 1981.

D. **Beddoe** and L. **Verrill-Rhys** (eds), *Parachutes and Petticoats: Welsh Women in the Second World War*, Honno, Cardiff, 1992.

C. R. **Berkin** and C. M. **Lovett** (eds), *Women, War and Revolution*, Holmes Meier, New York and London, 1980.

B. **Bousquet** and C. **Douglas**, *West Indian Women at War*, Lawrence & Wishart, London, 1991.

G. **Braybon**, *Women Workers in the First World War: the British Experience*, Croom Helm, London, 1981.

G. **Braybon** and P. **Summerfield**, *Out of the Cage: Women's Experiences in two World Wars*, Pandora, 1987.

M. **Brown**, *The Imperial War Museum Book of the First World War* (Part VI is on Women at War), Sidgwick & Jackson, London, 1991.

Cambridge Women's Peace Collective, *Anthology of Women's Work on Peace and War*, Pandora Press, London, 1984.

J. **Carmichael**, *First World War Photographers* (Chapter VI on the civilian at war), Routledge, London, 1989.

P. **Compton**, *Colonel's Lady and Camp Follower, The Story of Women in the Crimean War*, St Martin's Press, New York, 1970.

D. **Condell** and J. **Liddiard**, *Working for Victory? Images of Women in the First World War*, Routledge and Kegan Paul, London, 1987.

M. **Cosens**, *Lloyd George's Munitions Girls*, Hutchinson, London, 1916.

C. **Enloe**, *Does khaki become you: the militarisation of women's lives*, Pluto Press, London, 1983.

M. **Garrett Fawcett**, *The Women's Victory and after*, Sidgwick and Jackson, London, 1920.

N. L. **Goldman** (ed.), *Female soldiers – combatants or noncombatants?* Greenwood Press, Westport & London, 1982.

P. **Hamilton**, *Three Years or the Duration: the memoirs of a munitions worker 1914-1918*, Owen, London, 1978.

J. **Hartley** (ed.), *Hearts undefeated. Women's writing on the Second World War*, Virago Press, 1994.

E. **Hostettler**, *The Island at War: Memories of Wartime Life on the Isle of Dogs, East London*, Island History Trust, London, 1985.

L. **Jones** (ed.), *Keeping the peace*, Women's Press, London, 1983.

M. **Krippner**, *The quality of mercy: women at war*, David & Charles, London, 1980.

V. **Lynn, R. Cross,** and J. **de Grex**, *Unsung Heroines: the Women who won the War*, Sidgwick & Jackson, 1990.

L. **Macdonald**, *The roses of No Man's Land*, Michael Joseph, London, 1980.

S. **Macdonald, P. Holden** and S. **Ardener** (eds), *Images of women in peace and war: cross-cultural and historical perspectives*, Fontana, London, 1987.

A. **Marwick**, *The Deluge: British Society and the First World War*, The Bodley Head, London, 1965.

A. **Marwick**, *Women at War 1914-1918*, Croom Helm and the Imperial War Museum, London, 1977.

B. **McLaren**, *Women of the War*, Hodder and Stoughton, London, 1917.

Ministry of Supply/WLA Benevolent Fund, *Meet the Members, A Record of the Timber Corps of the Women's Land Army*, c.1945.

D. **Mitchell**, *Women on the Warpath*, Cape, London, 1976.

K. **Muir**, *Arms and the Woman. Female Soldiers at War*, Sinclair-Stevenson, 1992.

Parliament, *Report of the Committee of Women in Industry*, HMSO, London, 1919.

R. **Perks**, *Oral History: An Annotated Bibliography*, British Library Publications, London, 1990.

R. **Perks**, *Oral History: Talking about the Past*, The Historical Association, London, 1992.

R. R. **Pierson** (ed.), *Women and peace: theoretical, historical and practical perspective*, Croom Helm, London, 1987.

S. **Rowbotham**, *Women, resistance and revolution*, Penguin, London, 1972.

S. **Shepherd**, *Amazons and warrior women*, Harvester Press, Brighton, 1981.

N. St. J. **Williams**, *Judy O'Grady and the Colonel's Lady, The Army Wife & Camp Follower since 1660*, Brassey's, 1988.

P. **Summerfield**, *Women Workers in the Second World War*, Croom Helm, London, 1984.

R. **Terry**, *Women in Khaki, The Story of the British Woman Soldier*, Columbus Books, 1988.

D. **Thompson** (ed.), *Over our dead bodies: women against the bomb*, Virago, London, 1983.

P. **Thompson**, *The Voice of the Past*, 2nd. edn., Routledge, London, 1988.

M. **Trustram**, *Women of the Regiment, Marriage and the Victorian Army*, Cambridge University Press, 1984.

C. **Twinch**, *Women on the Land, Their Story during two World Wars*, Lutterworth Press, (this includes the WTC as well as the Women's Land Army), 1990.

K. **Walker**, *A piece of my heart: American women who served in Vietnam*, Ballantine, New York, 1985.

M. **Warner**, *Joan of Arc: the image of female heroism*, Penguin, London, 1981.

S. **Wilkinson and I. Hughes**, 'Soldiering On', *Museums Journal*, November 1991.

J. **Williams**, *The Home Fronts 1914-1918*, Constable, London, 1972.

M. **Williams**, *Lumber Jill*, Ex Libris Press, Bradford-on-Avon, 1994.

A. **Wiltshire**, *Most dangerous women: feminist peace campaigners of the Great War*, Pandora Press, London & Boston, 1985.

A. **Woodeson**, 'Going back to the Land. Rhetoric and Reality in Women's Land Army Memories', *Women's Lives, Oral History*, Autumn 1993, vol. 21, no. 2, 1993.

OTHER SOURCES
COLLECTIONS IN THE NATIONAL MUSEUMS OF SCOTLAND

Approximately 90 photographs

Recorded interviews:

T/1992/1	Alison McLure
T/1992/2-3	Nan MacLean
T/1994/3	Margaret Grant

Documents include: manuscript reminiscences, letters of thanks for war service, WLA membership card.

Artefacts:

W.1991.89-91 Beret badge, sharpening stone and book:

Hoppus's Measurer (for timber)

W.1992.33	Girthing tape
W.1992.34	Women's Forestry Service felt badge
W.1992.39	WTC uniform

W.1992.50	Screever or scribing knife, used to mark crosses on trees selected for felling
W.1993.96	WTC socks
H.1992.363	Women's Forestry Corps badge, 1914-16
H.1992.364	Women's Forestry Corps scarf, 1914-16

IMPERIAL WAR MUSEUM

The Imperial War Museum has extensive collections of material relating to twentieth century (and late Victorian) women's lives and work. The necessity to gather this was explicitly specified by the founders of the Museum. The reference departments comprise:

Art 0171-416 5211

Documents (personal papers) 0171-416 5222

Exhibits (objects) 0171-416 5271

Film 0171-416 5292

Photographs 0171-416 5333

Printed Books (also pamphlets & ephemera) 0171-416 5342

Sound Archive (both oral history & broadcasts) 0171-416 5363

There is no charge for visiting the reference departments but it is normally necessary to make an appointment in advance.

SOUND ARCHIVE
Imperial War Museum

Lambeth Road, London SE1 6HZ

Sound Archive   tel: 0171-416 5363
                 fax: 0171-416 5379

The Sound Archive holds some 2000 recordings (representing many thousands of hours) of women, both civilian and military, who have been witnesses to or participants in twentieth-century conflict from the Boer War to Bosnia. This includes wartime work on the land, in industry, in the arts, in medical and social services, in the armed forces and in the home as well as women involved with political activities or with the peace movement. Most of the contributors are British but there are also recordings of 'allied' and 'enemy' women. As well as oral history the Sound Archive also includes broadcasts and speeches.

The recorded extracts are all copyright and may not be reproduced without permission.

BRITISH LIBRARY
National Sound Archive

29 Exhibition Road, London SW7 2AS
            tel: 0171-412 7440

The collection has extended recently beyond its original specialisation in music and wildlife sound effects to encompass oral history including some tapes on industrial work.

ORAL HISTORY SOCIETY

Contact Rob Perks, Secretary,
National Sound Archive,
29 Exhibition Road, London, SW7 2AS
            tel: 0171-412 7405).

Membership of the Society includes an annual subscription to Oral History (a twice yearly journal), price reductions on conferences and publications, and specialist advice.

Part Two CHAPTER 6

Contemporary Collecting and Working Outside the Museum

A. Adburgham, *Shops and Shopping: 1800-1914*, Allen & Unwin, London, 1981.

S. Alexander, *Becoming a Woman and other Essays in 19th and 20th Century Feminist History*, Virago, London, 1994.

J. Ash and E. Wilson, (eds), *Chic Thrills: A Fashion Reader*, Pandora Press, London, 1992.

D. Atkinson, *Suffragettes in the Purple, White & Green, London 1906-14*, Museum of London, 1992.

D. Beddoe, *Discovering Women's History, a practical manual*, Pandora Press, London, 1983.

V. Bott, 'Collecting the 20th Century', in *Social History Curators Group News*, No. 13, pp12-14, 1985-6.

T. Campbell, *100 Years of Women's Banners*, Thalia Campbell, Wales, 1986.

R. Coles and B. Lancaster, (eds), *Geordies: Roots of Regionalism*, Edinburgh University Press, Edinburgh, 1992.

S. Davies, 'Collecting and Recalling the 20th Century', in *Museums Journal*, vol. 85, pp27-9, June 1985.

E. Ehrman, 'Putting on the Style', in *Museums Journal*, vol. 95, no. 10, p32, October, 1995.

O. Green, 'Our Recent Past: The Black Hole in Museum Collections', in *Museums Journal*, vol. 85, no. 1, p5, 1985.

Schnuppe Von Gwinner, *The History of the Patchwork Quilt. Origins, Traditions and Symbols of textile art*, 1987, reprinted Schiffer Publishing Ltd, Pennsylvania, 1988.

P. Hesketh, *My Aunt Edith*, 1966, reprinted Lancashire County Books, Preston, 1992.

J. Holmes, 'The 20th Century Folk Museum' in *Social History Curators' Group News*, no. 18, Summer 1988.

E. Hostettler, *The Island at War: Memories of Wartime Life on the Isle of Dogs, East London*, Island History Trust, London, 1985.

E. Hostettler, (ed.), *Memories of Childhood on the Isle of Dogs, 1870-1970*, Island History Trust, London, 1993.

C. Imlah, (ed.), *Biba: The Label, The Lifestyle, The Look*, Tyne & Wear Museums, Newcastle upon Tyne, 1993.

E. King, 'The Cream of the Dross: Collecting Glasgow's Present for the Future', in *Social History Curators' Group Journal*, vol. 13, pp4-11, 1985-6.

J. Liddington and J. Norris, *One Hand Tied Behind Us. The Rise of the Women's Suffrage Movement*, 1978, reprinted Virago Press Ltd, London 1985.

S. Miller, 'Collecting the Current for History Museums', in *Curator*, 28/3, 1985.

K. Moore and D. Tucker, 'Back to Basics', in *Museums Journal*, vol 94, no. 7, p22, 1994.

S. Mullins, 'Market Harborough. Building a Collection', in *Museums Journal*, vol. 85, pp20-1, 1985.

G. F. Newsham, *In a League of Their Own! Dick, Kerr Ladies' Football Club 1917-1965*, Pride of Place Publishing, Chorley, 1994.

R. Parker, *The Subversive Stitch: embroidery and the making of the feminine*, The Women's Press, London, 1984.

R. Perks, *Oral History: An Annotated Bibliography*, British Library Publications, London, 1990.

R. Perks, *Oral History: Talking about the Past*, The Historical Association, London, 1992.

A. Phizacklea, *Unpacking the Fashion Industry: Gender, Racism and Class in Production*, Routledge, London, 1990.

F. Robinson, (ed.), *Post Industrial Tyneside*, Newcastle upon Tyne City Libraries and Arts, 1988.

C. Ross, 'Great Idea, Even Better Execution', in *Social History in Museums*, vol. 20, pp42-6, 1993.

H. R. Rubenstein, 'Collecting for Tomorrow', *Museum News*, 60/1, March/April 1982.

T. J. Schlereth, 'Collecting Today for Tomorrow', *Museum News*, 60/1, March/April, 1982.

L. Taylor, *Through the Looking Glass: A History of Dress from 1860 to the Present Day*, BBC Books, London, 1989.

F. M. L. Thompson, (ed.), *The Cambridge Social History of Britain 1750-1950: Regions and Communities*, vol. 1, Cambridge University Press, Cambridge, 1993.

P. Thompson, *The Voice of the Past*, 2nd. edn., Routledge, London, 1988.

L. Tickner, *The Spectacle of Women, Imagery of the Suffrage Campaign 1907-14*, Chatto and Windus, London, 1993.

C. Walkley, *The Ghost in the Looking Glass*, Peter Owen, London, 1981.

E. Wilson, *Adorned in Dreams: Fashion and Modernity*, Virago, London, 1985.

L. Weerasngne and J. Silver, *Directory of Recorded Sound Resources in the United Kingdom*, British Library Publications, 1989.

PLACES TO VISIT AND FURTHER READING

Several recent permanent displays in British museums deal with broad histories of urban, industrial communities. All of the following attempt to communicate an inclusive history which, while acknowledging the importance of the industrial basis of the community, does not diminish the value of other spheres of life. All include recently acquired material.

THE PEOPLE'S STORY (opened July 1989)

Canongate Tollboth, Edinburgh, also see: H. Clark and S. Marwick, 'The People's Story – Moving On', *Journal of the Social History Curators Group*, vol. 20, pp54-65, 1993.

THE STORY OF HULL AND ITS PEOPLE!

(opened September 1990)

The Old Grammar School, Hull, also see: E. Frostick, 'The Story of Hull and Its People! a measure of success?', *Journal of the Social History Curators Group*, vol. 20, pp45-53, 1993.

THE MUSEUM OF LIVERPOOL LIFE

(opened May 1993)

Albert Dock, Liverpool, also see: L. Knowles, *Museum of Liverpool Life: Making a Living, Demanding a Voice*, Mersey Culture, National Museums & Galleries on Merseyside, 1993.

GREAT CITY! (opened June 1993)

The Newcastle Discovery Museum, Newcastle upon Tyne, also see: C. Ross, 'Great idea, even better execution?', *Journal of the Social History Curators Group*, vol. 20, pp42-6, 1993.

GODIVA CITY (opened June 1994)

Herbert Art Gallery, Coventry. S. Mileham, 'Godiva City: A Thousand Years in the Making', in *Museum Development*, p17, 1994.

'LIFETIMES' (opened January 1995)

The Clocktower, Croydon, S. Macdonald, 'Your Place or Mine', in *Social History Curators Journal*, vol. 19, pp21-7, 1992.

S. Macdonald, 'Changing our Minds: Planning a Responsive Museum Service', in E. Hooper-Greenhill, *Museum, Media, Message*, pp165-174, Routledge, London, 1995.

COLLECTIONS TO CONSULT:

1   The Museum of London has a collection of images of London Trades & Industries for the period 1975-1992. Many of the photographic images depict women at work; on the shop floor, in the office, etc. The majority of the collection, which comprises around 10,000 images, is in negative form, with contact sheets. Some prints do exist, and there is also a colour slide collection (around 2,000 images). This collection is kept at a Museum outstation at Poplar Business Park, East London. Call 0171-515 1162.

2   The Museum of London also has a collection of around fifty 16 x 12 colour prints depicting people at work in London office environments. The photographs were taken by Anna Fox in 1988 and formed the basis of an exhibition and book called *Workstations*. The collection is held by the Latter Department.

3   The Island History Photograph Collection is open to the public on Tuesday, Wednesday and Friday afternoons from 1.30pm to 4.30pm, at Island House, Roserton Street, London E14. Tel 0171-987 6041.

ADDITIONAL REFERENCES

M P G   Museum Professional Group
Publishes transactions and newsletters.

SHCG   Social History Curators Group publishes a newsletter and journal and holds annual conferences.

WHAM   Women, Heritage and Museums publishes Newsletters and Conference proceedings Also available is the 'WHAM! Resources List', 4th. edn., 1990.

Oral History Society publishes a Journal – For contact details, see 'Industry at War' sources section. Of particular interest are:

Vol. 14   no. 2. *Museums and Oral History*, 1986.
Vol. 5   no. 2, *Women's History Issue*, 1977.
Vol. 10   no. 2, *2nd Women's History Issue*, 1982.
Vol. 21   no. 2, *Women's Lives*, 1993.

Current contacts for Museum Specialist groups can be found in the *Museum Association Yearbook*.

ENDPIECE

WHAM, the First Ten Years

S. Davies, 'Social History Curators Group Review of the Year', *Museums Journal*, vol. 85, no. 3, December 1985.

R. Hasted, Quoted in 'The Way Forward: A National WHAM! Structure', *Women, Heritage and Museums Newsletter*, no. 8, p8, 8 June 1988.

Social History Curators Group, *Women, Heritage and Museums*, Report of the conference held on 7-8 April 1984, Woolton Hall, Fallowfield, Manchester, 1984.

Women, Heritage and Museums, *Working for Women's Heritage*, 1986. Proceedings of the Study Weekend held at Brighton Polytechnic, 5-7 July 1985.

Women, Heritage and Museums, *Women, Heritage and Museums*, Conference Proceedings 8-9 May 1983; Welsh Folk Museum, 1993.

Current contacts for WHAM can be found in the *Museums Association Yearbook*.

LIST OF ILLUSTRATIONS

Every effort has been made to contact the original copyright holders. The publishers would be pleased to make good any errors or omissions brought to our attention in future editions. The illustrations may not be reproduced without permission from the copyright holders.

INDEX